CiTY·SMaRT™
GUIDEBOOK

Pittsburgh

Doina N. Locke

John Muir Publications
Santa Fe, New Mexico

Acknowledgments

I would like to thank my wonderful husband, Michael, and my four children for their patience and support while I worked on this book. Tony LaRussa's help was invaluable, and he brought extra life to the sports, nightlife, and day trips chapters. For sharing their insiders' knowledge of Pittsburgh, I thank all my friends, including Betty Renier, "Jerry" Melzer, Pat and Chick Poshard, Edmonda Fives, Mary Alice Gorman, Tom and Linda Herward, Craig and Terra Koerpel, Dr. Durga Malepati, Michael Walsh, Sally Wharton, and Jane Wrenshall.

John Muir Publications, P.O. Box 613, Santa Fe, New Mexico 87504

Printed in the United States of America
First edition. First printing June 1999.

ISBN: 1-56261-349-9
ISSN: 1522-0516

Editors: Peg Goldstein, Nancy Gillan
Graphics Editor: Bunny Wong
Production: Rebecca Cook
Design: Janine Lehmann
Cover design: Suzanne Rush
Typesetting: Kathy Sparkes, White Hart Design
Map Illustration: Julie Felton
Printer: Publishers Press
Front cover photo: © Henryk T. Kaiser/Photo Network—View of the Golden Triangle
Back cover photo: © Jeffrey Greenberg/The Picture Cube, Inc.—South side neighborhood

Distributed to the book trade by
Publishers Group West
Berkeley, California

CONTENTS

MAP CONTENTS

See Pittsburgh the CiTY·SMaRT™ Way

The Guide for Pittsburgh Natives, New Residents, and Visitors

In *City•Smart Guidebook: Pittsburgh*, local author Doina Locke tells it like it is. Residents will learn things they never knew about their city, new residents will get an insider's view of their new hometown, and visitors will be guided to the very best Pittsburgh has to offer—whether they're on a weekend getaway or staying a week or more.

Opinionated Recommendations Save You Time and Money

From shopping to nightlife to museums, the author is opinionated about what she likes and dislikes. You'll learn the great and the not-so-great things about Pittsburgh's sights, restaurants, and accommodations. So you can decide what's worth your time and what's not; which hotel is worth the splurge and which is the best choice for budget travelers.

Easy-to-Use Format Makes Planning Your Trip a Cinch

City•Smart Guidebook: Pittsburgh is user-friendly—you'll quickly find exactly what you're looking for. Chapters are organized by travelers' interests or needs, from Where to Stay and Where to Eat, to Sights and Attractions, Kids' Stuff, Sports and Recreation, and even Day Trips from Pittsburgh.

Includes Maps and Quick Location-Finding Features

Every listing in this book is accompanied by a geographic zone designation (see the next page for zone details) that helps you immediately find each location. Staying in the Golden Triangle and wondering about nearby sights and restaurants? Look for the Downtown label in the listings and you'll know that statue or café is not far away. Or maybe you're looking for the Carnegie Museum of Art? Along with its address, you'll see an East Pittsburgh label, so you'll know just where to find it.

All That and Fun to Read, Too!

Every City•Smart chapter includes fun-to-read (and fun-to-use) tips to help you get more out of Pittsburgh, city trivia (did you know that palm trees grow in Pittsburgh?), and illuminating sidebars (to learn to talk *Pittsburghese*, for example, see page 175). And well-known local residents provide their personal "Top Ten" lists, guiding readers to the city's best places to take children, best restaurants, and more.

PITTSBURGH ZONES

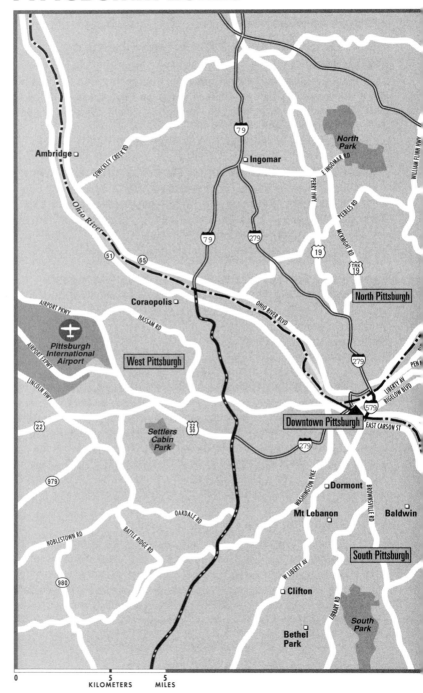

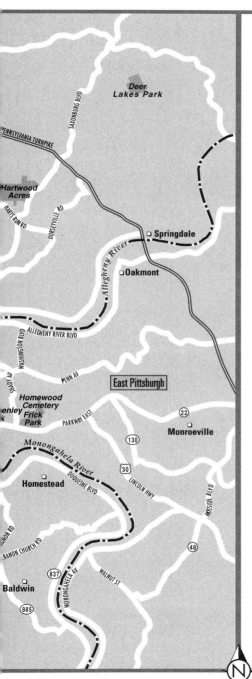

PITTSBURGH ZONES

Downtown (DP)
Bounded by the Allegheny, Monongahela, and Ohio Rivers and I-579. Downtown is also called the Golden Triangle.

North Pittsburgh (NP)
Bounded by the Allegheny and Ohio Rivers on the west, south, and east and roughly by the Red Belt on the north

East Pittsburgh (EP)
Bounded by the Allegheny and Monongahela Rivers and the Orange Belt (approximately the Pennsylvania Turnpike)

South Pittsburgh (SP)
The area west of the Monongahela River and east I-79. Includes the southern reaches of Allegheny County.

West Pittsburgh (WP)
The area south of the Ohio River and north of I-79. Includes the Pittsburgh International Airport.

Doina Locke

1

WELCOME TO PITTSBURGH

One of the country's most livable cities, believe it or not, was once known as Steel City and Smoky City. Modern Pittsburgh is now one of the country's most delightful suprises.

The surprises begin with your first glimpse of downtown Pittsburgh, while driving through the Fort Pitt Tunnel and across the Fort Pitt Bridge. As you head toward the Golden Triangle of downtown Pittsburgh, the vista of skyscrapers rising above the junction of three rivers is impressive. After dark, the sight is pure magic.

The Allegheny and Monongahela Rivers meet at the Golden Triangle to form the Ohio River, which continues on to the Mississippi. These three rivers are the reason for the city's existence and growth. They provided a strategic advantage for commerce, manufacturing, and early territorial expansion. The rivers have also made Pittsburgh a city of bridges—more than 700 of them join neighborhoods within the city. There are more than 1,500 bridges in Allegheny County as a whole.

Pittsburgh's terrain has also shaped its growth. Hills and valleys segment the city into a series of 88 distinctive neighborhoods, linked by winding streets, stairways up steep hillsides, and, at one time, as many as 16 inclines (inclined planes or hill-climbing trolleys) that carried workers to their jobs.

Pittsburgh is a city with its own unique character, richly flavored with the ethnic heritages of the immigrants who came primarily from Europe and the American South at the turn of the century. It is a city that prides itself on its strong work ethic. It is a city of sports champions and enthusiastic fans. It is a city redefining itself as a center of high technology, advanced research, and development in diverse fields—from robotics to surgical techniques.

Despite its muscular, brawling, blue-collar image of the past, today's Pittsburgh offers fine dining, cultural events, and top-class entertainment. A wealth of recreational choices, including large county parks, amusement parks, and a world-famous marathon, also make this a great visitor's town.

Getting to Know Pittsburgh

First, let's get one thing straight: Pittsburgh's days as "the Smoky City" are no more. Friends and relatives no longer need question your sanity in going to visit (or live in) Pittsburgh. Granted, it still ranks low among cities in terms of total sunshine, but not because of air pollution from belching smokestacks and fiery furnaces; they just aren't here anymore.

Officially, the Pittsburgh Metropolitan Statistical Area covers five adjacent counties in southwestern Pennsylvania: Allegheny, Butler, Beaver, Westmoreland, and Washington. Allegheny County contains 133 municipalities—Pittsburgh being the largest. Informally, most county residents describe themselves as Pittsburghers. The zones presented in this guidebook cover most of Allegheny County.

Pittsburgh History

In 1749 French explorer Celoron de Blainville proclaimed the point at which the Allegheny and the Monongahela Rivers met to form the Ohio River to be the most beautiful place along the river. This beautiful country was the destination of Delaware, Shawnee, Seneca, Fox, and Wyandot Indians, who migrated to western Pennsylvania between 1745 and 1760 to escape disease, famine, and European colonial expansion into their homelands. The area was reserved for Native Americans and officially closed to white settlers, who nevertheless moved in as squatters.

George Washington, on a scouting expedition in 1754, commented on the strategic advantage of the flat triangle of land at the meeting point of the Allegheny, Monongahela, and Ohio Rivers. The French seized the advantage

How Pittsburgh Kept Its "H"

In 1891 the U.S. Board of Geographic Names ruled that all city and town names ending in "burgh" should change the spelling (for mapmakers' sake) to "burg." The change was instituted nationally, but Pittsburghers officially hung onto their "h" and successfully petitioned the board to allow the spelling. Some isolated examples of Pittsburg *still exist, but they are tough to spot.*

first, building Fort Duquesne on that very site. A short while later, facing imminent defeat by a British force, the French abandoned the fort, setting it on fire before they left.

In 1759 the British built Fort Pitt on the ruins of the French structure. Both the fort and later the city of Pittsborough (soon to be called Pittsburgh) were named for British Prime Minister William Pitt.

By 1768 western Pennsylvania was officially opened to settlers. Instead of having provisions shipped over the Appalachians, Colonel George Morgan, commander of Fort Pitt during the Revolutionary War, contracted with local farmers and millers to provide the fort with goods.

Mounted police officers patrol downtown Pittsburgh.

In 1791 the U.S. government passed an excise tax on whiskey, creating hardships for western Pennsylvanian farmers, many of whom distilled and sold their own whiskey. By 1794, peaceful protests had failed, and sporadic armed resistance to the tax was called the Whiskey Rebellion. The rebellion withered at the sight of 13,000 troops led by George Washington and Alexander Hamilton.

Pittsburgh flourished and grew, despite many hardships. Cholera epidemics struck repeatedly throughout the 1830s. On April 10, 1845, fire destroyed 1,000 buildings and 700 homes in the city. The Monongahela Bridge, built in 1818, was completely destroyed.

In 1845 the Smithfield Street Bridge was designed and built by John A. Roebling, who later built the Brooklyn Bridge. Roebling's suspension bridge was replaced in 1883 by a lenticular truss bridge designed by Gustav Lindenthal. It is one of the oldest steel bridges in the United States. It was renovated in 1994.

In England in 1856, Henry Bessemer developed a process of blowing cold air through molten iron to convert it to steel. The process would transform Pittsburgh into a manufacturing giant. In 1868, Boston journalist James Parton described Pittsburgh as "Hell with the Lid Taken Off." He was amazed at the scale and energy of the city's 500 centers of production. Later, Lincoln Steffens used the same term scornfully.

In 1870, economic recession hit Pittsburgh hard and led to labor unrest. Protests over pay cuts, increased workloads, and unsafe working conditions grew into the Railroad Riot at Union Depot on July 21, 1877.

Andrew Carnegie brought the Bessemer process to Carnegie Steel's Edgar Thomson Works in Braddock in 1875. The works were named after

PITTSBURGH TIME LINE

1745-1760	Delaware, Shawnee, Seneca, Fox, and Wyandot Indians migrate to western Pennsylvania.
1754	George Washington comments on the strategic advantage of the flat triangle of land at the meeting point of the Allegheny, Monongahela, and Ohio Rivers.
1759	The British build Fort Pitt on the triangle, on the ruins of the French Fort Duquesne.
1764	Fort Pitt Blockhouse is built on the Point.
1768	Western Pennsylvania is officially opened to settlers.
1780s	The United States government expands its domain into the Northwest Territory, north and west of Pennsylvania.
1790	The population of Pittsburgh is 376.
1791	The U.S. government passes an excise tax on whiskey, creating hardships for western Pennsylvanian farmers.
1794	The Whiskey Rebellion is put down by a force of 13,000 soldiers led by George Washington and Alexander Hamilton.
1811	The first steamboat on western waters is built in Pittsburgh.
1818	The Monongahela Bridge is built, connecting downtown Pittsburgh to Birmingham on the south side of the river.
1830s	Cholera epidemics strike Pittsburgh repeatedly.
1834	The Pennsylvania Main Line Canal opens.
1845	Fire destroys homes, buildings, and the Monongahela Bridge.
1845	The Smithfield Street Bridge is built.
1849	The Perrysville–Zelienople Turnpike opens.
1849	Joseph Horne & Company is the first downtown department store.
1852	The Pennsylvania Railroad comes to Pittsburgh.
1862	H. J. Heinz Company is founded in Sharpsburg.
1870s	Economic recession hits Pittsburgh. Labor unrest ensues.
1870	The Monongahela Incline, first in the city, goes into service.
1871	The first streetcar lines are established in the South Hills.
1875	Andrew Carnegie brings the Bessemer process of making steel to Carnegie Steel's Edgar Thomson Works in Braddock.
1877	Railroad workers riot over pay cuts, increased workloads, and unsafe working conditions.
1877	The Duquesne Incline makes its first run.

Kaufmann's Department Store moves downtown to Fifth and Smithfield Streets.	**1879**
Economic recession, extensive layoffs, and pay reductions hurt Pittsburgh.	**1890s**
Henry Phipps builds Phipps Conservatory in Schenley Park.	**1893**
The Battle of Homestead takes place at Carnegie Steel's Homestead Works.	**1892**
U.S. Steel Company is formed.	**1901**
The Nickelodeon, the world's first movie theater, opens on Smithfield Street.	**1905**
The City of Allegheny is forcibly annexed by its neighbor the City of Pittsburgh.	**1907**
An explosion inside Pittsburgh Coal's Deer Mine kills 200 miners.	**1907**
Forbes Field is built in Oakland.	**1909**
The South Side's St. Clair Incline crashes to the bottom of the tracks. Two people are killed, eight are injured.	**1909**
"Grant's Hump" is lowered.	**1911**
William Penn Hotel opens with 1,000 guest rooms at $2.50 per night.	**1916**
The first radio broadcast ever is made from station KDKA in Pittsburgh.	**1920**
The Liberty Tunnels, the first automobile tunnels in the United States, are built.	**1924**
Renaissance I urban renewal program is initiated by Mayor David Lawrence and financier Richard King Mellon.	**Late 1940s**
Pittsburgh's population peaks at 676,806.	**1950**
WQED, the nation's first public television station, is founded.	**1954**
Pittsburgh Pirates win the World Series.	**1960**
USX Tower built.	**1970**
Forbes Field is torn down and the Pirates move to Three Rivers Stadium.	**1970**
Renaissance II urban renewal program is initiated under Mayor Richard Caliguiri.	**Late 1970s**
Both Pirates and Steelers win championships.	**1979**
U.S. Steel's Duquesne Works close.	**1985**
U.S. Steel's Homestead Works close.	**1986**
Penguins win Stanley Cup.	**1996**

> When the Steelers or the Penguins are on a roll, be sure to wear black and gold to join in on the fun. A Mario Lemieux or Jaromir Jagr jersey or a Steeler jacket is a treasure.

Carnegie's former boss, the president of Pennsylvania Railroad, which was by then one of Carnegie Steel's biggest customers. Throughout the 1880s, the steel industry brought Pittsburgh into international prominence and began to generate incredible fortunes.

The economic recession and subsequent layoffs and pay reductions of the 1890s hurt Pittsburgh, especially the people who were least able to survive hard times. On July 6, 1892, the Battle of Homestead took place at Carnegie Steel's Homestead Works when hundreds of workers rebelled against wage reductions. Forty died or were seriously injured in the bloody battle against 300 Pinkerton guards hired by Henry Clay Frick.

In 1907, the City of Pittsburgh forcibly annexed its neighbor, the City of Allegheny, located on the north bank of the Allegheny River. Allegheny City was the richest city in the country and, before its annexation, the third largest. Consequently, Pittsburgh became the richest city in the world.

But only a few held that enormous wealth. Andrew Carnegie, Henry Clay Frick, James Laughlin, Henry Phipps, George Westinghouse, and Thomas Mellon were some of the millionaires of Pittsburgh. Their sources of wealth included steel, railroads, banking, coal, iron, and real estate.

Pittsburgh's millionaires also became philanthropists, giving much to the city in cultural advantages. In 1893, Henry Phipps built Phipps Conservatory in Schenley Park, a 300-acre public park donated to the city by Mary Schenley. Andrew Carnegie established the Carnegie Institute. However, some people saw irony in the philanthropy of those who had proven to be brutal in the acquisition of their wealth. Nevertheless, the city benefitted, and its cultural institutions still rival those of larger cities.

At the turn of the century, Pittsburgh's millionaires began building the skyscrapers that would determine the city's unique skyline. The men seemed to be in competition, each trying to outdo the other with his building. Today, the buildings and streets of downtown Pittsburgh bear the names of those men in a chronicle of their achievements. In 1901, the Frick Building was built on Grant Street and the others soon followed.

Growth continued in the areas of industry, commerce, and technology. The U.S. Steel Company was formed in 1901. The Nickelodeon, the world's first movie theater, opened on Smithfield Street in 1905. In 1906, Russell H. Boggs founded the Pittsburgh, Harmony, Butler and New Castle Railway, an electric railroad that united Pittsburgh with the North Hills and outlying northern towns. In 1911, the first drive-through gas station opened in Pittsburgh.

Sports were important early in the city's history. In 1909 Forbes Field was built in Oakland. It was used not only for baseball but also for football, wrestling, fairs, daredevil shows, and concerts. The first modern World Series was played in 1903 in Pittsburgh's Exposition Park. The Pittsburgh Crawfords and the Homestead Grays, African American baseball teams in the Negro National League, were said to be among the best teams ever assembled.

Tragedy, common in the city's factories, mills, and mines, struck the inclines in 1909. The St. Clair Incline, crowded with workers heading home, broke a cable and crashed to the bottom of the track. Arthur Miller, 17, and Albert Klingenberger, 16, were killed when they jumped out of the car. Of the others who remained on board, eight were injured.

The downtown landscape continued to change. In 1911, "Grant's Hump," an elevation on Grant Street, was lowered. In the process, many old buildings were torn down. The Frick Building's original lobby became the mezzanine of a two-story lobby opening onto the lowered street. In 1916, the William Penn Hotel opened with 1,000 guest rooms. The rate was $2.50 per night.

On November 2, 1920, the first commercial radio broadcast ever was made from station KDKA in Pittsburgh. KDKA is still on the air in Pittsburgh, with a radio and a television station.

The year 1924 saw the opening of the Liberty Tunnels, called the Liberty Tubes, the first automobile tunnels in the country. Extending from the Liberty Bridge through Mt. Washington, the Tubes connected downtown with the South Hills.

More skyscrapers sprang up downtown. The Clark Building was

Carnegie Science Center overlooks the Ohio River.

constructed in 1928. The Grant Building, with a large aerial beacon at its summit that flashes P-I-T-T-S-B-U-R-G-H in Morse code, was built in 1929. For many years, pilots used the light as a navigational landmark. The Gulf Tower (1932) had a light on its pyramid-shaped top that changed color to indicate changes in the weather. The tower was the tallest building in the city until 1970, when the USX Tower surpassed it at 841 feet.

Allegheny University Hospital, long a North Side Landmark

In the late 1940s, Pittsburgh Mayor David Lawrence, backed by financier Richard King Mellon, initiated Renaissance I, an urban renewal program intended to revitalize the city. By 1950, Pittsburgh's population had reached its peak at 676,806. The nation's first public television station, WQED, was founded in Pittsburgh in 1954. It would become the home of the much-loved children's television program *Mister Rogers' Neighborhood.*

Sports continued as a local passion. In 1960, the Pittsburgh Pirates won the World Series when Bill Mazerosky hit a game-winning home run. In 1970, Forbes Field was torn down and replaced by Three Rivers Stadium—and "everybody cried." In 1979, when both the Pirates and the Steelers won championships, "the town went nuts." In 1996, the Penguins won the coveted Stanley Cup.

In the late 1970s, Mayor Richard Caliguiri introduced another urban renewal plan, Renaissance II. Through the early 1980s, the construction of PPG Place, CNG Building, One Oxford Center, and Fifth Avenue Place formed the basis of Pittsburgh's second renaissance.

In 1985, U.S. Steel's Duquesne Works closed. In 1986, its Homestead Works closed. Steelworkers were devastated. But Pittsburgh's economy appears to be on the upswing again—with a new focus. Its hope for the future lies in its universities, medical schools, and hospitals, which have collaborated in pioneering research and developments in areas such as robotics, micro-engineering, and medical techniques.

When to Visit

Pittsburgh is at its best in spring, when trees show their first haze of pale green. There's nothing brighter than a crystal-clear, frosty spring morning in Schenley Park. The Phipps Conservatory Spring Flower Show sets the tone, eagerly anticipating the daffodils and forsythia of late March and early April. Runners train for May's Pittsburgh Marathon. The Pittsburgh Folk Festival and the International Children's Festival offer less strenuous springtime pleasures.

Summer is the best time for walking the compact, 12-square-block Golden Triangle, admiring the architectural marvels of Renaissance II, and indulging in the timeless pleasures of people-watching. Market Square, Mellon Square, Gateway Center, PPG Place, and One Oxford Plaza are just some of many downtown spots rich in visual splendor. Summer is also the best time to indulge in guided city tours.

Summer is the season for the Three Rivers Arts Festival, the Mellon

Mayor Tom Murphy's Top 10 Reasons to Visit Pittsburgh

1. Pittsburgh's newest neighborhood and island community, Washington's Landing, which doubles as home base for rowing and river enthusiasts

2. A relaxed pleasure cruise along one of our three famous rivers—the Allegheny, the Monongahela, and the Ohio

3. Touring one or more of our city's 88 eclectic and inviting neighborhoods

4. Spending an afternoon watching one of our championship professional sports teams

5. Visiting one of our four regional parks for a fun-filled afternoon of swimming, biking, softball, tennis, golf, in-line skating, vintage car races, movies, concerts, or a picnic

6. A bike ride or run along our 25 miles of beautiful riverfront trails

7. A visit to the Cultural District to enjoy our world-class symphony or a ballet, opera, or theater performance

8. A trip aboard our famous Monongahela or Duquesne inclines to one of Mt. Washington's many wonderful restaurants and a breathtaking view of our downtown skyline and Golden Triangle

9. A visit to the Carnegie Museum of Natural History, which houses the world's foremost dinosaur fossil exhibit or to the Andy Warhol Museum, the world's largest museum dedicated to one artist

10. A freshly shaved flavored ice ball from Gus & Yia Yia's side walk cart on the city's North Side

Jazz Festival, the Cycling Classic, the Vintage Grand Prix, the Three Rivers Regatta, street fairs in the South Side and Shadyside, and farmers' markets in the Pittsburgh Zoo parking lot and on the North Side. It is the season for Pirates baseball games at Three Rivers Stadium, trips to Kennywood Amusement Park and Sandcastle Water Park, and outdoor concerts at the I. C. Light Amphitheatre, Hartwood Acres, and Coca-Cola Star Lake Amphitheatre.

If you enjoy fall foliage, then Pittsburgh should be your starting point for a spectacular color tour. You can take a river-cruise tour, with views of the Allegheny, Monongahela, and Ohio Rivers. If you prefer a road trip, head north on Route 19 into Butler County, take SR422 east into Butler, take Route 8 south to Wildwood Road, then head west on the Yellow Belt through North Park and around the lake. If you have more time, the Laurel Highlands offer wonderful vistas and a tour of Frank Lloyd Wright's Fallingwater, the home spanning a waterfall.

Winter is a great time to visit Pittsburgh for nearby skiing and wonderful Christmas displays at the Carnegie, Carnegie Science Center, PPG Place, Hartwood, and Pittsburgh Zoo. Ski runs are as close as Boyce Park or about an hour and a half drive away at Seven Springs or Hidden Valley in the Laurel Highlands.

Calendar of Events

JANUARY
Christmas at Clayton, Frick Art and Historical Center
Carnegie Tree Display, The Carnegie
Eckerd Drugs Celebration of Lights, Hartwood

FEBRUARY
Pittsburgh Auto Show, David L. Lawrence Convention Center

MARCH
St. Patrick's Day Parade, Downtown and Market Square
Spring Flower Show, Phipps Conservatory

APRIL
Pittsburgh Pirates season opener, Three Rivers Stadium

TRIVIA

Pittsburgh's St. Patrick's Day Parade is the second largest in the world after New York City's. Both are larger than any parade in Ireland.

MAY
Pittsburgh Marathon, Point State Park

International Children's Theater Festival, West Park

Pittsburgh Folk Festival, David L. Lawrence Convention Center

JUNE
Three Rivers Arts Festival, Point State Park and Gateway Center

Cycling Classic, downtown and Mt. Washington

Festa Italia, Strip District

Mellon Jazz Festival, various locations

Cathedral of Learning

Jeff Greenberg/GPCVB

JULY
Fourth of July Celebration and Fireworks, Point State Park

Pittsburgh Vintage Grand Prix Auto Race, Schenley Park

South Side Street Fair, East Carson Street

Bach, Beethoven and Brunch, Pittsburgh Center for the Arts

AUGUST
Three Rivers Regatta, Point State Park

Shadyside Arts Festival, Walnut Street

SEPTEMBER
The Great Race, Frick Park to the Point

Pittsburgh Steelers season opener, Three Rivers Stadium

Penn's Colony Festival, North Park

Oktoberfest, Penn Brewery

OCTOBER
Head of the Ohio Regatta, Washington's Landing to the Point

Halloween Celebration, Pittsburgh Children's Museum Haunted House

Halloween Fright Fest, Station Square

NOVEMBER
Light-Up Night and Sparkle Season Kick-Off, downtown

Christmas at Clayton, Frick Art and Historical Center

Christmas Tree Display, The Carnegie

Eckerd Drugs Celebration of Lights, Hartwood

Miniature Railroad Village, Carnegie Science Center

Carnegie Biennial International Art Exhibition, The Carnegie

Santas of the World Exhibit, Wintergarden in PPG Place

DECEMBER
Pitt Nationality Rooms Holiday Tours, University of Pittsburgh's
    Cathedral of Learning
Bach Choir Messiah Sing-In, borough of Carnegie
Pittsburgh First Night Celebration, Downtown

Pittsburgh's Weather

For a northern city, Pittsburgh has surprisingly temperate weather, often
similar to but less severe than weather in Detroit and New York City. When
snowstorms head east across the weather map, they often ease up on
Pittsburgh, dumping most of their snowflakes to the north or to the southeast and the mountains of the Laurel Highlands.

Get ready for cloudy days in Pittsburgh—most days are. The good
news is that even though the sun doesn't shine much in Pittsburgh, when
it does shine, everyone rejoices, and they really mean it when they say
"Have a nice day!" Note: you had better enjoy the sunshine, because it
never lasts very long.

A word of caution to allergy sufferers: High pollen counts and molds
(from the generally high humidity of the river valleys) can deliver a seasonal double whammy to the sensitive.

Dressing in Pittsburgh

Overall, Pittsburghers are very informal; people dress for comfort and util-
ity, not necessarily for high fashion or style. Pittsburgh is not on the cutting
edge of fashion—it may even be said that it meanders behind the trends at
a comfortable pace. On the corporate side, downtown office workers generally follow standard business dress codes.

From mid-autumn to late spring, it's best to dress in layers so you can
adjust to rapid changes in the weather. In winter, be ready with a heavy

As of April 30, 1998, Allegheny County has two area codes, 412 and 724.
Calls from one area to the other are considered local calls, but you
must dial a 1 when calling between the two areas.

Climate Chart

	Ave. Daily High (F)	Ave. Daily Low (F)	Ave. Monthly Precipitation (inches)	Percent Possible Sunshine
January	34	19	2.85	25
February	37	20	2.46	26
March	49	30	3.28	27
April	60	39	3.08	50
May	71	48	3.38	39
June	79	57	3.71	51
July	83	62	3.90	55
August	81	60	3.21	38
September	74	54	2.62	44
October	63	42	2.40	63
November	50	34	2.40	24
December	39	24	2.69	22

jacket, boots, and gloves (a hat and scarf wouldn't hurt). If the temperature doesn't get you, the windchill factor will.

The People of Pittsburgh

The best part of Pittsburgh is its people. But trying to make one blanket statement about them is as futile as trying to homogenize the neighborhoods and consolidate the boroughs.

The people of Pittsburgh, regardless of how long they've been here, are defined by family, hard work, and neighborhood. In general, they're very friendly, courteous, and helpful to newcomers and visitors.

Much of the city's social life revolves around the family and family-related activities, such as youth sports programs, school, church, and civic organizations. Newcomers, especially those without children, sometimes find it's harder to fit in here than elsewhere.

Pittsburghers tend to stay in Pittsburgh; a high percentage of the city's population was born here. If jobs or schooling take them away, Pittsburghers tend to gravitate back eventually. Pittsburgh also has a high number of senior citizens. It's second only to Florida's Dade County in average age of population.

Pittsburgh is its neighborhoods, all 88 of them, and Allegheny County has its 133 municipalities. Each of these areas is fiercely independent, proud of its differences (real and imagined), and insular. This independence

Macaroni production was one of the main Pittsburgh industries in the 1920s.

is reinforced by the hills, valleys, and highways that keep neighborhoods separated.

Ethnic pride is a strong force, unifying communities yet keeping people from blending into the larger community. Even today, Bloomfield is identified as Italian; Squirrel Hill, Jewish; and the Hill District, African American. Various ethnic days at Kennywood, the International Folk Festival, and other events demonstrate the strength of these bonds.

Pittsburghers are hard workers. Whether they hold blue-collar or white-collar jobs, whether they work in heavy industry or high technology, they always work hard. Even the Pirates promote themselves as a "hard-working team."

Pittsburgh is blessed with a relatively low rate of serious crime. A recent government study of safety in the country's 25 most populated metropolitan areas placed Pittsburgh at the top. Nevertheless, visitors should always use common sense when it comes to personal safety.

Business and Economy

In the early part of the twentieth century, the largest proportion of Pittsburgh's workers were employed in manufacturing. Gradually, the plants that made Pittsburgh an industrial giant disappeared. The workers who kept the steel mills and the coke ovens going stayed, but could not find work. As recently as twenty years ago, the city supported 19 Fortune 500 companies. Today, only seven Fortune 500s are left. Even Westinghouse pulled out.

On the positive side, an amazing 100,000 new jobs have been created in the last five years by approximately 3,600 high-tech Pittsburgh firms. Even that increase, however, is barely enough to balance the earlier loss of jobs.

Ten Top Reasons Cycloid Is Located in Pittsburgh

by Grant Renier, founder and chairman of the board, Cycloid Company

1. Center of high-precision, high-technology manufacturing
2. Center of plastics and associated industries
3. Highly trained personnel
4. State support for high-tech start-up companies
5. Low cost of living and doing business
6. System of three world-class research universities
7. Major interstate hub
8. International airport
9. World-class symphony orchestra and three professional sports teams
10. Bucolic hills and terrain with all four seasons

In addition, the jobs that are being created cannot provide employment for the industrial workers whose jobs were lost. The new jobs are either highly technical, requiring years of advanced education, or they are low-paying service jobs.

The city's largest employer is the federal government, followed by the Commonwealth of Pennsylvania, the University of Pittsburgh Medical Center, and US Airways. Thirteen of the top 50 Pittsburgh employers are in the health-care field.

The major source of revenue for Allegheny County is the real estate tax, which is based on a property's assessed value, or 25 percent of the amount for which a property can be sold. The current rate used to calculate county tax bills is 25.2 mills, with 1 mill equaling $1 for every $1,000 of assessed value ($25.20 for every $1,000).

Pittsburgh property owners also pay a city property tax of 184.5 mills for land and another 32 mills for buildings. A tax of 59.7 mills is collected on all properties to finance the public school system.

In Allegheny County, a 7 percent sales tax applies to all purchases except clothing and groceries. (The basic state sales tax is 6 percent, with the additional 1 percent going to finance regional assets such as sports stadiums, museums, and libraries.) County hotels and motels charge a 7 percent county tax in addition to the 7 percent sales tax.

City residents pay an earned income tax of 2.875 percent, with 1 percent going to the city and 1.875 percent going to the public school system. The city also collects an amusement tax of 5 percent, included in the price of sporting events, movies, concerts, and other recreational activities. A 26 percent parking tax is included in the price of parking in city garages and lots.

The cost of living is moderate in Pittsburgh compared to other American cities. Here's what you can expect to pay for the following goods and services:

five-mile taxi ride	$7.40
average dinner	$20, including tip
daily newspaper	$ .50 (*Pittsburgh Post-Gazette*)
hotel double room	$160 downtown; $123 near airport
movie admission	$6.50 first run; $3.50 bargain

Housing

Housing in the Pittsburgh area is both affordable and attractive. Throughout the area's urban and suburban neighborhoods, you'll find homes in all price ranges, from economical to high-end luxurious.

The average monthly rent in mid-1998 was about $400 for a one-bedroom apartment and $550 for a two-bedroom apartment. The average home price was about $91,000. Because the cost of living is lower in Pittsburgh than in many other large metropolitan areas, the same base price buys much more house in terms of quality and living space.

Schools

The Pittsburgh school district includes 93 schools serving 40,000 students. The rest of Allegheny County is divided into 42 school districts, ranging in size from the mammoth North Allegheny School District with 659 teachers and about 8,500 students to the relatively tiny Cornell School District with 54 teachers and 725 students.

Pittsburgh has a number of excellent universities and colleges, such as the University of Pittsburgh, Carnegie Mellon University, and Duquesne University. Smaller schools offering quality education include Chatham College, Carlow College, Point Park College, Robert Morris College, La Roche College, and four campuses of the Community College of Allegheny County.

Doina Locke

2

GETTING AROUND PITTSBURGH

Pittsburgh is not exactly an urban planner's dream city. The hilly terrain, rivers, and torturously winding suburban roads preclude any concept of a grid or of merely navigating with ease around town. Before venturing into the Golden Triangle or beyond, it's wise to acquaint yourself with the basics of the city layout—the freeways, belts, tunnels, and bridges. A good road map wouldn't hurt the effort.

Within the Golden Triangle are two subsystems of streets, oriented toward one of two rivers. Fort Duquesne Boulevard, Penn Avenue, and Liberty Avenue more or less parallel the Allegheny River, with the Sixth Street, Seventh Street, and Ninth Street Bridges crossing the river and continuing briefly up to Liberty Avenue. The Fort Duquesne Bridge crosses the Allegheny, and drivers have the choice of exiting at Fort Duquesne Boulevard or continuing on to the Fort Pitt Bridge, crossing the Monongahela ("the Mon"), and entering the Fort Pitt Tunnels for points south and west of the city. North of the Monongahela, the Boulevard of the Allies, Fifth Avenue, and Forbes Avenue run relatively parallel to the river. Immediately south of the Monongahela, Carson Street is the primary east-west roadway.

Leaving the North Side, East Ohio Street becomes Route 28 (Allegheny Valley Expressway) and runs along the north bank of the Allegheny River as far northeast as Tarentum and farther beyond the limits of Allegheny County.

From the West End Bridge, Ohio River Boulevard (Route 65) heads west toward Sewickley along the northern shore of the Ohio. On the southern shore, Route 51, as West Carson Street, heads west beyond McKees Rocks and east along the Mon as East Carson Street.

Pittsburgh's Belts

Far more logical than Pittsburgh's crazy-quilt pattern of streets and avenues are the belts—systems of streets and roads, somewhat like marked hiking trails for cars, that ring the city and traverse most of Allegheny County. Next to the rivers, the belts are the best way to orient yourself within the county.

The pattern begins with the newest belt, the Purple Belt, which loops around the Golden Triangle. The next one out is the Blue Belt, then the Green, the Yellow, the Orange, and the Red. The Green and Red Belts are not full loops: the Green extends from the north bank of the Ohio to the north bank of the Monongahela; the Red goes from the north bank of the Ohio east to the north bank of the Allegheny.

When driving in Pittsburgh, remember the bywords: You can't get there from here—but the belts help. They are marked with traffic signs that help keep you on track—at turns, at forks in the road, and when the street you are on temporarily merges with a larger roadway.

The system also helps you to make sense out of what could be a bewildering sequence of street names. For example, if you know a restaurant is on the Green Belt in the North Hills, that fact could be far more useful than knowing that the restaurant is in Ross. Amazingly, native Pittsburghers seem to be less familiar with the belts than newcomers.

Highways

Parkway East (also known as Interstate 376, US 22/30, and the Penn Lincoln Parkway) parallels the Monongahela River and connects downtown Pittsburgh with Monroeville. But don't call it the Penn Lincoln Parkway—no one will know what you're talking about, even though that name appears on all the maps. The name Parkway East does not appear on maps, but that is the road's designation in radio and television traffic reports.

Parking near Market Square in downtown Pittsburgh

Doina Locke

I-279 North is the relatively new (within the last ten years) and long anticipated (more than 20 years in the works) link between downtown and the North Hills. Soon after its completion, commuters were mystified to hear reports of congestion on "Parkway North." Happily, the confusion (but not the

My Favorite Things about Pittsburgh

by Louise Dickinson, member of the board of the Civic Light Opera

1. Pittsburgh's colleges and universities. The University of Pittsburgh Medical Center in Oakland, Phipps Conservatory, the Carnegie Museums, and the Carnegie Science Center all promote innovation and stimulate cultural growth.

2. The Strip District, with its multicultural offerings and produce and other food fresh off the loading docks, makes shopping an adventure.

3. The terrain, with lush greenery covering the hillsides, and the city skyline are delightful.

4. Pittsburgh's history, especially the stories behind Fort Pitt and the industrial barons, such as Frick, Mellon, and Carnegie, is endlessly fascinating.

5. The three rivers with their boats and bridges give Pittsburgh a dynamic vista.

6. The three major-league teams, the Steelers, Pirates, and Penguins, are fun to follow.

7. Heinz Hall and the Benedum, which has the largest, deepest stage this side of the Mississippi River, are theaters to be proud of.

8. The ethnic groups are uniquely Pittsburgh and are a force in the preservation of family unity, cultural identity, and civic pride.

9. Hillsides within the city create the physical boundaries that help define the multitude of neighborhoods.

10. The Civic Light Opera celebrated its 50th anniversary in 1997.

rush-hour congestion) cleared up, and the radio traffic reporter's nickname stuck.

Parkway North (I-279) supplements the primary North Hills north-south artery, Route 19, also known under various aliases. Heading north from the city, Route 19 is McKnight Road, and Truck Route 19 is Perry Highway. The two join in Wexford, where they are known as 19 or Perry Highway. The route continues north, following the path that Admiral Perry's forces took on their march to Lake Erie.

An unusual aspect of I-279 North is the HOV (High Occupancy Vehicle) lane, designed to encourage carpooling and bus travel between

Visitors should be aware that not all communities within Allegheny County have 911 emergency systems in place. Check the emergency numbers for your stay, area codes included.

downtown and the North Hills. The express lane connects the McKnight Road entrance/exit and a North Side exit/entrance that enables drivers to cross the Allegheny River into downtown either by way of the Fort Duquesne Bridge or the Seventh Street Bridge. The HOV lane is strictly in-bound in the morning and outbound in the afternoon and evening. The system is regulated by gates at either end that are closed manually by Pennsylvania Department of Transportation (PennDOT) workers.

I-279 North merges with I-79 at a point south of Wexford and continues north to Erie. Heading south on I-79, you may puzzle over signs indicating that Washington is roughly 30 miles away. Relax—they mean Washington, Pennsylvania, not Washington, D.C. (Incidentally, Washington, Pennsylvania, used to be nicknamed Little Washington.)

Parkway West (a.k.a. I-279 South, Route 22/30, and the Penn Lincoln Parkway) emerges from the Fort Pitt Tunnels and heads west to connect with Route 60, the Airport Parkway or Expressway. There is no "Parkway South."

Emerging from the Fort Pitt Tunnels, you can head south on I-279 to link up with I-79, you can take Banksville Road (Route 19 South), or you can take Sawmill Run Boulevard (Route 51). If you exit through the Liberty Tunnels (Tubes), you can head south on West Liberty Avenue (Truck 19 South) or Sawmill Run Boulevard.

The Pennsylvania Turnpike, I-76, is also a useful means of navigating around the area, particularly north and east of the city. Essentially, there are four Pittsburgh area exits: Exit 3 in Cranberry (Route 19, Perry Highway), Exit 4 in Gibsonia (Route 8, Butler Valley), Exit 5 in Harmarville (Allegheny Valley), and Exit 6 in Monroeville (Pittsburgh). Depending on the time of day, the turnpike is often the fastest route from the North Hills to Monroeville.

Tunnels

In 1924, Pittsburgh broke through its surrounding hills and became the first U.S. city to build an automobile tunnel, the Liberty Tunnels—known as the Liberty Tubes or simply the Tubes. The Liberty Tunnels together with the Liberty Bridge connect downtown Pittsburgh and the South Hills by way of I-579 on the north end and Truck 19 on the south.

The Fort Pitt Tunnels and the Fort Pitt Bridge connect the Golden Triangle, the North Hills, and the South Hills via I-279. Be careful in navigating your way through this area for the first time: Many signs are mounted under the overhead spans and you can't read them until you're practically underneath them. At least the signs marking the way to the airport are helpful. The Squirrel Hill Tunnel on Parkway East cuts through hillsides, bringing traffic into downtown from the eastern suburbs, Monroeville, and beyond.

Bridges

Pittsburgh is a city of bridges, from the "Bridge of Sighs" linking the Allegheny County Courthouse to the Old Jail, to the highway bridges spanning a multitude of valleys and creeks, to the majestic structures crossing the rivers. Pittsburgh's bridges are truly remarkable because of their variety and their beauty. Aside from the identical Sixth, Seventh, and Ninth Street Bridges, known as the Three Sisters, apparently no two bridges are alike in design. Even the colors of the bridges are different. The Hulton Bridge, which crosses the Allegheny to join Harmarville and Oakmont, is a delicate shade of lavender.

Major spans that are commonly mentioned on rush-hour traffic reports are the Fort Pitt Bridge, the Liberty Bridge, the 10th Street Bridge, the Birmingham Bridge, and the Homestead High Level Bridge across the Monongahela River; the Fort Duquesne Bridge, the Veterans' Bridge (I-579), the 16th Street Bridge, the 31st Street Bridge, the 40th Street (Washington Crossing) Bridge, and the Highland Park Bridge over the Allegheny; and the West End Bridge over the Ohio.

The country's oldest steel bridge, the Smithfield Street Bridge over the Monongahela River to Station Square, is over 110 years old. The first bridge at Smithfield Street was a coiled-steel cable suspension span designed and built in 1845 by John A. Roebling, who went on to design and build New York City's Brooklyn Bridge. Numerous complaints about swaying eventually led to Roebling's bridge's being replaced in 1883 by a lenticular truss (or through-truss) bridge designed by Gustav Lindenthal. The bridge underwent extensive renovation in the mid-1990s when the surface was so worn that the river was visible through holes in the roadway.

Public Transportation

Public transportation serves the city fairly well. It has to: Parking downtown is difficult, expensive, and severely limited. Drivers in the downtown area will encounter many one-way streets, construction obstacles, and heavy pedestrian traffic at times.

In Oakland, drivers and pedestrians alike must be alert to the fact that traffic is one-way inbound on Fifth Avenue but the left curb lane is an outbound, bus-only lane. Look both ways before you cross.

Buses

City buses are known as PAT buses, which stands for Port Authority Transit. The Port Authority stands as a reminder that Pittsburgh is, in fact, the country's largest inland port, which many Pittsburghers tend to forget.

The base PAT fare is $1.25; be sure to have exact change. Routes are divided into zones, and there is a 35-cent charge for crossing from one zone to another. Bus travel within the Golden Triangle is free.

Route information and passes are available at Giant Eagle supermarkets, at mall information centers, by calling 412/231-5707, or by going to PAT's downtown service center at 534 Smithfield Street. Reduced-rate and weekend passes are available.

PAT announced in the spring of 1998 that it would have 160 new buses in commission by spring 1999. The buses are "low floor" models that allow passengers to board and exit more easily. The new design eliminates the need for wheelchair lifts. The new buses are also air-conditioned and have onboard video cameras.

To facilitate bus travel, there are several "busways" around Pittsburgh. These are lanes that are reserved exclusively for buses; drivers should be aware that absolutely no automobile traffic is allowed on the busways. There are several Park-N-Ride locations in the suburbs that allow commuters to connect with bus lines more easily.

Subway and Light Rail

Pittsburgh has a delightful, if small, subway system called the T that serves the Golden Triangle with a three-stop loop. Rides within the Golden Triangle are free. The stations are light and clean, with classical music piped in. The Wood Street and Steel Plaza stations even have art galleries located above the subway stops. The T links at Station Square with a 10.5-mile light rail system to the South Hills, ending at the South Hills Village Mall. The T is managed by the Port Authority of Allegheny County, which has offices at 2235 Beaver Avenue. For further information, call 412/237-7429.

Taxis

With a fleet of 300 cars, Yellow Cab (412/665-8100) is one of the city's leading cab companies. Anywhere within a ten-mile radius of downtown, the base fare is $1.80, plus 40 cents per mile. Outside the ten-mile radius, add a $7 surcharge. A trip to the airport costs $30 from downtown.

Taxis wait at the airport outside the baggage claim area. At the Greyhound bus station, if a taxi isn't already there, a phone call will get one to you in five to ten minutes.

Driving in Pittsburgh

Visitors who intend to travel around the Pittsburgh area should be prepared to drive. Public transportation is good, but doesn't provide access to all parts of the city. While it is possible to take an airport shuttle to a hotel and walk to destinations within the Golden Triangle, it is very difficult to reach points beyond the bus and T lines. In the suburbs, many areas have no sidewalks to accommodate pedestrian traffic.

The most important driving aid in Pittsburgh, next to nerves of steel and the patience of a saint, is a good map. Many are available, including those in this guidebook. Others include the American Automobile Association's Pittsburgh, Pennsylvania Downtown & Vicinity map, which shows the Color Belt system, and the laminated Rand McNally Pittsburgh EasyFinder.

Newcomers will appreciate "Finding Yourself in Pittsburgh," by Bob Firth, who also developed an efficient system of directional signs, called the Wayfinder Sign System. Prominently posted within the city, the royal blue signs point the way to specific sites and also let you know where you are. A color code quickly establishes location: Purple represents downtown and the Strip District, aqua is for the North Side, green for the South Side, orange for Oakland, and gold for the East End.

Street signs within the city often carry the name of the neighborhood, such as Shadyside or Point Breeze, in addition to the name of the street. In

One of the Airmall shops at Pittsburgh International Airport, p. 26

GPCVB

the suburbs, many street signs are hard to find and hard to read. Also, many suburbs don't have street lights; it can get very dark out there.

Parking in Pittsburgh

Within the city, as in most cities, parking can be difficult and expensive. Downtown daily parking rates range from $6 to $17. The most economical downtown parking is offered by the Pittsburgh Parking Authority. And the farther you're willing to walk from the center of town, the less you'll pay. Bargain rates begin in the late afternoon and after 6 p.m. daily and all day Sunday at parking meters.

Parking at Three Rivers Stadium is affordable for commuters, but it is not available on game days. Parking spots on the Mon Wharf are also a bargain, but they have an unfortunate tendency to disappear underwater when the river is high.

Neighborhood parking can also be hard to come by. There are even stories of residents reserving curbside parking spots in front of their own

---

Driving Tips

- *Rule #1: You can't get there from here.*
- *Pittsburgh drivers can be overly polite; often they will stop the flow of traffic on a busy road to allow someone to enter from a side street or turn left in front of them. Be alert so you don't plow into the rear end of one of these generous souls.*
- *How to make a Pittsburgh merge: Come to a full stop at a Yield sign before merging slowly into the flow of traffic.*
- *Warning: Many Pittsburghers slow down inside tunnels to less than the 35-mile-per-hour speed limit.*
- *Note: There is a "runaway truck sandpile" on the Parkway West approach to the Fort Pitt Tunnel. Don't laugh. It is there for a good reason . . . a truck loaded with bananas once crashed into the tunnel entrance after losing its brakes.*
- *Elderly "Sunday drivers" like to get an early start in Pittsburgh; they're on the roads all week.*
- *Caution: Most roads have no shoulders, are narrow and winding, and have only two lanes. Watch out for foolhardy joggers and bikers in all kinds of weather, day or night.*

---

homes with lawn chairs. Some neighborhoods are posted with Resident Parking Permit signs and allow only an hour or two of parking without a permit.

Some boroughs also prohibit overnight on-street parking without police permission. Also, take note of designated street-cleaning days; signs announce when on-street parking is prohibited.

Parking in the suburbs is generally not a problem, except during the holidays. The malls offer free parking, but they attract overflow crowds of shoppers on major shopping days, such as the day after Thanksgiving.

Biking in Pittsburgh

Pittsburgh presents numerous challenges to bicycle riders, not the least of which are the hilly terrain, narrow roadways, and heavy traffic. Nevertheless, there are some urban cycling commuters; they cheered the opening of the "Jail Trail," running roughly parallel to the Monongahela River and connecting downtown with Greenfield. The nickname stems from the location of the downtown end of the trail, just beyond the Allegheny County Jail. The paved path, also available for walkers, joggers, and in-line skaters, snakes between heavily traveled roads, alongside Second Avenue and the Parkway East.

There is also a city bicycle route from Highland Park, connecting Mellon, Frick, and Schenley Parks. Call Citiparks at 412/255-2676 for information. Within Allegheny County as a whole, bike paths can be found in county parks. See Chapter 10: "Sports and Recreation" for more information. Some bikers enjoy the city's winding back roads despite their narrowness and lack of shoulders. Remember to follow the rules of bicycle safety at all times. Children 12 years of age and younger are required by law to wear helmets while riding a bicycle.

Airports

The Greater Pittsburgh International Airport (412/472-3500) is the major airport serving the region. Smaller planes also fly into the Allegheny County Airport in West Mifflin (412/461-4300).

Major Airlines Serving Pittsburgh
American 800/433-7300
British Airways 800/247-9297
Continental 800/525-0280
Delta 800/221-1212
Northwest 800/225-2525
TWA 412/391-3600
US Airways 800/428-4322
United 800/241-6522

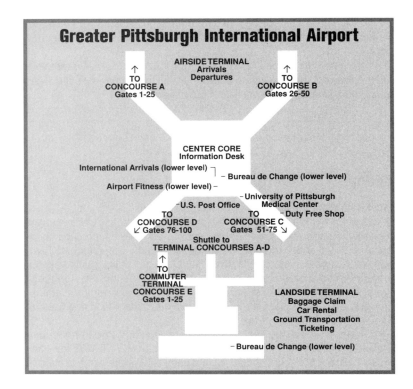

Train Service

The city's Amtrak station is located just east of Grant Street on Liberty Avenue, across from the Greyhound terminal. Three passenger trains serve Pittsburgh daily: the *Capitol Limited*, *Three Rivers*, and *Pennsylvanian*. Pittsburgh has access to the full Amtrak system, but some destinations require a bus/train combination. For more information contact Amtrak, 1100 Liberty Avenue, 412/471-6172 or 800/USA-RAIL.

Bus Service

There is a Greyhound bus terminal downtown at 11th Street and Liberty Avenue, 412/392-0194. A second bus terminal is located in Monroeville at 220 Mall Circle Drive, near the Monroeville Mall, 412/856-3080. For general Greyhound Bus Lines information, call 800/231-2222.

Hedrich Blessing

3

WHERE TO STAY

Pittsburgh has hosted its share of visitors, from its days as "the Gateway to the West" for early pioneers to its role today as a major hub for US Airways and international travelers. From Mars to Moon (Township) and beyond, from luxury hotels to charming bed-and-breakfasts to economical motels, Pittsburgh has accommodations of all types and in all locations. The special pleasures and treasures of Pittsburgh may take a little effort to find, but they are well worth it.

The following price-rating symbols indicate the cost of a double room per night:

Price-rating symbols:

$	Under $65
$$	$66 to $90
$$$	$91 to $135
$$$$	Over $135

DOWNTOWN PITTSBURGH

Hotels

DOUBLETREE HOTEL PITTSBURGH
1000 Penn Ave.
Pittsburgh
412/281-3700 or 800/222-TREE
$$$$
Located next to the David Lawrence Convention Center and a block away from the Federal Building, the Doubletree is convenient to the eastern end of the Golden Triangle. Two restaurants offer everything from buffets to fine dining. The 26-story hotel has 616 rooms and 42 suites. Six rooms have kitchens, and some are non-smoking. Out-of-town transportation is readily available, with shuttles to the airport or the nearby Greyhound Bus Terminal

DOWNTOWN PITTSBURGH

Where to Stay in Downtown Pittsburgh

1 DoubleTree Hotel Pittsburgh
2 Pittsburgh Hilton and Towers
3 Pittsburgh Marriott City Center
4 Ramada Plaza Suites
5 Westin William Penn

and Amtrak station. There is a charge for parking in the hotel garage. The hotel has an indoor swimming pool and exercise room. Chocolate-chip cookies are notable Doubletree amenities. Pets are allowed. Reservations can be guaranteed with a credit card. ♿ (Downtown Pittsburgh)

PITTSBURGH HILTON AND TOWERS
Gateway Center
Pittsburgh
412/391-4600 or 800/916-2221
$$$

The 24-story Hilton commands the best view in town, overlooking Point State Park, the three rivers, and downtown. There are 711 guest rooms and 35 suites. Guests can enjoy the health club. Multi-line phones are available for computer access, and there are in-room fax machines. The concierge can assist with any special arrangements. There is a charge for parking in the hotel garage. Small pets are allowed. The hotel has two restaurants and in summertime a charming sidewalk café. Special service is offered for the hearing impaired, and non-smoking rooms are available. A shuttle provides transportation to the airport. During the Three Rivers Arts Festival, food vendors set up shop opposite the Hilton, while exhibits, booths, and outdoor concerts fill the Gateway Center area. ♿ (Downtown Pittsburgh)

PITTSBURGH MARRIOTT CITY CENTER
112 Washington Place
Pittsburgh
412/471-4000
$$$$

On the outer edge of the Golden Triangle, on Centre Avenue near Crosstown Boulevard, the Marriott is located opposite the Civic Arena, home of the Pittsburgh Penguins hockey team. The hotel offers two suites, 401 guest rooms (some non-smoking), and a dining room. Banquet room capacity is 700; 14 meeting rooms can handle 1,000 people. The recently renovated 21-story hotel also offers guests a heated indoor pool, saunas, and health club. No pets are allowed. There is service for the hearing impaired. Roll-in showers are available. Fee parking and airport transportation are available ♿ (Downtown Pittsburgh)

RAMADA PLAZA SUITES
One Bigelow Square
Pittsburgh
412/281-5800 or 800/228-2828
$$$

Just blocks away from Steel Plaza, USX Tower, Allegheny Court House, Grant Street, and the Civic Arena, the Ramada offers walking-around accessibility to much of the eastern Golden Triangle. The hotel is best reached via the Seventh Street exit off I-579 or Seventh Street from downtown. There

Westin William Penn, p. 30

Hedrich Blessing

American Youth Hostels (AYH) is an organization for people of all ages who are interested in low-cost travel opportunities and recreational activities. Elderhostel offers travel, educational, and recreational activities for senior citizens at affordable prices. Contact AYH Pittsburgh at 412/431-1267 or AYH Activities Headquarters, 6300 Fifth Avenue, Pittsburgh, 412/362-8181.

is a fee for parking in the valet-attended hotel garage. The Ruddy Duck Restaurant and Lounge offers a clubby atmosphere for casual dining. The 311 suites are great for extended stays; the hotel provides room service and daily maid service for longer-term guests. There are two suites with wheelchair access; make advance reservations. The health club with a heated indoor pool is a real plus; use of the Downtown Athletic Club facilities is free for hotel guests. ♿ (Downtown Pittsburgh)

WESTIN WILLIAM PENN
530 William Penn Place
Pittsburgh
412/281-7100 or 800/937-8461
$$$$
Built in 1916, the William Penn is Pittsburgh's oldest hotel, a venerable but still viable institution. Guests in formal evening dress and wedding gowns are often seen passing through its elegant lobby to one of 25 ballrooms and meeting rooms. Banquet room capacity is 1,000. Nearby Mellon Square is a lovely little urban park, ideal for people-watching. Guests in one of the 550 rooms or 45 suites can luxuriate with 24-hour room service, voice mail, and a 24-hour fitness center. The full-service Terrace Restaurant features a daily high tea and Sunday brunch. Reservations are suggested; call 412/553-5235. The Tap Room offers a more informal sandwich and salad menu. Non-smoking

rooms available. Pets are allowed. ♿ (Downtown Pittsburgh)

NORTH PITTSBURGH

Hotels

HAMPTON INN
PITTSBURGH
4575 McKnight Rd.
Pittsburgh
412/939-3200 or 800/426-7866
$$
This Hampton Inn offers easy access to downtown but can be a little tricky to find: take the McKnight Road exit off I-275 heading north, make a dogleg turn right into the second driveway of the Amoco Station, turn left at the traffic light back onto McKnight Road; the hotel is on your right. Deluxe accommodations make the journey worthwhile: a full fitness center is open 24 hours a day, and three whirlpool suites are available. There are 61 rooms, and each has a computer modem hookup, cable TV and HBO, coffeemaker, hair dryer, and iron with ironing board. A laundry facility is on the premises. Guests get a complimentary continental breakfast. Non-smoking rooms are available. No pets are allowed. ♿ (North Pittsburgh)

THE PRIORY: A CITY INN
614 Pressley St.
Pittsburgh
412/231-3338

The Priory

$$$

Ask a Pittsburgher, "Where would you like to stay in Pittsburgh?" and chances are the answer will be The Priory, an historic landmark converted in 1986 into a European-style inn. A former parsonage, located only one-half mile from downtown, The Priory offers free parking and a free week-day shuttle to downtown, scheduled to accommodate guests' needs. There are only 24 rooms, a reservation deposit is required, and there is a cancellation fee. The three-story building has no elevator, but accommodations for the wheelchair-bound are available on the first floor. Complimentary continental breakfasts and evening wine are offered. In summer, wrought-iron tables near a fountain in the courtyard provide a marvelous setting for breakfast or for unwinding with a glass of wine. The Grand Hall at The Priory is a banquet facility with catering available for 125 to 650 people. Non-smoking rooms are available. The inn does not accommodate pets.
♿ (North Pittsburgh)

SEWICKLEY COUNTRY INN
801 Ohio River Blvd. (Rte. 65)
Sewickley
412/741-4300
$$

Sewickley, an affluent Pittsburgh suburb, is a world unto itself. It has wonderful mansions and fantastic turn-of-the-century architecture from castles to cottages, a quaint village atmosphere, and a charming shopping district. The inn has 149 rooms, including ten suites and a Jacuzzi suite. Ask about a senior discount. The two-story structure has no elevator but it does have an outdoor heated pool. Guests receive complimentary passes for the fitness center at the well-equipped Sewickley Y. Non-smoking rooms are available. Pets are allowed. The River Room and the Sweetwater Lounge are popular area dinner spots. Both Ohio River Boulevard and I-79 offer convenient access to the city and beyond. Be aware: Speed limits are strictly enforced along Ohio River Boulevard.
♿ (North Pittsburgh)

NORTH PITTSBURGH

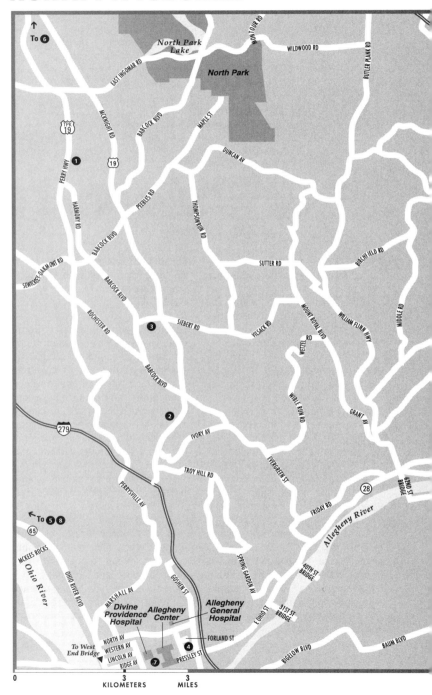

To 6

North Park Lake

North Park

EAST INGOMAR RD

MONTOUR RD

WILDWOOD RD

BUTLER PLANK RD

MCKNIGHT RD

BABCOCK BLVD

MAPLE ST

DUNCAN AV

TPK 19

19

PERRY HWY

1

HARMONY RD

PEEBLES RD

THOMPSON RUN RD

BABCOCK BLVD

SUTTER RD

BIRCHFIELD RD

SEWICKLEY-OAKMONT RD

BABCOCK BLVD

ROCHESTER RD

SIEBERT RD

3

VILSACK RD

MOUNT ROYAL BLVD

WILLIAM FLINN HWY

MIDDLE RD

WETZEL RD

BABCOCK BLVD

2

GRANT AV

WIBLE RUN RD

IVORY AV

279

TROY HILL RD

EVERGREEN ST

28

62ND ST BRIDGE

Allegheny River

PERRYSVILLE AV

FRIDAY RD

To 5 8

65

MCKEES ROCKS

Ohio River

OHIO RIVER BLVD

GOSHEN ST

SPRING GARDEN AV

40TH ST BRIDGE

31ST ST BRIDGE

MARSHALL AV

Divine Providence Hospital

Allegheny Center

Allegheny General Hospital

E OHIO ST

FORLAND ST

BIGELOW BLVD

BAUM BLVD

To West End Bridge

NORTH AV

WESTERN AV

LINCOLN AV

RIDGE AV

4

7

PRESSLEY ST

0   3   3
        KILOMETERS   MILES

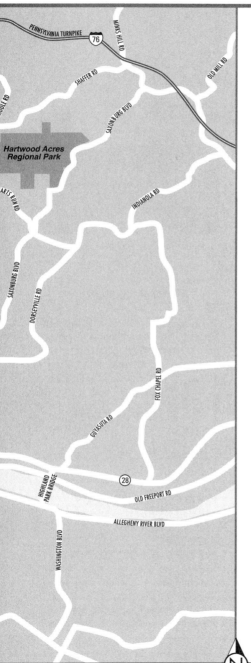

Where to Stay in
North Pittsburgh

1 Econo Lodge-Pittsburgh North
2 Hampton Inn Pittsburgh
3 Holiday Inn Pittsburgh-
  McKnight Road
4 The Priory: A City Inn
5 Sewickley Country Inn
6 Sheraton Inn-Pittsburgh North
7 Victoria House Bed & Breakfast
8 Whistlestop Bed & Breakfast

SHERATON INN-PITTSBURGH NORTH
910 Sheraton Dr.
Cranberry
724/776-6900 or 800/325-3535
$$$

The "Warrendale Sheraton," as many Pittsburghers call this hotel, is only minutes from the Pennsylvania Turnpike, I-79, and Route 19N. The five-story structure has a spectacular light-filled atrium, an "open-air" café with awninged tables and bar, and a glass-walled elevator. A fabulous Sunday brunch buffet draws crowds. A coffee shop, the Tremont House restaurant, a gift shop, and pricey boutiques are also located within the lobby. There are 191 rooms and four suites; non-smoking rooms are available. All rooms have coffee pots, hair dryers, irons, and ironing boards, in addition to voice mail. Interior rooms have small balconies overlooking the lobby and its fountain. There is both an indoor and an outdoor pool and an exercise room. No pets allowed. &. (North Pittsburgh)

Motels

ECONO LODGE-PITTSBURGH NORTH
107 VIP Dr.
Wexford
724/935-1000 or 800/553-2666
$

Just minutes from I-79, this two-story motel has 50 rooms but no elevator. Two wheelchair-accessible rooms are located on the first floor. Non-smoking rooms are available. Some rooms have kitchens. Ask for the senior discount. No pets allowed. &. (North Pittsburgh)

HAMPTON INN CRANBERRY
210 Executive Dr.

Appletree B&B

Appletree Bed & Breakfast, p. 38

Cranberry
724/776-1000 or 426-7866
$$

A heated indoor pool and hearing-impaired service make this Cranberry Hampton Inn distinctive. Extensive shopping is available along nearby Route 19, from books to bath accessories. Restaurants and fast food abound in the area. The four-story Hampton Inn has 117 rooms; four are wheelchair accessible, some are non-smoking. An exercise room is open daily. No pets allowed. &. (North Pittsburgh)

HOLIDAY INN PITTSBURGH-MCKNIGHT ROAD
4859 McKnight Rd.
Pittsburgh
412/366-5200 or 800/HOLIDAY
$$$

Perched on a hillside overlooking bustling North Hills traffic, this Holiday Inn offers direct access to downtown Pittsburgh, three large shopping malls, two cinema multiplexes, and scenic North Park. Longnecker's Restaurant offers full-service dining and a special Sunday brunch. Five luxury suites and 146 guest rooms have coffee service and phone message alert. Some rooms have microwave ovens and refrigerators. Non-smoking rooms and business services are available. Pets are allowed.

Finding this Holiday Inn requires steady nerves and sharp eyes, however. Head north from Pittsburgh about 2.5 miles on McKnight Road from the I-279 McKnight Road exit, turn left at the traffic light into North Hills Village Mall, and follow the signs beyond the mall. Approaching from the north is easier: 12 miles south on Route 19 (McKnight Road) from Pennsylvania Turnpike exit 3, turn right at the small Holiday Inn sign just past Siebert Road. ৬ (North Pittsburgh)

Bed-and-Breakfasts

VICTORIA HOUSE BED & BREAKFAST
939 Western Ave.
Pittsburgh
412/231-4948
$$$
Within the historic Allegheny West neighborhood on Pittsburgh's near North Side, Victoria House Bed & Breakfast is a magnificently restored, three-story, 27-room mansion and carriage house, fully furnished with high-Victorian antiques. Six guest rooms include four suites with private baths, the carriage house, and one standard guest room with a private hall bath. A full breakfast is served from 7:30 to 10. Depending on the weather or guest preferences, breakfast can be served in the dining room, guest rooms, or the back verandah—from which you can enjoy a private English garden surrounded by a brick wall. In the evening, a complimentary bar is open in the library. Guests get a 20 percent discount across the street at Cafe Victoria. A deposit or credit card guarantee is required for reservations. Free off-street parking is available for all guests. TVs are limited to a common viewing area in the library, one suite, and the carriage house. No pets allowed. (North Pittsburgh)

WHISTLESTOP BED & BREAKFAST
195 Broad St.
Leetsdale
724/251-0852
$$
The Whistlestop Bed & Breakfast is a restored 1888 house, originally built in affiliation with the communal Harmony Society, which built the towns of Economy and Harmony in western Pennsylvania. The house itself is about two

T
i
P

Four in-town bed-and-breakfasts—**Appletree Bed & Breakfast**, **Morning Glory Inn**, **Shadyside Bed & Breakfast**, and **Victoria House Bed & Breakfast**—participate in Light-Up Night Downtown at the opening of Sparkle Season (November). If you stay in one of the inns, you'll get first choice of tickets for the Holiday House Tour, which includes the inns, glorious in their Victorian holiday splendor. The Association of Pittsburgh Area Bed & Breakfasts and Molly's Trolleys joined forces for this charity benefit event.

miles north of picturesque Sewickley along Ohio River Boulevard. Whistlestop has two guest suites, each with a private bath, phone, air-conditioning, and cable TV. The entire house is smoke-free. A full hot breakfast is served each morning in the dining room, although a beautiful summer morning may call for outdoor dining. Pets are in residence; the owners prefer that guests not bring their own pets unless absolutely necessary. The Whistlestop is named and decorated with a railroad theme in honor of the trains that still travel along the banks of the Ohio River through Leetsdale. (North Pittsburgh)

EAST PITTSBURGH

Hotels

AL MONZO'S PALACE INN
2275 Mosside Blvd.
Monroeville
412/372-5500
$$
This highly personalized establishment emphasizes recreation, featuring a night club, game room, volleyball court, and indoor and outdoor pools. Nine suites, 262 guest rooms, and a coffee shop are available. The location offers an abundance of shopping malls, dining choices, and nearby Boyce Park. Getting there does require maneuvering through dense rush-hour traffic, however. ♿ (East Pittsburgh)

HAMPTON INN AT UNIVERSITY CENTER
3315 Hamlet St.
Pittsburgh
412/681-1000 or 800/426-7866
$$$
Free shuttle service to Oakland and downtown and free parking are real pluses here. A continental breakfast is complimentary. Pets under 40 pounds are allowed. There are 132 rooms, some are non-smoking. ♿ (East Pittsburgh)

HOLIDAY INN SELECT-UNIVERSITY CENTER
100 Lytton Ave.
Pittsburgh
412/682-6200 or 800/HOLIDAY
$$$
For real jazz lovers, Foster's, the Holiday Inn Select lounge, is THE place to be. Friday and Saturday, hear top local jazz players; Sunday, listen to Pittsburgh Jazz Society bands. Join the society and get food and drink discounts. Only a block away from Pitt's Cathedral of Learning, this Holiday Inn is in the heart of Oakland. In addition to the usual Holiday Inn amenities, Executive Edition-Business Traveler rooms feature two phones, in-room coffee service, hair dryers, irons, and ironing boards. There are 251 guest rooms and three suites. ♿ (East Pittsburgh)

RADISSON HOTEL PITTSBURGH
101 Mall Blvd.
Monroeville
412/373-7300 or 800/333-3333
$$$$
The Radisson offers 322 rooms and 46 suites. A business center, valet service, and in-room minibars are notable extras, in addition to in-room coffeemakers. The hotel features both indoor and outdoor pools. The dining room draws visitors and long-time Pittsburghers alike with its exciting dinner shows—from "you-solve-it" mysteries to Broadway-style reviews to "Pittsburgh Opry" silliness. The season runs March through December; call 412/856-5159 for reservations. Airport transportation and

EAST PITTSBURGH

Where to Stay in East Pittsburgh

1 Al Monzo's Palace Inn
2 Appletree Bed & Breakfast
3 Hampton Inn at University Center
4 Ramada Inn
5 Holiday Inn Select–University Center
6 The Inn at Oakmont
7 Radisson Hotel Pittsburgh
8 Red Roof Inn–Monroeville
9 Shadyside Bed & Breakfast
10 Sunnyledge Hotel & Tea Room

Most hotels in the Pittsburgh area routinely provide free local calling.

non-smoking rooms are available. No pets allowed. 👤 (East Pittsburgh)

RAMADA INN
699 Rodi Rd.
Monroeville
412/244-1600 or 800/321-2323
$$$
The Ramada has 152 guest rooms and "Junior Olympic-size" indoor and outdoor pools. Saunas and whirlpool baths add a touch of luxurious indulgence. Lighted tennis courts are an out-of-the-ordinary extra. On weekends, the dining room features live entertainment. Airport transportation, coffee, and a daily newspaper are free. Non-smoking accommodations are available; some rooms have roll-in showers. No pets allowed. Reservations must be put on a credit card. Ask about the senior discount and the very special weekend package. 👤 (East Pittsburgh)

SUNNYLEDGE HOTEL &
TEA ROOM
5124 Fifth Ave.
Pittsburgh
412/683-5014
$$$$
International leaders, visiting scholars, and celebrities can be found among the discerning clientele of this elegant and luxurious European-style hotel. Beautiful surroundings and superb service are hallmarks of the hotel, a significant historical landmark. Sunnyledge, built in the late 1880s, was the private home of Andrew Carnegie's personal physician.

The hotel has 10 guest rooms, including three suites. All rooms have the standard amenities and more: private phones, TV, minibars stocked with an assortment of beverages and delicacies. Each room has its own bath, renovated in white Corinthian marble, with an extra-deep bathtub. An exercise room is available for guests 24 hours a day. A lounge and dining room, which serves high tea, Sunday brunch, lunch, and dinner, are open to the public. Credit card guarantee is required for reservation; there is a fee for cancellation. No pets allowed. 👤 (East Pittsburgh)

Motels

RED ROOF INN-MONROEVILLE
2729 Mosside Blvd.
Monroeville
412/856-4738
$
The Monroeville location puts you right into Mall Heaven: shopping, movies, restaurants, acres of free parking. The three-story Red Roof Inn has 117 rooms; corridors are exterior. Small pets are allowed. Non-smoking accommodations are available. Guarantee reservations with a credit card. 👤 (East Pittsburgh)

Bed-and-Breakfasts

APPLETREE BED & BREAKFAST
703 S. Negley Ave.
Pittsburgh
412/661-0631
$$$

Shadyside's charming shopping districts (Ellsworth Shops and Walnut Street shops) are within walking distance and Oakland's University Center is minutes away. Once featured in *Gourmet* magazine, the three-story house, built in 1884, has been described as "an unusual combination of late Victorian and Italianate architecture." There are five guest rooms, one of which occupies the entire top floor and has a separate sitting room. Each room has a private full bath. A complete homemade breakfast is served each morning; a continental-style breakfast is also available. Complimentary tea, coffee, and cookies are always available. This is a non-smoking facility. No pets allowed. Free off-street parking. (East Pittsburgh)

THE INN AT OAKMONT
300 Rte. 909
Verona
412/828-0410
$$$

It was built just five years ago, but the

Shadyside Bed and Breakfast

Tom Cwenar

distinctive white clapboard building with black shutters, high ceilings, and abundant moldings is furnished with a blend of new pieces and family heirlooms that re-creates the stately, elegant tone of the Federal period. A full gourmet breakfast is served in the large dining room. Two guest rooms have fireplaces and whirlpool baths. Extras include private phones and separate modem jacks, TVs, radio alarm clocks, soothing white-noise "sleep machines," bathrobes, hair dryers, irons, and ironing boards. The inn is a non-smoking facility. Reservations must be guaranteed with a credit card; 48-hour notice required; full cancellation fee. No pets. ♿ (East Pittsburgh)

SHADYSIDE BED & BREAKFAST
5516 Maple Heights Rd.
Pittsburgh
412/683-6501
$$$

This 1903 stone manor house, the last of three mansions on a private lane, at one time was the private home of the prominent Oliver family of Pittsburgh (Oliver Street downtown is named for them.) The eight guest rooms are furnished with antiques. All have queen-size beds, and all but two have private baths. All guest rooms are on the second floor. A deluxe continental breakfast featuring fresh fruit, croissants, bagels, and muffins is available from 7 to 9 weekdays in the large formal dining room. On weekends, breakfast is available from 8 to 10 and includes quiche or various egg dishes. There is an informal evening Happy Hour on Friday and Saturday. On weekdays, complimentary evening wine is available. The Shadyside's hilltop site overlooks Fifth Avenue and is within walking distance of distinctive shops and public transportation. There is free off-street

Hampton Inn

parking, a treasure in this neighborhood. (East Pittsburgh)

SOUTH PITTSBURGH

Hotels

HAMPTON INN
1550 Lebanon Church Rd.
Pittsburgh
412/650-1000 or 800/426-7866
$$
Easy access to the Allegheny County Airport, South Park, and the rest of the South Hills make this Hampton Inn a prime choice. Just two years old, it's three stories tall and has 70 rooms. Access to and from the

city is also easy but allow plenty of time for rush-hour traffic. & (South Pittsburgh)

HOLIDAY INN-PITTSBURGH SOUTH
162 Fort Couch Rd.
Pittsburgh
412/833-5300 or 800/HOLIDAY
$$
Staying across the road from South Hills Village Mall means more than shopping 'til dropping. It also means that the T station at the mall makes it easy to get to the Golden Triangle and Station Square. The hotel has 210 guest rooms. Small pets are allowed. An outdoor pool is ready for summertime enjoyment. Hearing-impaired fa-

For a spectacular night in Pittsburgh, book a room downtown with a view of the Fourth of July, Regatta, or Light Up Night fireworks displays. Be sure to call well in advance for reservations—maybe even a year ahead. Ask about weekend packages for sporting events, special shows, or a super Christmas shopping and sightseeing expedition.

SOUTHWEST PITTSBURGH

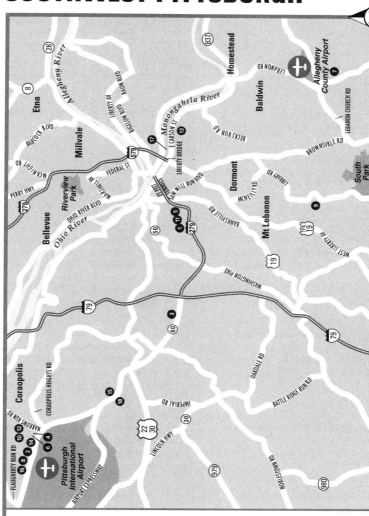

**Where to Stay
In Southwest Pittsburgh**

1 Best Western–Parkway Center Inn (WP)
2 Clarion-Royce Hotel (WP)
3 Clubhouse Inn (WP)
4 Courtyard by Marriott (WP)
5 Days Inn Pittsburgh (SP)
6 Embassy Suites Hotel (SP)
7 Hampton Inn (SP)
8 Hampton Inn Hotel Airport (WP)
9 Holiday Inn-Pittsburgh (SP)
10 Holiday Inn-Pittsburgh Airport (WP)
11 Holiday Inn-Pittsburgh Central (WP)
12 La Quinta Inn Airport (WP)
13 Morning Glory Inn (SP)
14 Motel 6 Airport (WP)
15 Pittsburgh Airport Marriott (WP)
16 Red Roof Inn Pittsburgh Airport(WP)
17 Sheraton Hotel Station Square (SP)
18 Wyndham Garden Hotel (WP)

*Note: This map includes South and
West Pittsburgh zone listings.*

cilities and non-smoking rooms are available. All rooms have microwave ovens and refrigerators. You'll wake up to a complimentary copy of *USA Today* and free coffee. The dining room, Georgine's Restaurant, provides full service for all meals. Airport transportation is available. & (South Pittsburgh)

SHERATON HOTEL STATION SQUARE
7 Station Square Dr.
Pittsburgh
412/261-2000 or 800/255-7488
$$$$

Staying at the Station Square Sheraton means easy access to wonderful dining, entertainment, shopping, and sightseeing. The spectacular light-filled atrium with its soaring girders gives the restaurant and lounge an open-air feel. Waterfall-fed pools and lush foliage add to the pleasant illusion. There is an indoor pool and fitness center. In-room coffee service is offered. On weekdays, a courtesy shuttle transports guests to the Golden Triangle. Small pets are allowed; security deposit or credit card imprint is required at check-in. Non-smoking accommodations are available. & (South Pittsburgh)

Motels

DAYS INN PITTSBURGH
1150 Banksville Rd. (Rt. 19)
Pittsburgh
412/531-8900
$

Located south of the city, this Days Inn is easily accessible to both downtown Pittsburgh and the airport, either by car or shuttle bus. The downtown shuttle is free, and the airport shuttle costs $8 one way. The Maharajah restaurant and lounge is conveniently located on-site. A free continental breakfast is available for all guests. The outdoor pool is a summertime plus. No pets are allowed. This two-story Days Inn has a total of 70 rooms. Only one room is wheelchair accessible. (South Pittsburgh)

Bed-and-Breakfasts

MORNING GLORY INN
2119 Sarah St.
Pittsburgh
412/431-1707
$$$

Located in the historic South Side neighborhood, the Morning Glory Inn is within walking distance of "the best restaurants and shops in Pittsburgh." The three-story brick Victorian of Italianate style was built in 1862 for John G. Fisher, owner of a prosperous brickyard across the street. Two porches overlook the garden, and the large front parlor has an antique grand piano, which guests are welcome to play. Each of the five guest rooms has a private bath, a private phone line, a digital answering machine, a computer hookup, TV, clock radio, desk, and reading chair. A full gourmet breakfast with freshly squeezed orange juice is served in the spacious breakfast room each morning; special diets can be accommodated. In the evening, complimentary sherry is available in the library. Fresh flowers throughout the house, a no-smoking rule, and valet parking are other special features. (South Pittsburgh)

WEST PITTSBURGH

Hotels

CLARION-ROYCE HOTEL
1160 Thorn Run Rd.

Coraopolis
412/262-2400
$$$

A Coraopolis (Corry-op-o-lis) location means good airport accessibility. Clarion-Royce guarantees that, with 24-hour airport shuttle service for guests. Four suites and 189 guest rooms are available in the elegant cream and burgundy structure. Non-smoking accommodations and roll-in showers are also available. Extras include concierge service and data ports. Remington's, the full-service restaurant and lounge on-site, is "Pittsburgh's Number One Home of the Oldies." There is a heated outdoor swimming pool. No pets allowed. Ask about the senior discount. &. (West Pittsburgh)

COURTYARD BY MARRIOTT
450 Cherrington Parkway
Coraopolis
412/264-5000
$$

Easy to reach off Business 60, this Courtyard has 148 rooms and nine suites. A fitness center offers a heated indoor swimming pool, whirlpools, and an exercise room. All rooms have coffeemakers, and guests get complimentary copies of *USA Today*. The small restaurant is open 6 to 10 p.m. weekdays; 7 to 11 a.m. Saturday, and from 7 a.m. to noon Sunday. No pets allowed. Airport transportation available. &. (West Pittsburgh)

EMBASSY SUITES HOTEL
550 Cherrington Parkway
Coraopolis
412/269-9070
$$$

The breathtaking atrium filled with trees and lush tropical plants, a trout stream, and a sparkling waterfall are sure to make any Pittsburgh stay a memorable one. Comfortable, well-appointed suites are equipped for the convenience of the business or vacationing traveler. Standard amenities include coffeemaker, microwave, and refrigerator. Full business services are available, and all suites have two-line phones. Complimentary extras begin with a super-fresh, cooked-to-order breakfast and end with an evening beverage reception. Guests are welcome to use the heated indoor swimming pool, sauna, whirlpool, and exercise center. Some suites have galley kitchens. A limited number of roll-in showers are available; request in advance. This air traveler–friendly facility also offers a free airport shuttle. Pets are welcome. Access from the airport is easy: take the Coraopolis-Sewickley Exit off Business Route 60, then immediately east onto the Cherrington Parkway. &. (West Pittsburgh)

HOLIDAY INN-PITTSBURGH AIRPORT
1406 Beers School Rd.
Coraopolis
412/262-3600 or 800/HOLIDAY
$$$

The largest Holiday Inn in Pittsburgh, this is also the closest to the Greater Pittsburgh International Airport, only one mile north of Business 60. The 11-story hotel has 256 rooms and one suite. It offers guests a large indoor pool and whirlpool. Through affiliation with nearby World Class Fitness, guests can work out for a discounted $5 fee. The Beef and Burgundy is a full-service restaurant. Data ports are in all rooms. Some rooms have a coffeemaker, microwave oven, and refrigerator, and there is a coin laundry on premises. Business services and non-smoking rooms are available, pets are allowed, and the hotel offers a free 24-hour airport shuttle. & (West Pittsburgh)

HOLIDAY INN-PITTSBURGH CENTRAL
401 Holiday Dr.
Greentree
412/922-8100
$$$

Guests enjoy privileges at the nearby Greentree Racquet Club, in addition to use of an on-site exercise room and outdoor pool. Harlan Longnecker's Restaurant and Lounge is a full-service restaurant open from 6 a.m. to 10 p.m. The hotel has 200 guest rooms. Microwaves and refrigerators are available on request. Small pets 30 pounds and under are allowed. Free area transportation includes airport and downtown shuttles. & (West Pittsburgh)

PITTSBURGH AIRPORT MARRIOTT
100 Aten Rd.
Coraopolis
412/788-8800
$$$$

In addition to indoor and outdoor swimming, the Pittsburgh Airport Marriott offers special services for the hearing impaired. The on-site dining room makes mealtimes convenient for those who choose not to explore the nearby restaurants. Small pets only are allowed in this 15-story, 314 room hotel. (West Pittsburgh)

WYNDHAM GARDEN HOTEL
1 Wyndham Circle
Coraopolis
724/695-0002
$$$$

This business-oriented hotel offers an office away from the home office—with in-room amenities such as coffeemakers, data ports, and high-quality lighting. Hearing-

impaired service is available on the telephones. There is an exercise room for working off workday tension. The Garden Cafe is open for weekday breakfast from 6:30 to 10 and for dinner from 5 to 10. The Lobby Terrace is the on-site lounge. Small pets are allowed by pre-arrangement. The hotel's 140 rooms on four floors have elevator service. & (West Pittsburgh)

Motels

BEST WESTERN-PARKWAY CENTER INN
875 Greentree Rd.
Pittsburgh
412/922-7070 or 800/528-1234
$$$

There are 138 rooms in this six-story facility; 44 are efficiencies. Some rooms have coffeemakers, microwave ovens, and refrigerators. Special extras include an exercise room, indoor pool, whirlpool, and sauna. There is a free evening beverage service from 5 to 7. Every morning is special, with a complimentary breakfast and a newspaper to enjoy with it. Weekly or monthly rates are available; there is a coin laundry. Small pets are allowed, with a $25 deposit at check-in. Non-smoking accommodations, hearing-impaired facilities, business services, and airport transportation are also available. The motel is located right on the way into Pittsburgh from the airport. Credit card guarantees reservation. & (West Pittsburgh)

CLUBHOUSE INN
5311 Campbells Run Rd.
Pittsburgh
412/788-8400 or 800/CLUB-INN
$$

An airport-handy location (right on I-279 and Route 22/30), an evening manager's reception with complimentary beverages, and a full breakfast buffet are benefits at this Clubhouse Inn. There are 152 rooms including 26 suites and executive rooms. The Clubhouse also has a heated outdoor pool and an indoor whirlpool spa. Coffeemakers, microwave ovens, and refrigerators are standard for the executive rooms and suites. No pets are allowed. Non-smoking rooms and free airport transportation are available. ♿ (West Pittsburgh)

HAMPTON INN HOTEL AIRPORT
1420 Beers School Rd.
Coraopolis
412/264-0020
$$

The hotel on Beers School Road, only one mile north of Business 60, is easily accessible to the airport, and free airport transportation is provided. All rooms have irons and ironing boards. Copier and fax service are available. ♿ (West Pittsburgh)

LAQUINTA INN AIRPORT
1433 Beers School Rd.
Coraopolis
412/269-0400
$

With 127 rooms on three floors, this motel has plenty of room to accommodate air travelers and other area visitors. Small pets are allowed to stay with their owners. (West Pittsburgh)

MOTEL 6 AIRPORT
1170 Thorn Run Rd.
Corapolis
412/269-0990
$

Easily accessible to the airport off Business Route 60 at the Coraopolis-Sewickley exit, Motel 6 fills the basic travelers' need for a clean, comfortable, secure place to spend the night. Small pets are welcome. (West Pittsburgh).

RED ROOF INN
PITTSBURGH AIRPORT
1454 Beers School Rd.
Coraopolis
412/264-5678
$

This economical, airport-accessible motel offers a free airport shuttle and 119 rooms on three floors. There is no on-site restaurant, but hungry guests have their choice of several nearby fast-food and casual restaurants. The motel's exercise room is an extra bonus. Pets are also welcome at this Red Roof Inn. ♿ (West Pittsburgh)

Doina Locke

4

Pittsburgh has more restaurants per capita than any other city of comparable size in the country. Within the Golden Triangle and the Cultural District, Oakland, Shadyside, Squirrel Hill, Station Square, and East Carson Street, the abundance of restaurants, nightclubs, and fast-food outlets is staggering. In recent years, the suburban restaurant scene has improved enormously, with a large numbers of restaurants gaining almost instant popularity.

Pittsburgh also has many expert chefs, with devoted fans who follow them from one restaurant to the next. Pittsburgh's diverse ethnic heritage, while not reflected as strongly in its restaurants as you might expect, nevertheless influences menus. You'll find international and regional specialties including kielbasa, antipasto, pierogies, grits, and barbecue ribs.

The following price-rating symbols reflect the cost of one meal (appetizer and entrée).

Price-rating symbols:
$ **Under $10**
$$ **$11 to $20**
$$$ **$21 and up**

American

Bobby Rubino's (SP) p. 72
Café Allegro (SP) p. 72
Café Victoria (NP) p. 53
Common Plea (DP) p 49

Damon's The Place for Ribs (NP) p. 53
James Street Tavern (NP) p. 57
Red River Barbeque & Grille (NP) p. 59
Seventh Street Grille (DP) p. 51
The Shiloh Inn (WP) p. 75

Vermont Flatbread Co. (EP) p. 71

Brewpubs
Church Brew Works &
  Restaurant (EP) p. 64

Caribbean
Kaya (EP) p. 65

Casual
Five Sisters New American Grill (NP)
  p. 56
Jergel's (NP) p. 57
North Park Lounge Clubhouse (NP)
  p. 57
Perrytowne Tavern (NP) p. 58
Sam Morgan's Clubhouse Inn (NP)
  p. 60

Chinese
China Palace (NP) p. 53
Great Wall Chinese Restaurant (NP)
  p. 57

Delis/Sandwiches
Delmonico's (DP) p. 49
Primanti Brothers (EP)p. 70
Rhoda's Deli Restaurant (EP) p. 70

Diners
Charlie's Diner (EP) p. 63
Eat 'n' Park (NP) p. 53
Original Hot Dog Shop (EP) p. 68
Pamela's (EP) p. 68
Ritter's Diner (EP) p. 70
Venus Diner (NP) p. 60

Fine Dining
Baum Vivant (EP) p. 61
Bravo! Franco (DP) p. 49
Cross Keys Inn (NP) p. 53
Davio (SP) p.72
Grand Concourse (SP) p. 72
Hyeholde (WP) p. 75
Iron Butterfly (DP) p. 49
Le Mont (WP) p. 75
Le Pommier (SP) p. 74
Mallorca (SP) p. 74

Morton's of Chicago (DP) p. 50
Pines Tavern (NP) p. 58
Poli's (EP) p. 70
Ruth's Chris Steak House (DP)
  p. 51
Stone Mansion (NP) p. 62

German
Penn Brewery (NP) p. 58

Italian
Bravo! Italian Kitchen (NP) p. 52
Bruschetta's (SP) p. 72
Juno Trattoria (DP) p. 50
Moonlite Café (SP) p. 74
Rico's (NP) p. 59
Spaghetti Warehouse (NP) p. 70
Tambellini's (SP) p. 75
Tuscan Inn (NP) p. 60

Japanese
Kotobuki (NP) p. 57

Middle Eastern
Ali Baba (EP) p. 61
Amel's (SP) p. 71
Christos Mediterranean Grill (DP)
  p. 49

Mexican
Mad Mex (EP) p. 68

Peruvian
La Feria (EP) p. 65

Pizza
Mineo's Pizza House (EP) p. 68

Seafood
Abaté Seafood Company (NP) p. 52
Benkovitz Seafoods (EP) p. 61
Original Oyster House (DP) p. 51
Wholey's (EP) p. 71

Steaks
Brendan's North (NP) p. 52
London Grille (SP) p. 74
Top of the Triangle (DP) p. 51

DOWNTOWN PITTSBURGH

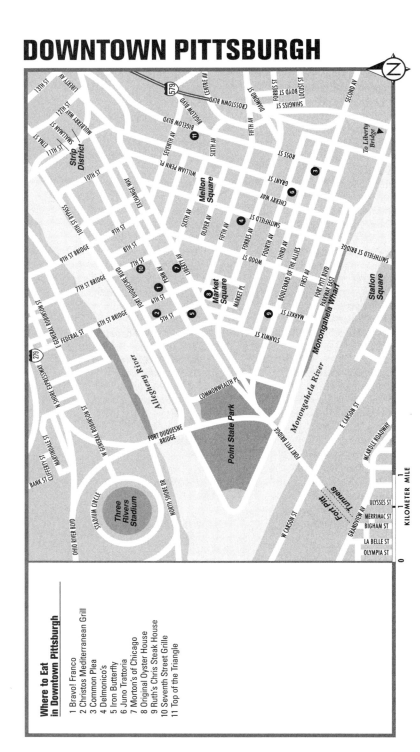

**Where to Eat
in Downtown Pittsburgh**

1 Bravo! Franco
2 Christos Mediterranean Grill
3 Common Plea
4 Delmonico's
5 Iron Butterfly
6 Juno Trattoria
7 Morton's of Chicago
8 Original Oyster House
9 Ruth's Chris Steak House
10 Seventh Street Grille
11 Top of the Triangle

DOWNTOWN PITTSBURGH

BRAVO! FRANCO
613 Penn Ave.
Pittsburgh
412/642-6677
$$$

Located across the street from Heinz Hall, Bravo! Franco caters to the before- and after-theater crowd with smooth, attentive service. The fine Italian cuisine includes veal dishes, pasta, seafood, and a famous fried zucchini appetizer. For a special post-performance treat, indulge in a light snack of appetizers and dessert. The cozy, intimate bar stays open until 2 a.m. Lunch, dinner daily. Open Sun only at show times. Reservations suggested. ♿ (Downtown Pittsburgh)

CHRISTOS MEDITERRANEAN GRILL
130 Sixth St.
Pittsburgh
412/261-6442
$

Don't be put off by its unwelcoming, hole-in-the-wall, stripped-down diner

Cross Keys Inn, p. 53

Doina Locke

appearance. This is the home of great authentic Greek food. The spinach pie and baklava can make the humble surroundings disappear. Sample the Middle Eastern or vegetarian dishes. Lunch, dinner daily. Open Sun only when there is a special event downtown. No credit cards accepted. (Downtown Pittsburgh)

COMMON PLEA
310 Ross St.
Pittsburgh
412/281-5140
$$$

THE lunch spot for Pittsburgh's legal eagles, the Common Plea is known for its seafood and veal. The three dining rooms are decorated with a Renaissance flair: wooden tables, high-backed chairs, and a "rococo decor." Lunch weekdays only, dinner Mon–Sat. Valet parking and limo service are available. Reservations recommended. (Downtown Pittsburgh)

DELMONICO'S
441 Smithfield St.
Pittsburgh
412/281-1212
$

A unique twist on the all-you-can-eat buffet: more than 60 hot and cold deli foods, plus Chinese. Pay by the pound at $4.29 per pound. You can eat in or take out—or eat as much as you can and then take the rest with you. Exercise restraint to pace yourself to dessert. Mon–Sat breakfast, lunch, dinner. (Downtown Pittsburgh)

IRON BUTTERFLY
212 Sixth St.
Pittsburgh
412/434-4766
$$$

Strategically located in the Cultural District across the street from Heinz

Best Ribs in the 'Burgh

1. **Hotlicks**, *Galleria Mall, Mt. Lebanon, 412/572-8090*
2. **Woodson's All-Star Grille**, *Station Square, 412/454-2600*
3. **Red River Barbeque & Grille**, *9805 McKnight Rd., North Hills, 412/366-9200*
4. **Sam Morgan's Clubhouse Inn**, *775 Freeport Rd., Harmarville, 724/274-2554*
5. **Bobby Rubino's**, *Commerce Court, Station Square, 412/642-7427*
6. **Damon's The Place for Ribs**, *Waterworks Mall, 412/782-3750*

Hall, the Iron Butterfly is the first stop for theatergoers in the know, who usually jam the elegant restaurant until just before curtain time. Non-theatergoers who wait out the rush can enjoy a leisurely meal in one of three multilevel dining rooms. Candlelit tables, fine table appointments, abundant flowers, and artwork add to the truly elegant atmosphere. The most popular items are the Crabmeat Hoelzel appetizer (lump crabmeat in fresh tarragon vinaigrette), osso buco, and the Iron Butterfly Strawberry Napoleon, a wicked concoction of Grand Marnier Zabaglione, strawberries, whipped cream, pecans, and chocolate. The bar is "cigar-friendly," which means that exhaust fans clear the air efficiently. Patrons at the bar are entertained with live piano music Sunday and Thursday; a singer entertains Tuesday, Friday, and Saturday. Park free in the Sixth Street and Penn Avenue garage after 4. Dinner only Sun. & (Downtown Pittsburgh)

JUNO TRATTORIA
One Oxford Centre
301 Grant St.
Pittsburgh
412/392-0225
$$
Marble tables, wood floors, and glass walls on the third floor of One Oxford Centre create a sophisticated setting for classic Italian food. One of the most popular items here is the Saltimbocca. From 5 to 9, an antipasto cart circulates with items that can be eaten as appetizers or combined to make a light meal. Pasta dishes are offered in two sizes: *piccolo* (small) or *tutto* (dinner-size portion). The menu also carries a "500 Club" (500 calories or less) section, but the selections are too delicious to be considered "diet" food. Closed Sun. & (Downtown Pittsburgh)

MORTON'S OF CHICAGO
CNG Tower, 625 Liberty Ave.
Pittsburgh
412/261-7141
$$$
Morton's is one place Pittsburghers choose for a very special dinner. The sumptuous elegance and impeccable

service are as much a part of the dining experience as the excellent food. Surrounded by luxury—dark paneling, candlelit tables, and fresh flowers—you know you're being pampered. As at other locations of the nationwide Morton's of Chicago chain, the entire dinner menu is arrayed on a tableside cart, including live lobster and tender steaks. Portions are generous, and ordering is à la carte. Tempting gourmet desserts tantalize the diner who "couldn't eat another bite." Jackets and ties are required men's attire. Dinner only. Valet parking. Reservations are recommended. ♿ (Downtown Pittsburgh)

ORIGINAL OYSTER HOUSE
20 Market Square
Pittsburgh
412/566-7925
$

Built in 1870 and a designated historic landmark, the Original Oyster House in Market Square is Pittsburgh's oldest saloon. As its name suggests, fried oysters are a specialty, but so are clams, and many rave about the "city's best $3 fish sandwich." Since Prohibition, buttermilk has been a standard accompaniment for fried oysters; after Prohibition ended, beer returned to the menu. Try the buttermilk, it's delicious, but be wary of the crab cake–sized fried oyster doughball; it can stay with you a long time. Things get pretty lively at times with the satellite TV showing major sporting events. If it's too crowded, park benches beckon from Market Square. There is a second location at 801 Liberty Avenue. Closed Sun. No credit cards accepted. ♿ (Downtown Pittsburgh)

RUTH'S CHRIS STEAK HOUSE
6 PPG Place
Pittsburgh

412/391-4800
$$$

Raising a great steak to the level of a ritual is part of the work of the Ruth's Chris chain of 57 restaurants across the nation. Only the best of U.S. prime beef is refrigerator-aged for 60 days, hand-cut, seared in a specially built, high-temperature broiler, and served in butter on a heated dish. Everything is á la carte. Dessert specialties include apple pie, pecan pie, and bread pudding with 80-proof whiskey sauce. Open for lunch weekdays only; open for dinner daily. Reservations recommended. Parking is free after 4 in the PPG Garage; enter off Third or Fourth Avenue. ♿ (Downtown Pittsburgh)

SEVENTH STREET GRILLE
130 Seventh St.
Pittsburgh
412/338-0303
$$

Popular for lunch, convenient to both the Benedum and Heinz Hall, and open every night until 2, the Seventh Street Grille is an attractive all-around downtown stop. The Wednesday feature is Mexican food; on Friday, prime rib and shrimp are the specials. Regulars can join the Back Bar Beer Club; a plaque carries the names of members who have sampled all 42 beers. ♿ (Downtown Pittsburgh)

TOP OF THE TRIANGLE
USX Tower, 600 Grant St.
Pittsburgh
412/471-4100
$$$

The steak, seafood, and wine list are excellent, but the main attraction here is the fabulous view of the city from 62 floors up. On windy days, the building sways noticeably. Don't worry, it's supposed to do that to relieve structural stress. Business or formal attire is appropriate. Parking is convenient in the USX Tower garage. The piano lounge is open until 11:30 on Saturday night. Open for dinner only on Sun. Reservations suggested. ♿ (Downtown Pittsburgh)

NORTH PITTSBURGH

ABATÉ SEAFOOD COMPANY
Waterworks, Freeport Rd.
Pittsburgh
412/781-9550
$$
Renowned throughout the area for its pasta, Abaté is one of the more popular places for special family dining at reasonable prices north of the city. Specialty seafood and Italian dishes are imaginative and well-prepared. Many pasta dishes can be ordered in smaller servings. Try for seating in the light and airy glass-walled front dining room, with white patio furniture and ceiling fans. Spacious and rambling, Abaté smoothly handles large groups as easily as couples. Casual

to business attire is the usual. ♿ (North Pittsburgh)

BRAVO! ITALIAN KITCHEN
4976 McKnight Rd.
Ross
412/366-3556
$$
Some of the best Italian food in town can be found at Bravo! Italian Kitchen, perched high above the perpetually jammed McKnight–Siebert intersection. However, those who brave the traffic can relax with the convivial ambience, attentive service, and stylized "Roman ruin" decor. You can savor warm focaccia and sourdough bread with herbed olive oil while you consider the menu. The hearty chopped Mediterranean salad is a great prelude to the wood-grilled pizza or any of the special pasta dishes. The highly polished dark-oak bar on the far side of the room has the requisite sports-channel TV and is a good spot to sit out a wait for a table. ♿ (North Pittsburgh)

Kotobuki, p. 57

Doina Locke

BRENDAN'S NORTH
9999 Kummer Rd.
North Hills
412/935-6566
$$$

Located on the Yellow Belt immediately west of North Park, Brendan's is popular with North Hills suburbanites for lunch, Happy Hour, and dinner. Rich, dark wood and a comfortable, upscale clublike atmosphere distinguish the main dining area while the adjoining lounge is used for more casual dining. The menu offers hardwood grilled Black Angus steaks, Virginia spots (a longtime Pittsburgh-favorite fish dish), and prime rib. Look for Early Dinner specials, but be prepared to wait. Reservations recommended, especially on weekends. ♿ (North Pittsburgh)

CAFÉ VICTORIA
946 Western Ave.
Pittsburgh
412/323-8881
$$$$

A charmingly restored Victorian house dating back to 1875, the aptly named Café Victoria sets the mood for elegant dining indoors or summertime dining outdoors in the garden courtyard. Two floors are dedicated to dining, including a tiny garret for a romantic dinner for two. Some of the menu items are house innovations, such as carrot bisque. Others, such as Victorian bread pudding, are evocative of times past. The historic structure has no wheelchair access. (North Pittsburgh)

CHINA PALACE
409 Broad St.
Sewickley
412/749-7423
$$$

The elegant "Chinese modern" decor of sleek black lacquer and frosted glass, sparked with a discreet golden dragon or two, provides a subtle and sophisticated backdrop for a business, social, or family meal. The special Weight Watchers Menu offers steamed selections that are light in oil and low in sodium, have no MSG, and are served with sauce on the side. The witty names sprinkled among the dinner entrées make choosing difficult, but fun. Other locations in Shadyside and Monroeville. Lunch and dinner daily, sushi bar closed Mon. ♿ (North Pittsburgh)

CROSS KEYS INN
599 Dorseyville Rd.
Fox Chapel
412/963-8717
$$$

Built in 1850, Cross Keys is a beautifully restored inn and stagecoach stop in a deceptively rural setting, the wooded hills of suburban Fox Chapel. The large continental menu includes appetizers such as house pâtés, pastas such as lobster ravioli, and a zucchini/lamb sausage lasagne, made with spicy lamb sausage. Entrées range from seafood to beef to fowl, including game hen, quail, and duck. Lunch and dinner Tue–Sat, Sun dinner only. Reservations recommended, necessary on weekends. (North Pittsburgh)

DAMON'S THE PLACE FOR RIBS
Waterworks Mall, Freeport Rd.
Pittsburgh
412/782-3750
$$

Damon's is a casual, sports-bar restaurant for the whole family—famous for its barbecued ribs and chicken. Four TV screens provide sports, and a table speaker can be tuned to the TV screen of your

NORTH PITTSBURGH

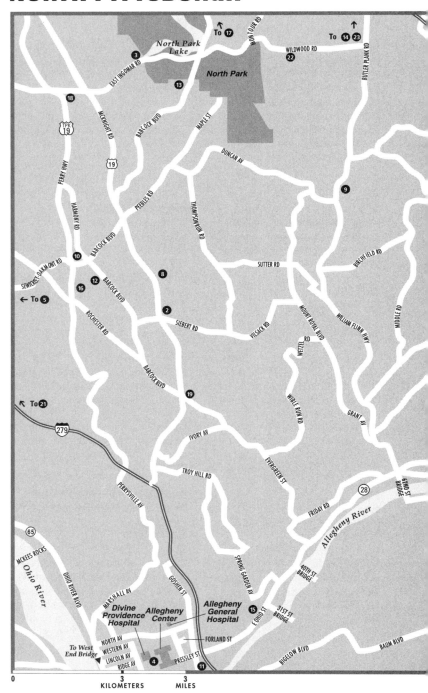

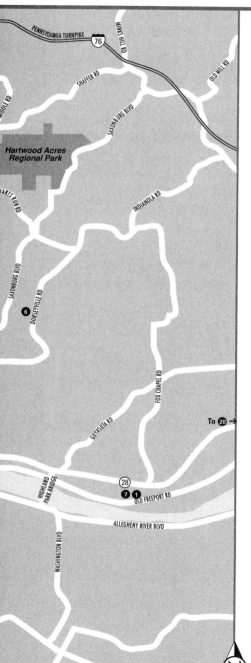

Where to Eat in North Pittsburgh

1 Abaté Seafood Company
2 Bravo! Italian Kitchen
3 Brendan's North
4 Café Victoria
5 China Palace
6 Cross Keys Inn
7 Damon's The Place For Ribs
8 Eat 'N' Park
9 Five Sisters New American Grill
10 Great Wall Chinese Restaurant
11 James Street Tavern
12 Jergel's
13 Kotobuki
14 North Park Lounge Clubhouse
15 Penn Brewery
16 Perrytowne Tavern
17 Pines Tavern
18 Red River Barbeque & Grille
19 Rico's
20 Sam Morgan's Clubhouse Inn
21 Stone Mansion
22 Tuscan Inn
23 Venus Diner

Tastes Ex-Pittsburghers Yearn for After They Leave

Chipped chopped ham: Thinly shaved then chopped ham for heaping in a dense clump on a sandwich, perfected by the Isaly deli section

Funnel cakes: A Pennsylvania Dutch treat made of deep-fried dough; made of batter drizzled through a funnel into hot oil, then sprinkled with sugar.

Ham barbecue sandwich: Usually made with chipped chopped ham mixed with bottled barbecue sauce.

French fries from the Potato Patch at Kennywood Park: Melted cheese or gravy can be added to increase the saturated-fat level or a dash of vinegar to give the fries tang.

Primanti's sandwich: Huge piles of meat, fried eggs, or fried fish, plus coleslaw and French fries, crammed between two slabs of Italian bread and served on a piece of waxed paper

Original Hot Dog's hot dog and fries: A full dose of artery-clogging taste delights from "the O"

Oyster House fish sandwich: Huge slabs of fried fish on a sandwich roll, often accompanied by a "fried oyster,"—an oyster buried in a golf ball–size lump of dough.

choice. The trivia competition is great fun for all. The special house appetizer is fried onion loaf. Damon's has other locations on McKnight Road in the North Hills and in Monroeville. ♿ (North Pittsburgh)

EAT 'N' PARK
7671 McKnight Rd.
North Hills
412/364-1211
$
The Eat 'n' Park chain originated in

Pittsburgh as a drive-in restaurant with carhops. The Ross Park location is popular because of its excellent breakfast buffet, with a good selection of fresh fruit, scrambled eggs, meats, French toast or waffle sticks, muffins, and a hearty, stick-to-your-ribs sausage gravy. Service is very good; coffee cups and the buffet are always filled. There's an on-premises bakery and bake shop. Pies are a specialty, and small children get a delicious "Smile" cookie free. Open 24 hours.

Discounts for seniors and children. &
(North Pittsburgh)

FIVE SISTERS
NEW AMERICAN GRILL
3982 Rt. 8
Hampton
412/487-1755
$
Located at the intersection of Route 8
and the Green Belt (Duncan Avenue),
this casual pub in a small brick building backed up against a big hill is in
fact owned and operated by five sisters. Start with the tortilla chips and
salsa; Five Sisters makes its own, so
they're fresh and delicious. The sandwiches are hearty and the soups are
homemade. & (North Pittsburgh)

GREAT WALL CHINESE
RESTAURANT
1130 Perry Hwy.
Ross
412/481-5913
$$
The best General Tso's chicken
around can be found at this quietly
sophisticated restaurant tucked
among the stores in the Pines Plaza
Shopping Center. The egg drop soup
and wonton soup are especially deli-
cious ways to begin a meal. In fact,
if you prefer soup as your entrée, the
noodle soup with vegetables is so
hearty and generously portioned
that it can easily serve two. Mongo-
lian chicken is another savory de-
light from the extensive menu.
Sixteen Heart Healthy Specials, pre-
pared without oil, salt, sugar, corn-
starch, or MSG, are delicious and
will appeal to everyone. The service
is always cordial, fast, and efficient.
& (North Pitttsburgh)

JAMES STREET TAVERN
422 Foreland/James St.

Pittsburgh
412/323-2222
$$
Known for its jazz on Friday and Sat-
urday and at the upstairs James
Street Pub Wednesday through Saturday, the James Street Tavern offers
a wide selection of Cajun dishes,
seafood, chargrilled chicken, and
steaks. It even has alligator for the
adventurous. (North Pittsburgh)

JERGEL'S
3855 Babcock Blvd.
Ross
412/364-9902
$$
This casual, friendly combination
restaurant and bar has TVs running
constantly. The dining area, two steps
up from the bar, feels spacious yet
cozy, especially in winter when
there's a fire in the large fireplace.
There is a great selection of delicious
sandwiches, many with clever names.
Seekers of the "perfect French fries"
rate these among the best. Old-
fashioned chicken croquettes are a
house specialty. Live entertainment at
the bar brings in the young crowd.
(North Pittsburgh)

KOTOBUKI
9801 Old Babcock Blvd.
Allison Park
412/369-7885
$$$
Many members of Pittsburgh's Asian
community are regulars at this sophisticated restaurant, nestled close to
North Park. Sit at the sushi bar to
watch Mr. Shin prepare sushi and
sashimi. Friendly waitstaff assist
novices through the mysteries of the
authentic Japanese and Korean offerings, with teriyaki and tempura likely to
be the only familiar items. Head Chef
Debbie Cho's house salad with a light

orange and ginger dressing can be addictive. "Happy Fish" signs will lead you from McKnight Road and Babcock Boulevard to Kotobuki's off-the-beaten-path location. Lunch and dinner Mon–Sat. ♿ (North Pittsburgh)

NORTH PARK LOUNGE CLUBHOUSE
5301 Ranalli Dr.
Gibsonia
724/449-9090
$$

This large, popular spot overlooking Route 8 is great for casual, friendly dining. It was voted "most popular with kids" in a very informal poll. The secret of its popularity lies in the plentiful arcade games, kids' favorite foods on the menu, and the fact that nobody much cares about the noise. Another secret: grownups love the games, too. Adult favorites from the full-service menu are the large fish sandwich, fries, and beer. (North Pittsburgh)

PENN BREWERY
Troy Hill Rd.
Pittsburgh

Café Victoria, p. 53

Doina Locke

412/237-9402
$$

Located on Pittsburgh's North Side in the old Deutschtown section, the former Eberhardt & Ober Brewery revels in its German origins. Diners in the German-style pub sit at long tables with picnic benches, in full view of the Penn Pilsner brewing process in huge copper vats. House specialties include freshly brewed Penn Pilsner, sauerbraten, the best wurst you've ever had, sauerkraut, spaetzle, and German potato salad. The menu also includes a good selection of American entrées. The cozy downstairs Rathskeller and the summertime outdoor beer garden offer alternate seating. Lively music from the Dixieland jazz–style Boilermakers or German oompah bands keeps the place hopping from Tuesday through Saturday. Dress casually and be ready for fun. ♿ (North Pittsburgh)

PERRYTOWNE TAVERN
1002 Perry Hwy.
Ross
412/367-9610
$

Set in the charming Perrysville business district, the Perrytowne Tavern puts forth an old-time theme with dark wood floors, tables, and booths, walls and rafters lined with antiques, and large multi-paned windows facing the street. The tavern boasts of 26 draught beers on tap. Fans of great French fries rate Perrytowne's among the best. The menu offers a large selection of sandwiches, including the New Yorker, with kielbasa, cheese, and corned beef, and the Black Forest, a Reuben on marbled rye. ♿ (North Pittsburgh)

PINES TAVERN
Bakerstown Rd.

'Burgh's Best Fish Sandwiches

1. *Original Oyster House,* *20 Market Place, 412/566-7925*
2. *Nied's Hotel,* *5438 Butler St., 412/781-9853*
3. *Armand's,* *4755 Liberty Ave., 412/681-3967*
4. *Robert Wholey and Company,* *1711 Penn Ave., 412/391-3737*
5. *Benkovitz Seafood,* *23rd and Smallman Sts., 412/263-3016*
6. *Fox Trot Inn,* *9566 Perry Hwy., North Hills, 412/366-3544*
7. *Abaté Seafood Company,* *Waterworks Mall, 412/781-9550*
8. *Cheese Cellar,* *Station Square, 412/471-3355*

Gibsonia
724/625-3252
$$$
This rustic country inn nestled securely on the Red Belt between Route 19 and Route 8 is an idyllic spot for a long, leisurely lunch or a special dinner. The best time to visit is December, when every nook and cranny is decorated for Christmas, the fireplaces are blazing, and the tavern offers its exquisite holiday menu. During November, the restaurant serves special wild game dishes. The Pines Tavern is famous for its excellent turtle soup and delicious raspberry pie. Reservations suggested. &
(North Pittsburgh)

RED RIVER BARBEQUE & GRILLE
Pine Creek Shopping Plaza
9805 McKnight Rd.
Wexford
412/366-9200
$$
It serves seriously delicious, slow-cooked barbecued meat in a laid-back Western style, but Red River Barbeque & Grille is a Pittsburgh original. Its own barbecue sauce was such a hit with Pittsburghers that it is now bottled and available in supermarkets. The number-one best-seller is sliced beef brisket, cooked up to 16 hours over hickory wood. Award-winning baby back ribs and "Smokin' Joe's" pulled-pork BBQ with dried cherry coleslaw served in a cherry tortilla cup with crispy and colorful tortilla strips are can't-miss choices. Wings come in five degrees of heat, right up to Desert Fire, and are served with fresh jicama sticks and Cactus Ranch Dipping Sauce. Each table has its own roll of paper towels for quick cleanups after savory, but messy, feasts. The menu offers a full range of margaritas, "Riveritas," and 24 beers on tap, including two house brews, Red River Amber Lager and Black and Tan. & (North Pittsburgh)

RICO'S
Park Place off Babcock Blvd.
Ross
412/931-1989
$$$
A favorite of North Hills residents, this hilltop restaurant is really hidden away. Many first-timers get lost trying

to find it. Ease off McKnight Road carefully onto Babcock Boulevard heading east. Park Place is on the left, immediately after the Deily Moving Company office. Go up the hill on the winding drive. It's worth the trip. Rico's has a strong reputation for fine Northern Italian cuisine, even if it can get a little pricey. For a heavenly treat, try Rico's signature angel hair pasta with pine nuts and a light cream sauce. Closed Sun. (North Pittsburgh)

SAM MORGAN'S CLUBHOUSE INN
775 Freeport Rd.
Harmarville
724/274-2554
$$

This golf-themed restaurant is the place for big appetites. Sam Morgan's house specialty is smoked Bedrock Ribs, a large slab named for its resemblance to the mammoth cartoon rack from *The Flintstones*. Entrées ranging from homemade Italian dishes, to steaks, ribs, pizza, and sandwiches are also featured. Diners relish the bucket of jumbo chicken wings that can be topped with a half dozen different sauces. The casual golf theme is reminiscent of the nearby famed Oakmont Country Club. A large game room features vintage arcade games and more than a dozen satellite-linked televisions for a sports-bar feel. (North Pittsburgh)

STONE MANSION
Stone Mansion Dr.
Franklin Park
724/934-3000
$$$

The Stone Mansion is synonomous in the North Hills with excellent continental cuisine in a beautifully renovated stone house. The bar is located in the stunningly handsome great room, which has a cathedral ceiling and an enormous stone fireplace. The dining area is divided into small cozy rooms, each with its own working fireplace. One of the house specialties is delicate duck strudel, wrapped with crisp phyllo pastry and served with a light sauce. The desserts are definitely worth saving room for. Closed Sun. (North Pittsburgh)

TUSCAN INN
2684 Wildwood Rd.
Allison Park
412/486-7696
$$$

The secret is out: the rustic stone building out in the middle of nowhere on the Yellow Belt is the home of excellent northern Italian cuisine. Inside, the dining area is also rustic, comfortable, and unpretentious. The food is sublime. The salad of baby greens, goat cheese, and toasted pine nuts with an orange vinaigrette is a Tuscan Inn specialty. Pasta choices include Pasta Roberto, a fiery mixture of sea scallops, anchovies, and hot peppers; and Pasta Luigi, a vegetarian blend of grilled Portobello mushroom, spinach, and Gorgonzola. Dinner Mon–Sat. (North Pittsburgh)

VENUS DINER
5315 William Flynn Hwy.
Gibsonia
412/443-2323

As Pittsburghers love to say, "You can't miss it!" Between Mars and Moon (Township), what else is there but Venus? This beautifully maintained authentic 1957 diner is located immediately south of Pennsylvania Turnpike Exit 4 on the southbound side of Route 8. The coffee is great, and the ten kinds of homemade pies, including egg custard and raisin, make dessert

The Original Oyster House, p. 51

an important part of any meal. The menu includes the expected diner foods, but the specialties are home-style pork and sauerkraut, roast lamb, stuffed peppers, and stuffed cabbage. Breakfast, lunch, and dinner daily. ♿ (North Pittsburgh)

EAST PITTSBURGH

ALI BABA
404 S. Craig St.
Pittsburgh
412/682-2829
$$
This long and narrow restaurant is usually jammed with a lunchtime crowd from the university and the medical center. It is known for its authentic Middle Eastern menu. Tabouli (a salad of bulgur wheat, tomato, and onion), baba ghanoush (roasted eggplant puree), and hummus (mashed chickpeas) taste best when scooped up with a piece of warm pita bread. Lamb and rice and shish kebab are the

specialties in this light-filled contemporary restaurant. A sweet, honey-soaked diamond of baklava and a cup of Arabic coffee is the perfect ending to a fine meal. ♿ (East Pittsburgh)

BAUM VIVANT
5102 Baum Blvd.
Pittsburgh
412/682-2620
$$$$
A tiny, elegant restaurant specializing in haute cuisine with distinctive Portugese and Italian influences, Baum Vivant is a gourmet delight. The decor, excellent service, and chef's personal attention to any special dietary requirements create an intimate, yet sophisticated ambience. Innovative menu items include pork tenderloin with clams in red pepper sauce. Every meal comes with complimentary house pâté and herbed cream cheese with bread for starters. While the hearty soups and gourmet entrées win raves, the desserts are exceptional. Complimentary after-dinner almond

EAST PITTSBURGH

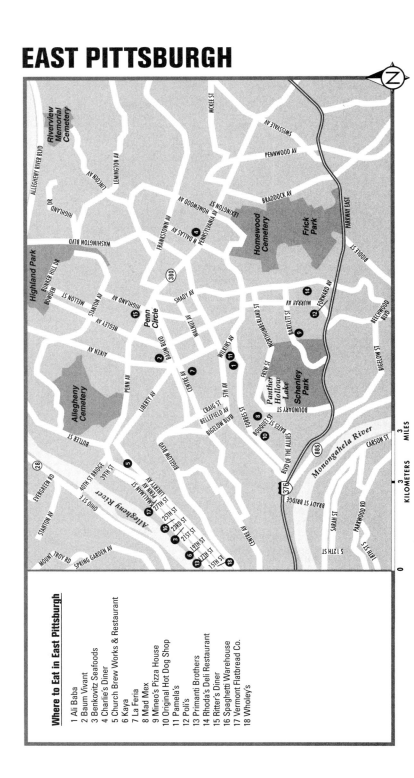

Where to Eat in East Pittsburgh

1 Ali Baba
2 Baum Vivant
3 Benkovitz Seafoods
4 Charlie's Diner
5 Church Brew Works & Restaurant
6 Kaya
7 La Feria
8 Mad Mex
9 Mineo's Pizza House
10 Original Hot Dog Shop
11 Pamela's
12 Poli's
13 Primanti Brothers
14 Rhoda's Deli Restaurant
15 Ritter's Diner
16 Spaghetti Warehouse
17 Vermont Flatbread Co.
18 Wholey's

Top Ten Restaurants from "Someone in the Business"

by Cynthia Tuite, president of the Chef's Association and culinary director at Bidwell Training Center/ Manchester Craftsmen's Guild

1. **Wooden Angel, Beaver:** Wonderful food, atmosphere, service, and wine list
2. **Top of the Triangle, Mount Washington:** Great view and good food
3. **Cafe Mimi's, Edgewood:** From filling entrées to sandwiches, it's always good
4. **Cafe Baci, Highland Park:** Relaxed European dining
5. **The Tavern, New Wilmington:** Very good homestyle cooking and baking in Amish country; reservations needed
6. **Tara, Sharon:** Takes you back to *Gone With the Wind*; the meal was great from start to finish
7. **Bravo! Italian Kitchen, Ross:** Great pasta combinations, bread with herbed olive oil is delicious
8. **Kaya, Strip District:** Caribbean cuisine—fried plantains my favorite; plenty of vegetarian items
9. **Johnston House, Mars:** Serves high tea in an elegant style
10. **Franklin Inn, Franklin Park:** Authentic Mexican cooking, very good refried beans

liqueur is the perfect finishing touch. Reservations are required. Closed Sun. (East Pittsburgh)

BENKOVITZ SEAFOODS
23rd and Smallman Sts.
Pittsburgh
412/263-3016
$

Benkovitz offers real stand-up dining—at narrow waist-level counters. Join the lunch crowd for an inhaled repast. If you can get past the pervasive oily mist of frying fish, join the line to order a hearty fried fish sandwich: three crispy, flaky fillets on a hoagie bun. To get all the fixings, order a fried fish hoagie. Broiled fish sandwiches, softshell crab (in season) sandwiches, fried fish by the pound, and dinners to go are just some of the listed items. After eating, browse around for high-quality fresh seafood, prepared deli offerings, frozen seafoods, and gourmet items. If you're not angling for cooked fish, try the sushi bar which is open 11:30 to 2 only. (East Pittsburgh)

CHARLIE'S DINER
7619 Penn Ave.
Pittsburgh

Joltin' Joe, or
Great Coffeehouses about Town

Beehive Coffeehouse & Dessertery, *1327 E. Carson St., 412/488-4483. The atmosphere is funky and hip. You'll find the largest concentration of young adults and college students outside of Oakland.*

Beehive Coffeehouse & Theatre, *3807 Forbes Ave., 412/683-4483. The exterior looks like a hokey make-believe castle, but the coffeehouse inside is pretty much back-to-basics Formica diner-style. A movie screening room is in the back of the building, and the counter carries an array of snacks.*

Bookworks Café, *3400 Harts Run Rd., Glenshaw, 412/767-0344. Reclaimed architectural details provide the visual interest for leisurely browsing among the books or lingering over a cappuccino and gourmet muffin.*

Cappuccino City & Gourmet Coffee, *441 Beaver St., Sewickley, 412/749-0766. Linger a while at tiny tables with a newspaper, caffeine in any one of its many guises, and a friend. This coffeehouse equivalent of a neighborhood bar has an almost bohemian atmosphere.*

Coffee Express Shop, *Station Square Shops, 412/765-1086. In keeping with the tradition of Station Square, the Coffee Express Shop is*

412/241-9506
$

Renowned for its breakfast, Charlie's Diner draws enough eager eaters to form lines outside the building on Sunday morning. Breakfast includes eggs, homefries, grits, sweet Italian sausage, and, most importantly, baked ham cut right there fresh off the bone. Of course, you needn't be an early riser to enjoy; breakfast is served round the clock, seven days a week. Charlie's also has a full menu of diner food, such as hamburgers, French fries, and gallons of hot coffee. 24 hours daily. ♿ (East Pittsburgh)

**CHURCH BREW WORKS &
RESTAURANT**
3525 Liberty Ave.
Pittsburgh
412/688-8200
$$$

The awe-inspiring beauty of the renovated St. John the Baptist Church, built in 1902, may be a distraction at first, especially with enormous copper vats and stainless steel where the altar used to be, but eventually the *located in a renovated freight car. Drink your coffee at one of the tiny tables in front of the shop, take it outside, or buy gourmet beans to brew at home.*

Coffee Tree Roasters, *5840 Forbes Ave., 412/422-4427. This coffeehouse should come with a warning label: "This shop can be hazardous to an insatiable sweet tooth." The pastries and sweets are that good. Coffee beans, teas, brewing accessories, and mugs are also for sale.*

Darla's Coffee House & Desserts, *8501 Perry Hwy., North Hills, 412/ 367-8151. Coffees, desserts, and light lunches are offered in this renovated one-floor house that takes you back to the 1930s with its overstuffed furniture in the charming back sitting room.*

Ebenezer's Coffeehouse, *Duncan Manor Shopping Plaza, North Hills, 412/369-3931. Large, overstuffed seating and coffee tables in the front invite casual newspaper reading. Tables are also available in the well-lit dining area for conversation with coffee, light lunch, and desserts.*

Mystery Lovers Bookshop Café, *514 Allegheny River Blvd., Oakmont, 412/681-3700. Luxuriate among thousands of mystery novels as you enjoy your espresso or latte and nibble on fabulous gourmet dessert or light entrées.*

business of dining requires full attention. The menu is adventurous, offering such delicacies as quinoa pilaf and buffalo steak, but those who are looking for the old standbys won't be disappointed. One other offering bears mentioning: the Untraditional Pittsburgh Pierogies, with fillings that vary daily, are worth a try. Without being too punnish, the desserts are sinfully delicious. (East Pittsburgh)

KAYA
2000 Smallman St.
Pittsburgh

412/261-6565
$$
According to a recent Miami transplant, who will have to suffice as an expert, the secret to an authentic Cuban sandwich is in the bread. And, according to her, the bread at Kaya is "great" and its Cuban sandwich is the best she's ever had. The rest of the menu lives up to the standard set by the aforementioned Cuban sandwich, and the Caribbean specialties will make your taste buds think they've left Pittsburgh for the tropics. Such tropical treats as sauteed mango

Pure Pittsburgh:
The Things That Mean Pittsburgh to Me
by Rick Sebak, producer and narrator at
Pittsburgh's WQED public television station

One of the best ways to survey Pittsburgh is from high atop Mount Washington on the South Side. Getting there is half the fun if you take one of two inclines—the Duquesne or Monongahela. I prefer the Duquesne Incline, about a mile from Station Square. Built in 1877, the Duquesne Incline's cars are the oldest mass-transit vehicles in daily operation in America. The fare is only $1 each way, and the ride is thrilling.

While the Andy Warhol Museum is a must-see for anyone visiting Pittsburgh, there is a special experience tucked away in its basement. An old-fashioned photo booth that spits out a vertical strip of four black-and-white photos is pure pop art and a great souvenir of Pittsburgh, Andy Warhol's hometown.

To pay your respects at Warhol's grave, jump on a Shannon Drake or Shannon Library streetcar and ride out to Washington Junction in Bethel Park. Walk across the parking lot and onto Route 88, turn left (north), walk two blocks to Cochran Road, turn left again, and cross the tracks. The cemetery is on the left. Warhol's unpretentious grave is in the center of the cemetery, about halfway up the hill in the Warhola plot. Sometimes you'll find cans of Campbell's Tomato Soup and other pop memorabilia left there in tribute.

On Saturday, take a stroll through the Strip District, a mecca for food lovers, serious cooks, and bargain hunters. While there, consider lunch at Primanti's on 18th between Smallman and Penn Avenues. The restaurant's big sandwiches include the most curious ingredients you are likely to find—French fries and coleslaw loaded right in there with the meats and cheeses.

Downtown, stop by the Original Oyster House in Market Square for a fried oyster. Wash it down with a cold Iron City beer or, if you're adventurous, a tall glass of buttermilk. The tavern has an incredible collection of photos from Miss America contests lining its walls.

In Oakland, be sure to walk along South Craig Street (which ends at the Carnegie Museums). There you will find several book shops, including Caliban Books at number 410, Townsend Booksellers at 4612 Henry Street, and the Bryn Mawr-Vassar Book Store at 4612 Winthrop. At the Carnegie Museums and Library, a great little room called Andrew's Alcove sells donated and discarded books at rock-bottom prices. Bargains and treasures are plentiful at the shop, open between 11 and 3 Monday through Saturday.

If you're really lucky, your visit will include the last Sunday of the month (February through November) and a stop at the huge antique flea market at the Meadows race track in Washington County. Before 8 a.m. it's dealers only, with a $35 admission fee. After 8 a.m., admission is just $2 per person. Prices vary from excellent to outrageous, but tend toward "western Pennsylvania reasonable."

Western Pennsylvania has a chain of stores that are a bargain hunter's dream. Known simply as Gabe's by locals, these are big discount clothing stores where you can get designer labels, seconds, rejects, and last season's styles—all at incredible prices. Nothing's very organized, so be prepared to sift through mounds or racks. Stores are located about an hour east of Pittsburgh on Route 30 in Greensburg, along Route 19 in Washington, and on the Route 40 bypass at Uniontown.

For a sweet treat, head northeast of downtown near Springdale for some Glen's Custard at 400 Freeport Road. The drive-in stand serves real, old-fashioned, ultra-creamy frozen custard, not some ersatz soft dairy product. On the South Side, stop by Page Dairy Mart at the corner of Carson and Beck's Run Road. In Oakland, don't miss Dave & Andy's Ice Cream at 207 Atwood Street, where you may get to taste some of Andy's experimental ice creams like Golden Ale Vanilla. If you're near Millvale, step into a time warp at Regis Steedle & Sons, one of those old ice-cream and sandwich places that feels as though it hasn't changed since the 1940s.

plantains, conch fritters, alligator on a stick, and jerked chicken breast with banana-guava ketchup (not one of Heinz's 57!) are well worth a try. ♿ (East Pittsburgh)

LA FERIA
5527 Walnut St., Second Floor
Pittsburgh
412/682-4501
$$

La Feria is a pleasant surprise at the end of a climb upstairs. Homey with a clutter of colorful Peruvian decorations and clothing, the small dining room feels cozy, yet exotic, definitely the place to try some new foods. Start with the crispy sweet potato chips. First-time La Feria diners can't go wrong with either of the two daily specials—one vegetarian, the other "carnivorian"—served with rice and a wonderful salad of red leaf lettuce, Swiss and Parmesan cheeses, walnuts, Bermuda onions, olives, and tomatoes in a homemade vinaigrette dressing. When in doubt, follow your server's recommendations; everything is delicious. (East Pittsburgh)

MAD MEX
370 Atwood St. and Bates St.
Pittsburgh
412/681-5656
$$

The abstract dancing Native American figure sets the southwestern theme for this popular restaurant and nightspot. The music is loud, the crowd is noisy, and there's an impressive selection of microbrewed and imported beers to wash down the great tortilla chips with salsa and black-bean dip. Tex-Mex staples become 'Burgh-Mex treats when the usual ingredients are given a new twist. Try a whole-wheat quesadilla topped with chickpeas, peppers, onions, marinated mushrooms,

tomatoes, and Monterey Jack or a vegetarian enchilada stuffed with zucchini, roasted peppers, tomatoes, red onions, and mushrooms. There is another Mad Mex on McKnight Road in the North Hills. ♿ (East Pittsburgh)

MINEO'S PIZZA HOUSE
2128 Murray Ave.
Pittsburgh
412/521-9864
$

If there's such a thing as Pittsburgh-style pizza, Mineo's has it. The hand-tossed pies have gobs of cheese and rich, tangy sauce. Expect to wait; this tiny Squirrel Hill pizzeria is usually jammed on weekends. Mineo's other location in Mt. Lebanon is just as popular. (East Pittsburgh)

ORIGINAL HOT DOG SHOP
Forbes Ave. and Bouquet St.
Pittsburgh
412/621-7388
$

"The O" is where Pittsburghers go when they need an injection of grease—straight into the arteries. And it's not as if they didn't know any better: the shop's Oakland neighborhood is the university and medical center in Pittsburgh. But when the siren call of pizza, burgers, hot dogs, and fries is heard, caution is tossed to the winds. The original Original Hot Dog opened in East Liberty in 1928 with a foot-long hot dog. The hot dog is now about seven inches long, but still well loved. Open 24 hours. (East Pittsburgh)

PAMELA'S
5813 Forbes Ave.
Pittsburgh
412/422-9457
$

On Sunday, they're lined up out the

Tea for Two (or More) about Town

Tea Pot, *10850 Perry Hwy., Wexford; 724/934-0730* • *Browse through the small shop filled with imported British treats, then go to the cozy tea room in back. The service is cordial, the ambience is definitely non-stuffy, and the food is delicious.*

Johnston House, *907 Route 228, Mars; 724/625-2636* • *The beautifully renovated Victorian farmhouse offers boutique items on all three floors. The tearoom is exquisitely decorated for a total-immersion experience of all things Victorian—from the demurely covered table legs to the server's wonderful white lace-trimmed dress. With only two seatings, at 11 a.m. and 1:30 p.m., advance reservations are required (at least a week ahead).*

Persephone's, *643 Allegheny River Blvd., Oakmont; 412/828-2310* • *After a few hours of strolling and shopping in Oakmont's delightful business district, cross the railroad tracks at the wrought-iron waiting platform and go a about a block upriver. Relax with a light tea. Persephone's takes you back to a less raucous time.*

Sewickley Victorian Tea Parlour, *433 Beaver St., Sewickley; 412/749-0525* • *Up the handsome wooden stairway overlooking the interior of the Nickelodeon Mall, the marvelous Victorian atmosphere is relaxing and enchanting. The service is also enchanting, and the food is delicious. Open 11 to 3 Tuesday through Saturday.*

Starbuck's, *717 Cochran, Mt. Lebanon, 412/563-7813* • *This national chain is renowned for its coffee specialties. However, the chai latte (Indian-style sweet spiced tea with steamed milk) is a major treat. Try it for a bracing change of pace. Lingering over a steaming cup and a sweet is encouraged; comfy seating and reading materials are available. Starbuck's has shops in downtown Pittsburgh, the Strip District, Squirrel Hill, Monroeville, the North Hills, and Sewickley.*

Westin William Penn Hotel, *Palm Court Lobby, 530 William Penn Place, Pittsburgh; 412/553-5235* • *High tea is served daily from 3 to 6. Elegant and luxurious surroundings add to the enjoyment of dainty tea sandwiches, scones, and pastries with tea or coffee. Piano music provides a soothing background.*

door, waiting for breakfast. Service is fast and the wait is usually not too long. Lingering over the Sunday paper, however, is not encouraged (at least not by those waiting in line for your table). The food is very good. In fact, Pamela's serves the best breakfast in town, according to a vote conducted by *Pittsburgh Magazine*. The pancakes are impressive: dinner-plate size and melt-in-your-mouth delicious. The omelets are hearty and heaped with fillings such as spinach and feta cheese or traditional Western ham, cheese, and onion. (East Pittsburgh)

POLI'S
2607 Murray Ave.
Pittsburgh
412/ 521-6400
$$$

Famous for its seafood, Poli's has become the standard by which many of the city's restaurants are judged. The restaurant has an elegant atmosphere but still serves its hearty meals at reasonable prices. With room for 400 customers in its various dining rooms, Poli's is a popular spot for large groups and special events such as wedding rehearsal dinners and graduation parties. Its striking lounge and services such as valet parking add to the experience. & (East Pittsburgh)

PRIMANTI BROTHERS
46 18th St.
Pittsburgh
412/263-2142
$

Talk about no-frills: you get no silverware, no plate, and no glass for your beer unless you ask. But this is the home of legendary, immense, Pittsburgh-style sandwiches: huge piles of roast beef, corned beef, kielbasa, or fried fish, plus coleslaw and fries, crammed between two slabs of Italian bread and served on a piece of waxed paper. Open 24 hours, Primanti's is jammed with the late-night crowd after last call and with breakfasting Strip District workers in the wee hours of the morning. Whenever you go, don't be shy—grab a chair when you see one. Other locations include Market Square and South Side. & (East Pittsburgh)

RHODA'S DELI RESTAURANT
2201 Murray Ave.
Pittsburgh
412/521-4555
$$

Matzo ball soup, potato pancakes, pickled herring, smoked salmon, blintzes, and sandwiches heaped high with corned beef and other kosher meats make Rhoda's one of the finest Jewish delis in Pittsburgh. The restaurant also is a popular breakfast spot, featuring fresh bagels with an impressive selection of toppings. The deli does a brisk take-out business and has a nice selection of imported and domestic beers. & (East Pittsburgh)

RITTER'S DINER
5221 Baum Blvd.
Pittsburgh
412/682-4852
$

Efficiency and good plain cooking served without delay 24 hours a day keep businesspeople, workers, and late-nighters coming back to Ritter's again and again. As in diners everywhere, everyone gets to know everyone else's business because they're all talking over the noise. Breakfast any time, day or night, is hearty and delicious; try the dark, dense buckwheat cakes from the griddle. The large menu offers everything from burgers and sandwiches to steaks, deep-fried seafood, country-cooking, Italian favorites—even pierogies and gyros. Parking is available behind the building and in the lot across the street. Ritter's is open 24 hours. (East Pittsburgh)

SPAGHETTI WAREHOUSE
2601 Smallman St.
Pittsburgh
412/261-6511
$

Believe it or not, there's a trolley car in the middle of this family-favorite restaurant. The converted warehouse has a large dining hall loaded with tons of memorabilia that will keep the kids (and adults) fascinated while you're waiting for your food. This fun place offers generous portions at bargain prices. Basic family-style Italian food such as antipasto, pasta, veal or chicken Parmesan, and pizza is guaranteed to satisfy. Portions are hearty, so if you start with soup and salad, you may not have room left for dessert. ♿ (East Pittsburgh)

VERMONT FLATBREAD CO.
2701 Penn Ave.
Pittsburgh
412/434-1220
$$

Vermont Flatbreads have been described as "design-your-own pizzas, but not really pizzas." To explain: flatbread is a thin, crispy Italian bread called focaccia, baked in a specially built wood-burning clay oven to achieve just the right texture, and finished off with your choice of toppings or with the chef's gourmet creations. The desserts are not to be missed; prepared by a neighboring caterer, they're all irresistibly scrumptious. Lunch and dinner Mon–Sat. Reservations not accepted. ♿ (East Pittsburgh)

WHOLEY'S
1711 Penn Ave.
Pittsburgh
412/391-3737
$

Wholey's is famous for its fish sandwich, done Pittsburgh-style, where they like 'em big! The hardest part is finding your way into the parking lot: turn into the alley between Penn and Liberty off 16th Street, pass McDonald's parking lot, and you're there. Other offerings include shrimp in a basket and a full range of deli options. The seafood is ultra-fresh because Wholey's big business is in wholesale and retail fish. It's usually jammed with the lunchtime crowd from nearby office buildings and the Strip. Seating is available upstairs in the Pittsburgh Room or on the Captain's Deck. Closed by 6 p.m. (East Pittsburgh)

SOUTH PITTSBURGH

AMEL'S
435 McNeilly Rd.
Pittsburgh
412/563-3466
$$$

A tradition in Pittsburgh, Amel's has maintained its reputation for good Middle Eastern food, yet also serves Italian and seafood dishes. Don't look for a Middle Eastern atmosphere, however. The appetizers and entrées are excellent, and the homemade desserts are definitely worth saving plenty of room. ♿ (South Pittsburgh)

BOBBY RUBINO'S
Commerce Court, Station Square
Pittsburgh
412/642-7427
$$

At this popular spot for casual dining, you can wait for a table at the bar or outside the restaurant, watching the crowds at The Shops at Station Square. Ribs are deliciously messy, served in slabs, with plenty of napkins. When washed down with an ice-cold beer, hearty is a word that inadequately describes the meal. The house specialty is the "humongous" fried onion ring loaf. Closed Sun. &. (South Pittsburgh)

BRUSCHETTA'S
1831 E. Carson St.
Pittsburgh
412/431-3535
$$
Squeezed into a tiny Carson Street corner storefront, Bruschetta's has built a large reputation among lovers of country Italian cuisine. Closed Sun. Reservations recommended for 6 or more. &. (South Pittsburgh)

CAFÉ ALLEGRO
12th and Carson Sts.
Pittsburgh
412/481-7788
$$$
Imaginative combinations of the freshest ingredients available make for a great dining experience at Café Allegro. The closest description of the delectable dishes may be "California cuisine"—prepared with a light touch and beautifully presented. The casual yet elegant ambience is bistrolike and welcoming. Reservations are a must on weekends. &. (South Pittsburgh)

DAVIO
2100 Broadway Ave.
Beechview
412/531-7422
$$$
A real treasure for diners in the know, this tiny restaurant has only seven tables, but it boasts one of the finest chefs in the city. No liquor is sold, but

diners may bring their own wine. Lunch is the best bargain. Lunch, dinner Mon–Sat, dinner only Sun. Reservations required. No credit cards accepted. &. (South Pittsburgh)

GRAND CONCOURSE
One Station Square
E. Carson St. at Smithfield Street
Bridge
Pittsburgh
412/261-1717
$$$
Everyone should eat at the Grand Concourse at least once, just for the experience. It provides a breathtaking setting for elegant gourmet dining in the marvelously renovated PL&E Railroad station. The main hall's vaulted stained-glass ceiling and marble staircase sweep diners back to Victorian splendor. Even a trip to the ladies' rest room is a charming step back in time. Visit again for the most fabulous Sunday brunch in the city. The early dinner special Monday through Saturday is moderately priced. The children's menu has discounted prices. For a wonderful view of downtown across the Monongahela River, try the River Room. &. (South Pittsburgh)

LE POMMIER
2104 E. Carson St.
Pittsburgh
412/431-1901
$$$
Le Pommier combines the charm of a plain French country inn with the sophistication of a high-powered gourmet chef in the kitchen and one of the finest wine lists around. The decor is simple, with works by local artists creating a comfortable, intimate setting. A good way to sample the cuisine is at the monthly wine tastings. Valet parking takes the worry out of parking on crowded South Side streets. Dinner

SOUTHWEST PITTSBURGH

Note: This map includes South and West Pittsburgh zone listings.

Tue–Sat. Reservations required. ♿
(South Pittsburgh)

LONDON GRILLE
First Level, Galleria
500 Washington Rd. at Gilkeson
Mt. Lebanon
412/563-3400
$$

A quietly refined "gentlemen's club"
atmosphere heightens the fine dining
experience at the highly rated London
Grille. Excellently prepared traditional
offerings include prime rib and York-
shire pudding, steak, chops, fowl, and
lobster. The intimate garden patio of-
fers a full menu, plus a Sunday brunch,
in delightful surroundings. Even more
dining options can be found in the Pub,
where British pub fare shares the card
with casual American food. Bangers
(grilled sausage) and shepherd's pie
(not your usual Pittsburgh choices),
fish and chips, steak, and sandwiches
are available. You'll find London Grille
on the first level inside the upscale
Galleria mall. ♿ (South Pittsburgh)

MALLORCA
2228 E. Carson St.
Pittsburgh
512/488-1818
$$$

If rustic and jewel are words that can
be used together in describing an ele-
gantly renovated historic building,
then Mallorca, with its scenic murals,
columns, polished oak, and ceramic
tiles, is a rustic jewel. The sophisticated Spanish cuisine and impressive
wine list provide counterpoints to the
rustic feel. Summertime dining at an
umbrella-covered table in the side
courtyard charmingly transports you
from Carson Street to somewhere in
southern Europe. The paella is outstanding—do not miss it! Lobster in a
very light cream sauce is a specialty.

Stone Mansion, p. 60

Doina Locke

The finishing touch to each meal is
the complimentary glass of Spanish
almond liqueur. Valet parking is provided. ♿ (South Pittsburgh)

MOONLITE CAFÉ
530 Brookline Blvd.
Pittsburgh
412/531-2811
$$

Moonlite Café is plain and simple—a
neighborhoord restaurant with delight-
fully good original Italian cuisine.
Decor is uncluttered Formica; the
focus is on the food and the service.
Getting to the dining room requires
snaking through a dark, narrow path-
way past the very busy, very crowded
bar, with darts players to the right of
you and convivial drinkers to the left of
you. It's worth the walk, whether for
Chef Louie's exquisite Veal Pizzaiola or
for a piece of Chocolate Confusion
Cake or Sticky Pecan Cheesecake. ♿
(South Pittsburgh)

TAMBELLINI'S
860 Saw Mill Run Blvd.

Pittsburgh
412/481-1118
$$$

Tambellini's has been a famous Pittsburgh name in seafood for 50 years. Billed as the city's largest restaurant, the building can accommodate 800 diners in six dining areas, and it draws amazing crowds. The nightly seafood special is moderately priced. House specialties include Shrimp or Scallops Louie in garlic sauce, baked stuffed Imperial Crab, and a large seafood platter brimming with lobster, shrimp, oysters, crab cakes, sole, and scallops. Lunch is the best time to enjoy this popular spot because the crowds are smaller, the portions are generous, and the prices are lower than at dinner. ♿ (South Pittsburgh)

WEST PITTSBURGH

HYEHOLDE
190 Hyeholde Dr.
Coraopolis
412/264-3116
$$$$

An elegant atmosphere, plush surroundings, and fine food make dining at Hyeholde a memorable occasion. Gourmet meals can be accompanied by fine wines selected from an extensive list. Diners may enjoy the hanging tapestries, fireplaces, and flagstone floors, which make it easy to imagine being transported to an Elizabethan castle. In summer, you can eat unusual gourmet picnics outdoors while enjoying the surrounding four acres of woodlands. Another unusual dining option is available: groups of two to six diners can sit in the kitchen and observe their meals being prepared. Lunch weekdays, dinner Mon–Sat. Reservations required. (West Pittsburgh)

LE MONT
1114 Grandview Ave.
Pittsburgh
412/431-3100
$$$

A breathtaking view, fine continental cuisine, attentive service, and one of the best wine cellars in town make the award-winning Le Mont one of Pittsburgh's premiere restaurants. Subdued lighting and rich burgundy-and-green decor direct attention to the endlessly fascinating view beyond the windows—the Golden Triangle and Pittsburgh's three rivers seen from Mount Washington. Nevertheless, when the dessert cart laden with chocolate pecan pie and macadamia nut cheesecake appears, everyone manages to tear their eyes away from the view long enough to choose a sweet ending for a delicious meal. ♿ (West Pittsburgh)

THE SHILOH INN
123 Shiloh St.
Pittsburgh
412/431-4000
$$$

Dress is casual and the attitude is cordial at the Shiloh Inn, a meticulously restored two-story, 125-year-old house, where the emphasis is on delicious food and the Civil War–era atmosphere. You can usually find a crowd gathered around the piano bar Monday through Friday from 9 to 1. Twice a year, Broadway revues are presented upstairs on weekends at 9. Because of the building's age, there is no handicapped access. Dinner Mon–Sat. Available for parties of up to 65. (West Pittsburgh)

Doina Locke

5

SIGHTS AND ATTRACTIONS

Pittsburgh offers visitors and residents many interesting attractions: educational, cultural, and entertaining. Pittsburgh also offers an abundance of natural scenic attractions because of its rugged, wooded terrain, rivers, and solutions to the problems they pose—namely, the bridges of Allegheny County, all 2,000 of them.

The sights of Pittsburgh include historic landmarks, towering office buildings, and churches with diverse architectural styles, reflecting the rich variety of the city's spiritual beliefs and ethnic origins.

The sights of Pittsburgh include large county parks, landscaped city parks, heavily wooded "unbuildable" city hillsides and ravines, and the intense green of the surrounding hills and valleys.

The sights of Pittsburgh include its three rivers and its bridges, hills, and tunnels. More than the steel mills that no longer exist, the bridges and tunnels stand as monuments to the people who labored hard and risked their lives building the City of Pittsburgh and bringing it to industrial greatness.

Finally, the sights of Pittsburgh include its pastoral and parklike cemeteries, with their abundant trees, shrubs, and grasses and their beautiful monuments, memorials, and headstones. Contemplating the names and brief histories on the stones is like visiting an outdoor historical museum.

DOWNTOWN PITTSBURGH

BENEDUM CENTER FOR THE PERFORMING ARTS
719 Liberty Ave.

Pittsburgh
412/456-6666
This theater lends glamor to every performance, from its elegant sweeping staircases to the enormous amber

DOWNTOWN PITTSBURGH

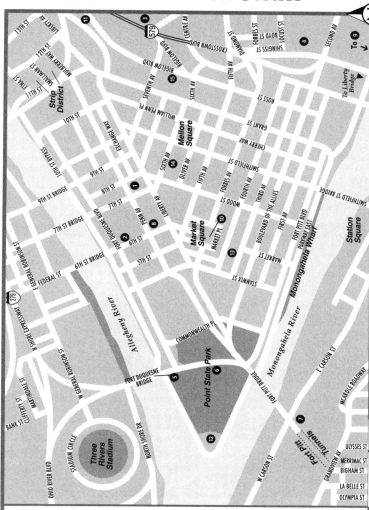

Sights in Downtown Pittsburgh

1 Benedum Center for the Performing Arts
2 Byham Theater
3 Civic Arena
4 Duquesne University Campus
5 Fort Duquesne Bridge
6 Fort Pitt Museum and Blockhouse
7 Fort Pitt Tunnel and the Fort Pitt Bridge
8 Heinz Hall
9 Liberty Tunnels and the Liberty Bridge
10 Market Square
11 *The Pennsylvanian*
12 Point State Park and Fountain
13 PPG Place
14 Trinity Episcopal Cathedral
15 USX Tower

crystal chandelier in its domed ceiling. But the exterior of the Benedum gives little indication of the opulence to be found inside the former Stanley Theater, a movie palace built in 1927. (See also Chapter 11: "Performing Arts.") ᑐ (Downtown Pittsburgh)

BYHAM THEATER
101 Sixth St.
Pittsburgh
412/456-6666
Recently renovated and renamed, the Byham Theater is the former Fulton Theater, Pittsburgh's first vaudeville house. It is located in the distinctive Fulton Building, built in 1906, with a seven-story arch facing the North Side and the Sixth, Seventh, and Ninth Street Bridges across the Allegheny River. The theater's brightly lit marquee lends an air of show-biz excitement to Sixth Street and Fort Duquesne Boulevard. (See also Chapter 11: "Performing Arts.") ᑐ (Downtown Pittsburgh)

CIVIC ARENA
66 Mario Lemieux Place
Pittsburgh
412/642-2062
Even though it's not a skyscraper, "The Igloo" is a unique part of Pittsburgh's downtown skyline. The roof of this silvery half-sphere retracts for open-air performances on beautiful summer nights. Civic Arena is the home of Pittsburgh's championship ice hockey team, the Penguins. (See also Chapter 11: "Performing Arts.") ᑐ (Downtown Pittsburgh)

DUQUESNE UNIVERSITY CAMPUS
600 Forbes Ave.
Pittsburgh
412/396-6000
Built on The Bluff, a plateau overlooking the Monongahela River, the venerable Duquesne University Campus is well worth a walking tour. The University was founded in 1878 by the Fathers of the Holy Ghost. (Downtown Pittsburgh)

FORT DUQUESNE BRIDGE
I-279 at the Allegheny River
Pittsburgh
The Fort Duquesne Bridge crosses the Allegheny River and smoothly continues over the Point to connect with the Fort Pitt Bridge. It was built in 1968 and carries I-279 traffic, connecting downtown Pittsburgh with the North Side and the northern suburbs. (Downtown Pittsburgh)

FORT PITT MUSEUM AND BLOCKHOUSE
Point State Park
Pittsburgh
412/281-9284
The Blockhouse of 1764 is the last vestige of Fort Pitt, built by the British on the Point in 1759. Fort Pitt was built on the site of Fort Duquesne, which was abandoned and burned by the French in their retreat from the British in 1758. The museum is located in one of the excavated bastions of Fort Pitt. Displays and exhibits cover the frontier history of the region. Wed–Sat 10–4:30, Sun 12–4:30. Blockhouse closes at 3:45. Museum: $4 adults, discounts for seniors and children. Blockhouse admission is free (See also Chapter 6: "Museums and Art Galleries.") ᑐ (Downtown Pittsburgh)

FORT PITT TUNNEL AND BRIDGE
I-279 and Route 22/30 at the Monongahela River
Pittsburgh
The Fort Pitt Tunnel and Bridge together frame the view that no visitor to Pittsburgh should miss: The Golden Triangle in all its glory, by day or by

TIP

For outings and return trips to the museums, family membership in the Carnegie is a real bargain. With a family membership, there's no need to rush to visit the entire collection in one exhausting day. Shorter visits allow you to get closer looks at displays with less chance for young children to get tired or bored. A family membership also makes it easier to check out the Rangos Omnimax Theater's latest feature movies and to visit special holiday displays. Members get discounts at museum gift shops, too.

night, with its tightly meshed pattern of skyscrapers. Emerging from the semi-twilight of the tunnel to the sight of the city across the river offers surprising drama and sophistication. The Fort Pitt Bridge carries I-279 and Route 22/30 traffic across the Monongahela River. From the far side of the tunnel, traffic continues west toward the airport via the Parkway West or south via Route 19 (Banksville Road). (Downtown Pittsburgh)

GOLDEN TRIANGLE
Allegheny River, Monongahela River, and Grant Street
Pittsburgh
The 12 square blocks of downtown Pittsburgh are known as the Golden Triangle. Armed with a map from the Greater Pittsburgh Tourist and Convention Bureau information booth at Gateway Center, take a walking tour of the Golden Triangle, noting the energetic activity in the Cultural District and the many restaurants of all sizes and price ranges. Note: "Lift thine eyes"—don't just scan the first-floor establishments. Allow about three hours to cover the area at a leisurely pace. (Downtown Pittsburgh)

HEINZ HALL
600 Penn Ave.
Pittsburgh
412/392-4900

Attending a performance at Heinz Hall is like stepping back in time to Old World elegance and beauty. Today's Heinz Hall was built in 1926 as Loew's Penn Theater, a vaudeville and movie palace. It closed in the 1960s but in 1971 was renovated and renamed. Opera, ballet, and musical performances are featured. Heinz Hall Plaza, a serene "parklet" is nestled next to Heinz Hall on Sixth Street. (See also Chapter 11: "Performing Arts.") & (Downtown Pittsburgh)

LIBERTY TUNNELS AND BRIDGE
I-579 and the Monongahela River
Pittsburgh
The Liberty Tunnels, often called the Liberty Tubes or the Tubes, were the first tunnels built strictly for automobiles in the United States. Built in 1924, they link the suburbs south of the city with downtown Pittsburgh. The Liberty Tunnels and the Liberty Bridge cross the Monongahela to connect with I-579 on the north and Truck Route 19 (West Liberty Avenue) and Route 51 (Sawmill Run Boulevard) on the south. (Downtown Pittsburgh)

MARKET SQUARE
Smithfield St.
Pittsburgh
This square dates back to the late eighteenth century as the site of a city market. Now the commerce and

restaurant trade occurs at its perimeter, while park benches, patio tables and chairs, and high-backed rocking chairs lure people-watchers. The small covered stage is the site of political rallies and musical entertainment. Some of the stores and restaurants ringing the square are historic landmarks—such as Original Oyster House and the 1902 Landmark Tavern. Others, such as Primanti's, are city traditions. It's a great spot to watch the world go by—just watch out for the pigeons. (See also Chapter 8: "Parks, Gardens, and Recreation Areas.") ♿ (Downtown Pittsburgh)

THE PENNSYLVANIAN
1100 Liberty Ave.
Pittsburgh
412/391-2272

Sharing an address with the Amtrak station, The Pennsylvanian is now a luxury apartment building and commercial office building. It comes with a long history. Before its recent renovation, the elegant 12-story building was the Pennsylvania Railroad Station, built at the turn of the century. The location was the site of Union Station, burned down in the riot of 1877. A lavishly decorated domed rotunda with dramatic arches covers the entrance to the building's lobby. (Downtown Pittsburgh)

POINT STATE PARK AND FOUNTAIN
Allegheny and Monongahela Rivers
Pittsburgh

Point State Park is the smallest state park in Pennsylvania, covering 36 acres where the Allegheny and Monongahela Rivers converge to form the Ohio River. The park contains a museum and fountain and is the site of concerts, festivals, and fireworks displays. Designated as a park in the Pittsburgh Renaissance of the 1950s, the Point was previously covered with warehouses and railroad yards. A paved walkway follows the riverbanks, but some areas are not easily wheelchair accessible. The entrance to the park is a tunnel passing under Fort Pitt Bridge.

Built in 1974, the Point State Park Fountain, with its spectacular column of water shooting 150 feet straight up, provides a dramatic counterpoint to the city skyline. Pumps draw the water from a subterranean "river," the Wisconsin glacial flow (which has no connection to city's three rivers), from 54 feet below the surface. The fountain operates daily, weather permitting, spring through fall. (See also Chapter 8: "Parks, Gardens, and Recreation Areas.") (Downtown Pittsburgh)

PPG PLACE
Market Square
Pittsburgh

An eye-catching standout on the downtown skyline, PPG Place is a dazzling complex of five aluminum and reflective glass buildings clustered around an open plaza. Their rooftop peaks and imposing presence bring to mind battlements of a fantasy-world fortress or perhaps a fairy-tale castle. The open plaza, surrounded by the skyscraper and four smaller glass office buildings of PPG Place, is the site of free lunchtime concerts every Friday in May. Wintergarden, a stunning three-story glass-walled atrium, with the crystal castle towering overhead, is the location of the Santas Around the World display at Christmas. The Shops are located in Two PPG Place. (See also Chapter 8: "Parks, Gardens, and Recreation Areas" and Chapter 9: "Shopping.") (Downtown Pittsburgh)

The National Aviary, p. 87

TRINITY EPISCOPAL CATHEDRAL
Sixth Ave.
Pittsburgh
412/232-6404

The intricate Gothic Revival design of Trinity Cathedral makes a powerful visual impact and the surrounding, towering skyscrapers don't overwhelm it. The cathedral was built in 1872. It shares space with a small graveyard that holds the remains of early Native Americans, French, and British. The cathedral and graveyard make an interesting stop on walking tours of downtown. (Downtown Pittsburgh)

USX TOWER
600 Grant St.
Pittsburgh

Originally called the U.S. Steel Building, the USX Tower is covered entirely in steel—it was designed to showcase the company's namesake product. Because steel rusts and weakens, it is generally not used for outer walls. However, the USX Tower is covered with Cor-Ten, a special U.S. Steel product with a self-limiting rusting process. As this steel rusts, the first rust layer protects the steel beneath it. When the tower was built in 1970, it became the tallest building in downtown Pittsburgh, with a height of 841 feet. The triangular structure is one of downtown's more unusual landmarks, and visitors and residents alike relish a trip to the Top of the Triangle, a fine restaurant located (where else?) on top. (Downtown Pittsburgh)

NORTH PITTSBURGH

ALCOA BUILDING
River Ave. between the Seventh and Ninth Street Bridges
Pittsburgh

With its smoothly undulating face turned toward the Allegheny River, the new Alcoa Building seems to mimic the river's waves, at the same time reflecting them. This striking addition to the North Shore should not be overlooked on any tour. Perhaps the best view of the structure is

NORTH PITTSBURGH

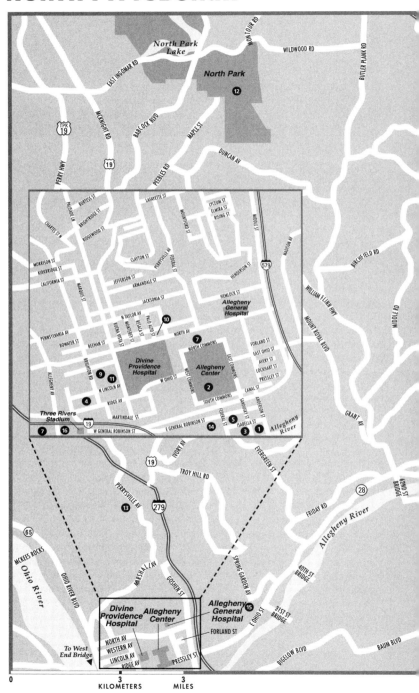

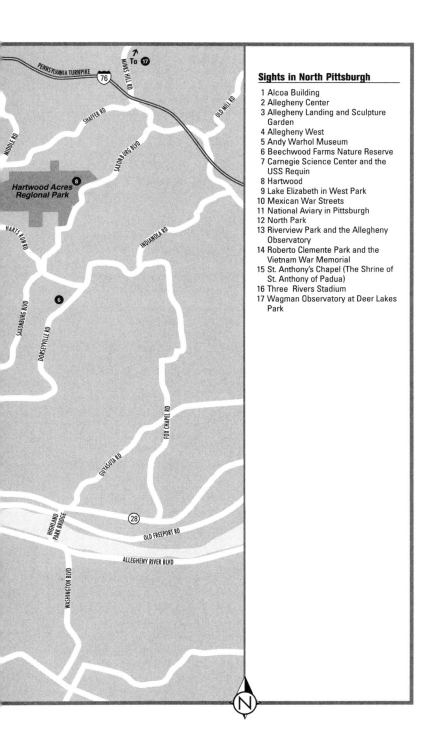

Sights in North Pittsburgh

1 Alcoa Building
2 Allegheny Center
3 Allegheny Landing and Sculpture Garden
4 Allegheny West
5 Andy Warhol Museum
6 Beechwood Farms Nature Reserve
7 Carnegie Science Center and the USS Requin
8 Hartwood
9 Lake Elizabeth in West Park
10 Mexican War Streets
11 National Aviary in Pittsburgh
12 North Park
13 Riverview Park and the Allegheny Observatory
14 Roberto Clemente Park and the Vietnam War Memorial
15 St. Anthony's Chapel (The Shrine of St. Anthony of Padua)
16 Three Rivers Stadium
17 Wagman Observatory at Deer Lakes Park

Literary Pittsburgh: Recommended Reading

African American in Pennsylvania, Shifting Historical Perspectives, Joe William Trotter Jr. and Eric Ledell Smith, editors (1997)

The All New GO GUIDE: Two-Day Getaways from Pittsburgh by Jane and Wingenbach Clark (1997)

Ghost Stories of Pittsburgh and Allegheny by Beth E. Trapani and Charles J. Adams (1994)

The Johnstown Flood by David McCullough (1987)

Only in Pittsburgh by S. Trevor Hadley (1994)

Pittsburgh: The Story of a City 1750–1865 by Leland D. Baldwin (1995)

Pittsburgh: An Urban History by Franklin Toker (1986)

The Pittsburgh Pirates: An Illustrated History by Bob Smizik (1996)

Pittsburgh: Views into the 21st Century by Joel B. Levinson, Susan Negra, and others (1996)

A Rich/Poor Man's Guide to Pittsburgh by Dorothy Miller (1997)

Seeing Pittsburgh by Barringer Fifield (1996)

The Tongue-in-Cheek Guide to Pittsburgh by Ken and Jackie Abel (1992)

---

the changing perspective you get as you move across the Seventh Street Bridge. From the walkway alongside the water, the angled view of the successive waves of glass is also spectacular. (North Pittsburgh)

ALLEGHENY CENTER
North, East, West, and South

Commons Rds.
Pittsburgh
Allegheny Center is a complex of modern apartment buildings, office buildings, and a shopping mall. It also holds the first Carnegie Library, the Old Post Office, the Buhl Planetarium, and the Institute of Popular Science. The library building includes Carnegie

Hall, home of the Pittsburgh Public Theatre. The Old Post Office no longer sees any mail but still has hordes of visitors to the Children's Museum of Pittsburgh.

The center's broad, tree-lined walkways lead past sculptures rescued from demolished buildings and bridges, as well as fine examples of modern and traditional art. The square contains a fountain within an amphitheatre setting that encourages children to play in its spray. (North Pittsburgh)

ALLEGHENY LANDING AND SCULPTURE GARDEN
Allegheny River North Shore between Federal and Sandusky Sts.
Pittsburgh
Allegheny Landing is a small park on the riverfront between the Sixth and Seventh Street Bridges. The Sculpture Garden consists of artwork scattered throughout the park. A colorful abstract metal installation invites children to explore and climb. Nearby, a noble effort in marble, an anatomically correct Grecian stylized frieze, has, unfortunately, already succumbed to vandals. A life-size pair of figures is so realistic that a plaque identifying it as *The Builders* is almost unnecessary. A paved walkway includes a water-taxi landing and extends along the Allegheny River to Three Rivers Stadium. (See also Chapter 8: "Parks, Gardens, and Recreation Areas.") ⅊ (North Pittsburgh)

ALLEGHENY WEST
Allegheny Ave., Ridge Ave., and Brighton Rd.
Pittsburgh
This small neighborhood was once the wealthiest in the North Side—formerly Allegheny City. Industrial giants

such as Andrew Carnegie, H. J. Heinz, and Henry Oliver—some of Pittsburgh's wealthiest citizens—lived here before moving on to grander mansions. Famed painter Mary Cassatt, modern dance great Martha Graham, and world-class mystery writer Mary Roberts Rinehart also lived here, and author Gertrude Stein was born at 850 Beech Avenue in 1878. A leisurely drive through Allegheny West, comparing the architecture to that along the Mexican War Streets, can cap off a visit to the nearby National Aviary of Pittsburgh. (North Pittsburgh)

ANDY WARHOL MUSEUM
117 Sandusky St.
Pittsburgh
412/237-8300
An ornate turn-of-the-century building, a renovated former warehouse built in 1910, seems an unlikely location for a collection of pop art, but it is appropriate for the contradictions and complexities of Andy Warhol's world. He was a native son, but he achieved international fame. His

PPG Place, p. 80

Doina Locke

artwork and a small part of his vast personal collection are on display in this museum dedicated solely to his work and life. Thur–Sat 11–8, Sun and Wed 11–6. $6 adults, discounts for children and seniors. (See also Chapter 6: "Museums and Galleries") ♿ (North Pittsburgh)

BEECHWOOD FARMS NATURE RESERVE
614 Dorseyville Rd.
Fox Chapel
412/963-6100
Abundant wildlife flourishes in this 90-acre reserve, a treat for bird-watchers and hikers on its five miles of carefully laid out trails. The large education center, housed in a comfortable wood-frame building, is used for talks, classes, and summer camp activities. Trails open daily from dawn to dusk. Education Center open Tue–Sat 9–5, Sun 1–5. Free. (See also Chapter 7: "Kids' Stuff" and Chapter 8: "Parks, Gardens, and Recreation Areas.") (North Pittsburgh)

CARNEGIE SCIENCE CENTER AND THE USS REQUIN
One Allegheny Ave.
Pittsburgh
412/237-3400
With more than 250 hands-on exhibits demonstrating scientific principles and technological advances, the Science Center might sound too much like school. But in fact the complex is never boring and is a fun place to visit. The nationally respected Henry Buhl Jr. Planetarium and Observatory, SciQuest, Early Learners' Landing, the SeaLife Aquarium, and the Miniature Railroad and Village are just some of the Science Center's attractions. One of only a few Omnimax theaters in the country, the Rangos Omnimax surrounds you with wraparound sights

Duquesne Incline, p. 98

and sounds. The USS *Requin*, a decommissioned submarine moored outside the Science Center in the Ohio River, offers an astounding glimpse of life aboard a World War II sub. Imagine yourself going underwater in that! Sun–Fri 10–5, Sat 10–9. $6–12 adults, discounts for children and seniors. Parking: $3 (See also Chapter 6: "Museums and Galleries" and Chapter 7: "Kids' Stuff.") (North Pittsburgh)

HARTWOOD
215 Saxonburg Blvd.
Hampton
412/767-9200
Located just off the Green Belt on Saxonburg Boulevard, this former estate is now a 639-acre county park. Attractions include a Gothic Tudor mansion and formal gardens, dinner theater, outdoor concerts, charity polo matches, and show-horse jumping competitions. Large, ultra-modern abstract installations are scattered about the grounds, in stark contrast to the imposing, historic landmark stone

mansion dominating the hilltop and its formal gardens. The annual winter light show draws huge crowds. April–Dec Wed–Sat 10–3, Sun 12–4. $3 adults, discounts for seniors and children. Reservations required for guided tours. (See also Chapter 8: "Parks, Gardens, and Recreation Areas.") (North Pittsburgh)

LAKE ELIZABETH IN WEST PARK
W. North Ave., Brighton Rd., and Ridge Ave.
Pittsburgh
This pretty little artificial lake provides a serene setting for strollers, picnickers, and children. Beyond the water and the surrounding treetops, the skyline of the Golden Triangle is visible. The double arch of the small bridge is a graceful addition to the scene. (North Pittsburgh)

MEXICAN WAR STREETS
North of W. North Ave.
Pittsburgh
History is preserved in this neighborhood of row houses built between 1850 and the 1890s in what used to be Allegheny City. Named after heroes and battles of the Mexican War, these streets and avenues bear such names as Palo Alto, Monterey, Buena Vista, Resada, Jacksonia, Sampsonia, and Taylor. The homes, most of which are built in the Greek Revival style, were originally owned by businesspeople, who commuted to downtown by horsecar. (North Pittsburgh)

NATIONAL AVIARY IN PITTSBURGH
Allegheny Commons West
Pittsburgh
412/323-7235
More than 250 species of birds, some endangered, are sheltered in 23 different habitats at the only national aviary in the country. In the Marsh Room, visitors stroll on an elevated walkway over a small pond and through lush vegetation to observe native birds as they swim, feed, and fly overhead. American bald eagles solemnly watch the colorful parade of visitors behind the glass walls of their outdoor enclosure. Exotic and potentially endangered species such as Bali mynahs, pink pigeons and red-crowned cranes survive and flourish in habitats dedicated to their preservation. Daily 9–5. $4 adults, discounts for children and seniors. (See also Chapter 7: "Kids' Stuff.") &. (North Pittsburgh)

NORTH PARK
E. Ingomar Rd. (Yellow Belt)
North Hills
724/935-1971
Encompassing 3,010 acres, North Park is the largest of Allegheny County's nine parks. Most of its buildings and extensive woods were Depression-era WPA and CCC projects. The park has many facilities for recreation, including the Latodami Nature Center, which has a full-time naturalist on staff. The beautiful and well-maintained park swimming pool is one of the largest in the world. The park also has a golf course, tennis courts, an ice-skating rink and a boathouse. The fishing on North Park lake is excellent. (See also Chapter 8: "Parks, Gardens, and Recreation Areas" and Chapter 10: "Sports and Recreation.") &. (North Pittsburgh)

RIVERVIEW PARK AND THE ALLEGHENY OBSERVATORY
Brighton Rd.
Pittsburgh
Riverview Park is located on the North Side, off Perrysville Avenue (Route 19) or Brighton Road. It is a 250-acre city

Clayton, p. 92

park with a swimming pool, tennis courts, and ball fields. Riverview Drive within the park leads to the Allegheny Observatory, which, when it was built in 1856, housed the third-largest telescope in the country. During this research facility's brief public season, tours are available by reservation only; call 412/321-2400. (See also Chapter 8: "Parks, Gardens, and Recreation Areas.") (North Pittsburgh)

ROBERTO CLEMENTE PARK AND THE VIETNAM WAR MEMORIAL
Allegheny River
Pittsburgh
The riverside walkway that extends from Three Rivers Stadium to just short of the Sixth Street Bridge combines the visual impact of the Allegheny River and some of its bridges, the Point, the far shore of the Monongahela River, and large-scale works of art. Near the stadium, the walk embraces the Vietnam War Memorial, an emotional depiction of homecoming

with realistic life-size figures. It is an accessible monument that viewers can walk through and around and contemplate from all sides. (See also Chapter 8: "Parks, Gardens, and Recreation Areas.") & (North Pittsburgh)

ST. ANTHONY'S CHAPEL (THE SHRINE OF ST. ANTHONY OF PADUA)
1704 Harpster St.
Pittsburgh
412/231-2969, ext. 5
Built between 1880 and 1890, the Shrine of St. Anthony of Padua, or St. Anthony's Chapel, was financed by the private fortune of Father Suitbert Mollinger, son of a wealthy Belgian family. The chapel holds a collection of more than 5,000 sacred relics, perhaps the largest in the Western Hemisphere. Sadly, Father Mollinger died shortly after the completion of the chapel. The Suitbert Mollinger House, built in 1876, is nearby on Harpster Street. Tue, Thur, Sat, Sun

EAST PITTSBURGH

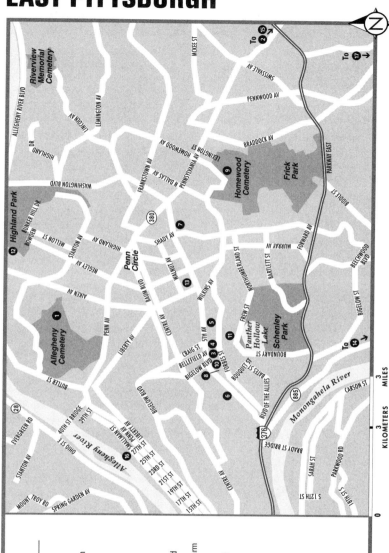

Sights in East Pittsburgh

1 Allegheny Cemetery
2 Boyce Park
3 Carnegie Institute
4 Carnegie Library of Pittsburgh
5 Carnegie Mellon University
6 Cathedral of Learning
7 Clayton
8 Heinz Memorial Chapel
9 Homewood Cemetery
10 Nationality Classrooms
11 Phipps Conservatory
12 Pittsburgh Zoo
13 Rodef Shalom Synagogue and Bibical Gardens
14 Round Hill Park and Exhibit Farm
15 Sri Venkateswara Temple
16 Strip District
17 George Westinghouse Bridge

TIP

The ballgame parking lot crush can be avoided by planning ahead. Get an early start, park at Station Square, and take the Gateway Clipper shuttle to Three Rivers Stadium.

1–4; tours at 1, 2, and 3. Chapel opens at 12:15 Sun. For information from the Chapel Shop, call 412/323-9504. (North Pittsburgh)

THREE RIVERS STADIUM
400 Stadium Circle
Pittsburgh
412/321-0650 (tour information)
Home of the Pittsburgh Steelers and the Pittsburgh Pirates, Three Rivers Stadium is a distinctive part of the North Shore riverfront. It is located on the site of Exposition Field, where the Pirates played in the first World Series in 1903. Across the Allegheny River from the Point, the stadium is accessible on foot by way of the Fort Duquesne Bridge pedestrian walkway, by boat (either private or Gateway Clipper shuttle) at Allegheny Landing, by chartered buses, or by car. Guided tours are available; call for information. (See also Chapter 10: "Sports and Recreation.") & (North Pittsburgh)

WAGMAN OBSERVATORY AT DEER LAKES PARK
Mahaffey Rd.
Frazier Township
724/265-3520 (park)
724/224-2510 (observatory)
Deer Lakes county park is the home of Wagman Observatory, which houses several major telescopes. The observatory hosts free public "star parties," at which people can gaze at the stars through more powerful tele-

scopes than generally are available to the public. (See also Chapter 8: "Parks, Gardens, and Recreation Areas.") (North Pittsburgh)

EAST PITTSBURGH

ALLEGHENY CEMETERY
4734 Butler St.
Pittsburgh
Pittsburgh's history and some of its most intensely personal public art can be found in its cemeteries. The largest, Allegheny Cemetery and Homewood Cemetery, are parklike and elegant. Allegheny Cemetery was designed in 1844 and was the fourth rural cemetery in the United States, after those in Boston, Philadelphia, and Brooklyn. The graves of many famous people can be found here, including Stephen Foster, Lillian Russell, and Harry Thaw. (East Pittsburgh)

BOYCE PARK
Frankstown Rd.
Plum
412/271-2717
Boyce Park covers 1,096 acres, and it is the only Allegheny County park with downhill ski facilities, including a ski lodge, a snow-making machine, four tow ropes, rental equipment, and instruction. The lodge is available year-round for rental and on-site catering. The Boyce Park Nature Center is staffed by a full-time natu-

ralist. Other facilities include a wave pool, basketball courts, lighted ball fields, and a variety of trails, including bridle paths. The Carpenter Homestead, a replica of a log house originally built on the site, is used for historical society programs. (See also Chapter 8: "Parks, Gardens, and Recreation Areas.") (East Pittsburgh)

CARNEGIE INSTITUTE
4400 Forbes Ave.
Pittsburgh
412/622-3131
Andrew Carnegie made his fortune in Pittsburgh and gave away $350 million around the world. His gift of the Carnegie Institute established Oakland as Pittsburgh's cultural center in 1895. Today, the massive structure forms the foundation of the Carnegie Museums, which include the Carnegie Museum of Art and the Carnegie Museum of Natural History, both located here, and the Carnegie Science Center and Andy Warhol Museum, located on the North Side. The Carnegie Music Hall and the Carnegie Library are also part of the institute. Don't miss it, but don't expect to cover everything in one visit. (See also Chapter 6: "Museums and Galleries.") & (East Pittsburgh)

CARNEGIE LIBRARY OF PITTSBURGH
4400 Forbes Ave.
Pittsburgh
412/622-3116
The Carnegie Library of Pittsburgh is the city's main library and has 18 branches in Pittsburgh. It contains a collection of 4.5 million books, periodicals, and audio visual materials and is a good spot to start any research project. The library system was instituted by Andrew Carnegie at the turn of the century and now has 2,500

Carnegie libraries around the world. & (East Pittsburgh)

CARNEGIE MELLON UNIVERSITY
Schenley Park
Pittsburgh
412/268-2000
Carnegie Mellon University (CMU) has established an international reputation as a leader in robotics and software. Its campus is tucked behind Schenley Park. If you stand at the Forbes Avenue entrance to the Carnegie's parking lot and look across the wooded ravine, you will have a wonderful view of the university's impressive Hammerschlag Hall, topped with a tower of pillars and arches surrounding a smokestack. It's worth taking a leisurely walking tour of the campus to enjoy the parklike setting and the early twentieth-century buildings. & (East Pittsburgh)

CATHEDRAL OF LEARNING
Fifth Ave. and Bigelow Blvd.

Phipps Conservatory, p. 93

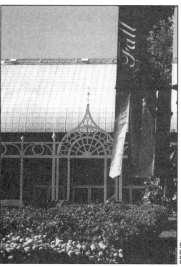

GPCVB

(University Of Pittsburgh)
Pittsburgh
412/624-6000
Reputed to be the tallest college classroom building in the Western Hemisphere, the University of Pittsburgh's Cathedral of Learning is 42 stories high. When you're in Oakland, as Pittsburghers love to say, "You can't miss it." The Commons Room, with its soaring three-story ceiling, is used as a study hall. But the lighting is so dim that, even with a desk lamp at every table, it's a wonder anyone can read here. Stop at the information counter for a map of the Nationality Classrooms before you take a look around. ৬ (East Pittsburgh)

CLAYTON
7227 Reynolds St.
Pittsburgh
412/371-0600
Henry Clay Frick's mansion in Point Breeze was one of many millionaire's homes in that neighborhood when the wealthy industrialist and philanthropist bought it in 1882. Today it is the only one left. Clayton was built in 1872 and was remodeled several times and then completely restored to its turn-of-the-century condition, along with many of the original family belongings. The house is the base for the six-acre Frick Art and Historical Center. Frick's daughter, Helen Clay Frick, lived in the mansion until her death in 1984 at the age of 96. Tue–Sat 10–5:30, Sun 12–5. $6 adults, discounts for students and seniors. (See also Chapter 6: "Museums and Galleries" and Chapter 7: "Kids' Stuff.") ৬ (East Pittsburgh)

HEINZ MEMORIAL CHAPEL
Fifth and Bellefield Aves.
(University of Pittsburgh)
Pittsburgh

412/624-4157
Heinz Memorial Chapel is an architectural jewel set in the center of the University of Pittsburgh campus. Light streaming in through the enormous stained-glass windows is the only interior illumination; the chapel was never wired for electricity. An inspirational marble altar, carved stone- and woodwork, and an organ are other notable features. The stylized French Gothic interdenominational chapel is a wonderful setting for a wedding, but it is available only to Pitt alumni, employees, and their families. Concerts, recitals, and programs are also held here. Mon–Fri 9–4, Sun 1–5. Free. Guided tours available only by appointment. (East Pittsburgh)

HOMEWOOD CEMETERY
Beacon St. and Beechwood Blvd.
Pittsburgh
The cemetery is the prestigious resting place of H. J. Heinz, Henry Clay Frick, members of the Mellon family, and many other wealthy Pittsburghers. The grounds cover 205 acres. (East Pittsburgh)

NATIONALITY CLASSROOMS
Fifth Ave. and Bigelow Blvd.
(University of Pittsburgh)
Pittsburgh
412/624-6000
The Nationality Classrooms are deep within the Cathedral of Learning, on both the first and third floors, ringing the central Commons Room. Each of the 23 working classrooms was sponsored, designed, and decorated by architects and artists with the same ethnic heritage as the room they worked on. The Christmas decorations are superb. Mon–Fri 9–3, Sat 9:30–3, Sun 11–3. Guided tours Apr–Aug, Dec, and Sat and Sun. Guided tours: 50 cents–$2. Reserva-

tions recommended at least two weeks in advance for guided tours. ♿ (East Pittsburgh)

PHIPPS CONSERVATORY
Schenley Dr., Schenley Park
Pittsburgh
412/622-6914

The distinctive, graceful curves of the Victorian-era glass structure enhance the natural beauty of Schenley Park and the plants within the conservatory. When the conservatory was built in 1893, it was the first large-scale enclosed botanical garden in the country. At 2.5 acres, it is still the largest greenhouse in the country. Several specialty gardens are maintained inside, and seasonal exhibitions draw large crowds. Do not ignore the exterior of the building; the landscaping includes flowering annuals, lily ponds, and three exuberant leaping dolphin topiaries. Tues–Sun 9–5. $4 adults, $5 for special shows, discounts for children and seniors. (See also Chapter 8: "Parks, Gardens, and Recreation Areas.") (East Pittsburgh)

PITTSBURGH ZOO
1 Hill Rd.
Pittsburgh
412/665-3640

The Pittsburgh Zoo opened in Highland Park in 1898, one of the first zoos in the country. The 77-acre park now includes natural habitats for many of its 4,000 animals, including 38 endangered species. Just entering the zoo is an adventure—you ride an outdoor escalator from the parking lot and pass through a tunnel. A winding pathway takes you past the new interactive Discovery Pavilion, where fish swim by overhead in an aquarium; past Kids' Kingdom, where children can play like the animals; and past the Carousel, Asian Forest,

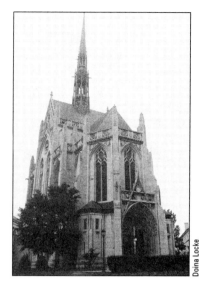

Heinz Memorial Chapel

African Savannah, Tropical Forest, Cheetah Valley, AquaZoo, and Niches of the World, an underground zoo. Memorial Day–Labor Day daily 10–6, rest of year daily 9:30–4. $6 adults, discounts for children and seniors. (See also Chapter 7: "Kids' Stuff") ♿ (East Pittsburgh)

RODEF SHALOM SYNAGOGUE AND BIBLICAL GARDENS
4905 Fifth Ave.
Pittsburgh
412/621-6566

Built in 1907, Rodef Shalom Synagogue is one of Oakland's architectural treasures, yet it is radically different in style than the rest of Oakland. Its intricate decoration is exotic and more typical of the East than the West. As with other houses of worship, the serious visitor who would like to look more closely should call in advance for permission. The synagogue grounds are the setting for the

Doina Locke

Rodef Shalom Biblical Gardens. Gardens open June–Sept 15 Sun–Thur 10–2, Sat 12–1, Wed 7 p.m.–9 p.m. Free. (See also Chapter 8: "Parks, Gardens, and Recreation Areas.") (East Pittsburgh)

ROUND HILL PARK AND EXHIBIT FARM
Rt. 48
Elizabeth Township
412/384-8555

Children can check out the green eggs laid by Polish show chickens and judge for themselves if they were the inspiration for Dr. Seuss's *Green Eggs and Ham.* This 1,100-acre county park has the added attraction of an exhibit farm, set up in 1968 at the site of the historical Scott House, which lets kids experience the operations of a real, working farm. The farm has both dairy and beef cattle and several varieties of chickens. Guided tours are available with advance reservations. There are also picnic areas and ball fields for public use. (See also Chapter 8: "Parks, Gardens, and Recreation Areas.") (East Pittsburgh)

SRI VENKATESWARA TEMPLE
1230 S. McCully Drive
Penn Hills
412/373-3380

A Hindu temple may be the last thing you'd expect to see in suburban Pittsburgh, but the beautiful, intricately carved white walls and towers rising from a tree-filled hillside are part of the Penn Hills landscape. Sri Venkateswara Temple is one of only 10 Hindu temples in the United States. Mon–Fri 10–4. Free guided tours available by appointment only; call for reservations. (East Pittsburgh)

STRIP DISTRICT
Smallman St. and Penn Ave.

Pittsburgh
The former industrial warehouse area, where trains once brought in fresh produce and carried out specialty steel, is still a bustling district selling the freshest produce, meat. and seafood. Extending for several blocks along Smallman Street and Penn Avenue east of the Veterans Bridge and I-579, the Strip provides a wealth of stores, street vendors, restaurants, and nightspots. Fresh foods, ethnic foods, exotic ingredients, and specialty imports are all jammed together, so shoppers can search and comparison shop, then be satisfied that they got "such a deal." Saturday is the Strip's busiest retail day, and you can get the best bargains in the afternoon as grocers try to unload their perishable leftovers. But if you can't handle crowds, try shopping during the week. (See also Chapter 9: "Shopping.") (East Pittsburgh)

GEORGE WESTINGHOUSE BRIDGE
Route 30 at Braddock Avenue
Turtle Creek

The sheer immensity of the George Westinghouse Bridge makes it awe-inspiring. When it was built in 1932, it was the longest concrete arch in the country. It crosses Braddock Avenue in Turtle Creek near the site of the two-mile-long electric works that Westinghouse opened in 1894. The Westinghouse company has left Pittsburgh, but the bridge stands as a reminder of the enormous role that George Westinghouse played in the days of Pittsburgh's industrial giants. (East Pittsburgh)

SOUTH PITTSBURGH

EAST CARSON STREET
South bank of the Monongahela

SOUTHWEST PITTSBURGH

Sights in Southwest Pittsburgh

1 Duquesne Incline and the West End
   Overlook (WP)
2 E. Carson Street (SP)
3 Kennywood Park (SP)
4 Monongahela Incline (SP)
5 Pittsburgh International Airport and
   Airmall (WP)
6 Sandcastle (SP)
7 Settler's Cabin Park (WP)
8 South Park and the Oliver Miller
   Homestead (SP)
9 Station Square (SP)

Note: This map includes South and
West Pittsburgh Zone listings.

Light Up Your Life: Holiday Displays

Zoolights, when the Pittsburgh Zoo sports thousands of sparkling lights in the evening during November and December, is a genuine holiday treat. Walking tours delight all ages.

The **Celebration of Lights** at Hartwood is a drive-through spectacular, with lighted display figures throughout the Hartwood estate grounds. Admission fees are donated to area charities. The dazzling display attracts huge crowds, so be prepared to wait in traffic on your way in and out.

Light Up Night in downtown Pittsburgh attracts huge crowds for fireworks and entertainment before the lighting of the city's Christmas tree. Downtown traffic is re-routed to ease rush-hour congestion for commuters and celebrants alike. Be on the lookout for free parking and free refreshments.

River
Pittsburgh

Carson Street is the "Main Street" of the South Side, formerly known as Birmingham and now designated a National Historic District, one of only seven Main Street USA Centers in the country. Restaurants, bookstores, nightspots, antique shops, tattoo and piercing parlors, fashions for skateboarders and slackers, and specialty shops fill the nineteenth- and early twentieth-century storefronts here on the south bank of the Monongahela River. Ongoing restoration includes peeling back facades to reveal wonderful art deco and Victorian buildings that were covered with brick, wood, and aluminum years ago. Parking is predominantly on-street metered parking; there is a small, metered public lot. (South Pittsburgh)

KENNYWOOD PARK
4800 Kennywood Blvd.

West Mifflin
412/461-0500

One of only two amusement parks in the country to be named a National Historical Landmark, Kennywood Park is more than 100 years old. Five roller coasters provide plenty of state-of-the-art thrills. These include the impressive Thunderbolt, the 80-mile-an-hour Steel Phantom, and the old-favorite Jack Rabbit. Lacking curves but still giving a major thrill is the aptly named Pitt Fall. Live entertainment, midway games, sideshow attractions, kiddie rides, and plenty of food stands keep every member of the family happy. Ethnic days and community days always draw large crowds, but no one ever feels left out. Pittsburgh favorites are Potato Patch fries, served with gravy, cheese, vinegar, or whatever, and the enormous funnel cakes, delicious Pennsylvania Dutch treats. Mid-May–Sept 1 daily 10:30–10. $4.95–$19.95, discounts for seniors. (See also Chapter 7: "Kids' Stuff.") & (South Pittsburgh)

MONONGAHELA INCLINE
Carson Street across from Station Square
Pittsburgh
412/442-2000

The tracks ascending Mt. Washington are an unmistakable part of Pittsburgh's unique landscape. At one time, Pittsburgh had as many as 17 working inclines moving passengers up and down the steep slopes of the city. The Mon Incline connects Station Square with Mt. Washington, a distance of 635 feet. It was the city's first, built in 1870, and was designated a National Historic Landmark in 1970. The UFO-like observation platform at the top offers a great view—don't forget your camera. Mon–Sat 5:30 a.m.–12:45 a.m., Sun 8:45–12. $1 adults, discount for seniors and children. (South Pittsburgh)

SANDCASTLE
1000 Sandcastle Dr.
West Homestead
412/462-6666

Sandcastle water park is one of Pittsburgh's most popular summer attractions. The site, an abandoned steel mill on the Monongahela River, has been converted into a long boardwalk linking 15 breathtaking water slides, assorted pools, hot tubs, a Lazy River, sand volleyball, food booths, and a Sandbar for adults. Wet Willie's Waterworks is a special playground for children, and the Tad Pool is for smaller children. An 18-hole miniature golf course and two Formula One tracks are located adjacent to the water park. Admission to each is separate. June–Aug daily 11–6. $8.50–14.50, discounts for seniors. (See also Chapter 7: "Kids' Stuff.") (South Pittsburgh)

SOUTH PARK AND THE OLIVER MILLER HOMESTEAD
Corrigan Dr. and Brownsville Rd.
South Hills
412/ 835-5710 (park information)
412/835-1554 (homestead)

South Park's 1,999 acres include a wave pool, skating rink, tennis courts, nature center, and golf course. In addition, the grounds hold the South Park Conservatory Theatre, which produces the Summer Straw Hat theatre program; call 412/831-8552 for information. South Park also is the site of a newly renovated game preserve with a small herd of buffalo, white-tailed deer, pheasants, partridges, quail, ducks, and geese.The Oliver Miller Homestead dates back to the Whiskey Rebellion of 1794 and includes special exhibits and tours of a stone house, log house, and blacksmith shop. Sun 1–4. (See also Chapter 8: "Parks, Gardens, and Recreation Areas" and Chapter 10: "Sports and Recreation.") (South Pittsburgh)

STATION SQUARE
Carson St. at the Smithfield Street Bridge
Pittsburgh

Station Square is a shopping, dining, and entertainment complex that is popular with visitors and Pittsburghers alike. Located on the far side of the Monongahela River across the Smithfield Street Bridge from downtown, it covers about forty acres of former railroad yards. The terminal, with its fabulous domed, stained-glass ceiling, has been converted into the Grand Concourse restaurant. The warehouse is now Commerce Court, home of the Shops of Station Square. Visit Bessemer Court, a small outdoor museum, for a peek at Pittsburgh's industrial past. (See also Chapter 3: "Where to Stay," Chapter 4: "Where

to Eat," and Chapter 9: "Shopping.") &
(South Pittsburgh)

WEST PITTSBURGH

DUQUESNE INCLINE AND
THE WEST END OVERLOOK
**Carson St. between the Fort Pitt
Bridge and Station Square
Pittsburgh
412/381-1665**
The Society for the Preservation of
the Duquesne Heights Incline operates this historic incline, one of only
two left in Pittsburgh. The 1877 cable
railway and station were carefully restored, although electricity, rather
than steam, drives the incline now.
The Duquesne Incline is 800 feet long
and travels to a height of 400 feet at
an angle of 30 degrees. Once at the
top, visit the observation platform for
a magnificent view of Pittsburgh and
its rivers. Mon–Sat 5:30 a.m.–12:45
a.m., Sun and holidays 7 a.m.–12:45
a.m. $1 adults, discounts for children
11 and under. (West Pittsburgh)

PITTSBURGH INTERNATIONAL
AIRPORT AND AIRMALL
**Airport Expressway (Route 60)
Findlay Township
412/472-3525**
Even if you don't fly into town, a visit
to the Pittsburgh International Airport,
one of the best airports in the country,
is definitely worth the drive. The airport itself is divided into two portions:
Landside and Airside. They are very
efficiently linked by an express subway train. Ticket counters and airport
security dominate Landside. US Airways Express gates are also Landside. All other airlines use the four
Airside concourses. Airmall is located
Airside, and its approximately one
hundred shops, restaurants, and services can be found along the concourses and at their hub. (See also
Chapter 9: "Shopping.") & (West Pittsburgh)

SETTLER'S CABIN PARK
**Greer Rd. southeast of Rt. 22/30
and Rt. 60
Imperial
412/787-2750**
Located in the western corner of the
county, Settler's Cabin Park covers
1,290 acres. In addition to a wave
pool, it has a diving pool with both
springboard and platform diving. To
use the high boards, a swimmer has
to pass a test of diving ability. Settler's
Cabin also has six tennis courts. (See
also Chapter 8: "Parks, Gardens, and
Recreation Areas" and Chapter 10:
"Sports and Recreation.") (West
Pittsburgh)

CITY TOURS

GATEWAY CLIPPER FLEET
**9 Station Square Dock
Pittsburgh
412/355-7980**
The Gateway Clipper Fleet offers
standard two- to two-and-a-half-hour
narrated sightseeing tours and special tours such as Lock and Dam, Twilight Fountain, and romantic
moonlight dance cruises. The fleet
consists of the 1,000-passenger *Majestic*, the 600-passenger *Gateway
Party Liner*, two 400-passenger
Belles, and the 150-passenger *Good
Ship Lollipop*, which offers delightful
child-oriented cruises. Memorial
Day—Labor Day daily. Times vary;
call for information. $8.50 adults, dis-
counts for seniors and children.

GRAY LINE OF PITTSBURGH
110 Lenzner Court

Sewickley
412/741-2720

Gray Line offers four tours of Pittsburgh: a two-hour Historic Pittsburgh Tour, a three-hour Cultural Pittsburgh Tour, a combination tour of Historic and Cultural Pittsburgh, and a five-hour combination of Historic Pittsburgh with a three-hour cruise on Pittsburgh's three rivers. All tours begin at Station Square; pickups can be made at major downtown hotels. Cultural Pittsburgh Tour April–Oct daily at 1, all other tours at 9:45. Pittsburgh and Its Rivers Tour June–Labor Day daily. $18–28 adults, discounts for children. Reservations required at least one hour before tour begins.

GREAT PITTSBURGH SIGHTSEEING AND EXPEDITION COMPANY
Pittsburgh
412/922-8833

This company customizes its tours to suit the sightseer's interests. Large groups or individuals can take a comprehensive tour of the city in as little or as much time as they want to take. Experienced guides give overviews of the city with historical perspectives, background information, and anecdotes to make each tour unique. Translators are available. Tours given year-round; reservations must be made in advance.

JUST DUCKY TOURS INC.
Station Square
Pittsburgh
412/928-2489

Being one of the sights as well as a sightseer is part of taking a Just Ducky tour of Pittsburgh: the bizarre, lime-green, restored WWII amphibious truck/tour bus is a sure head turner. A sense of humor also helps when the truck splashes into the Allegheny River for a cruise past Three Rivers Stadium. Starting and ending at Station Square, the hour-long narrated Duck tour outlines the Golden Triangle, goes to the Strip, then turns into a boat. Although the Duck is heated and has a canopy for "inclement" weather, the wind and spray on any day can spoil good clothes and hairdos. The tour is best suited to the truly young at heart. April–Nov daily 10:30–6, closed Tue in April, May, Oct, and Nov. $12 adults, discounts for seniors and children. &

Jeff Greenberg/GPCVB

6

MUSEUMS AND GALLERIES

Thanks to the philanthropy of the industrial barons of Pittsburgh's Gilded Age, the city is graced with some of the country's finest museums, libraries, and public art. While Pittsburgh is a relatively small city, it has a vast number of cultural activities. The Pittsburgh region has one of the most extensive library systems in the country because of Andrew Carnegie's belief that all children should have free libraries readily available. In the area of art, Carnegie believed that too much attention was being paid to the old masters. He therefore established a collection of contemporary modern art that rivals any other collection in the world.

Many of the buildings erected by industrial giants such as the Fricks, Schenleys, Scaifes, and Phippses are works of art in themselves. They have been preserved as museums not only for their historical significance but also to hold the art collections that were amassed by their owners.

A number of early benefactors ensured that their contributions would endure by establishing charitable foundations. Continuing this tradition, most of Pittsburgh's large corporations today support the arts through foundations that underwrite restoration projects, new collections, and other cultural activities.

ART MUSEUMS

ANDY WARHOL MUSEUM
117 Sandusky St.
Pittsburgh
412/237-8300
Andy Warhol was a Pittsburgh native

acclaimed as "one of the most influential artists of the second half of the twentieth century." There are more than 500 of his works on display here. The Andy Warhol Museum is the largest museum in the country dedicated to the works of a single artist.

The Warhol is also part of the Carnegie Museums of Pittsburgh. Thur–Sat 11–8, Sun and Wed 11–6. $6 adults, discounts for seniors, students, and children. ＆ (North Pittsburgh)

CARNEGIE MUSEUM OF ART
4400 Forbes Ave.
Pittsburgh
412/622/3131

Commissioned as part of Andrew Carnegie's gift to the city, the Carnegie Museum of Art was the first museum in the country dedicated to modern art. It holds an impressive collection of Impressionist and post-Impressionist paintings, sculpture, and decorative works of the nineteenth and twentieth centuries. The museum's film and video collection is nationally recognized. The Carnegie Museum of Art also contains the Heinz Architectural Center, which chronicles the history of architecture and the development of various architectural styles. Tue–Sat 10–5, Sun 1–5; Mon-Sat 10–5 in July and Aug. $6 adults, discounts for seniors, students, and children. ＆ (East Pittsburgh)

FRICK ART MUSEUM
7227 Reynolds St.
Pittsburgh
412/371-0600

The Frick Art Museum is part of the Frick Art and Historical Center located at Clayton, the former estate of Henry Clay Frick, wealthy Pittsburgh industrialist and philanthropist. The art museum was built in 1969 by his daughter, Helen Clay Frick, for her collection of French, Italian, and Flemish paintings from the Renaissance through the eighteenth century. Sixteenth-century Chinese tapestries, Chinese porcelains, Renaissance panels, and bronzes are also on exhibit. The

museum is not recommended for children under 10. Tue–Sat 10–5:30, Sun 12–6. Free with admission to the Frick Art and Historical Center, which is $5 adults, discounts for seniors and students. ＆ (East Pittsburgh)

MATTRESS FACTORY LTD. MUSEUM
500 Sampsonia Way
Pittsburgh
412/231-3169

One of the few locations in the city with enough open space to feature large installations, the Mattress Factory is known for taking chances with art. In fact, according to urban critic Barringer Fifield, artists consider this to be the finest installation art facility in the country. The avant-garde and contemporary can be found here, in a former factory/warehouse. There are 11 permanent installations, including James Turell's light works and *Ship of Fools* by Bill Woodrow, housed a block away at 1414 Monterey. Ongoing showings of temporary installations guarantee a steady influx of controversy and excitement. Tue–Sat 10–5, Sun 1–5. $4 adults, discounts for students, children, and seniors. Free on Thur. ＆ (North Pittsburgh)

SCIENCE AND NATURAL HISTORY MUSEUMS

CARNEGIE MUSEUM OF NATURAL HISTORY
4400 Forbes Ave.
Pittsburgh
412/622-3131

The Carnegie Museum of Natural History should be on everyone's "not to be missed" list, but too many Pittsburghers overlook the nationally known treasure in their own neighborhood.

The name is pronounced car-NAY-ghee, as Andrew pronounced his name, not CAR-neg-ghee, as New Yorkers call their hall. The Carnegie, "Home of the Dinosaurs," includes the following exhibits and more:

- Dinosaur Hall: has 10 full skeletons, including one T. rex.
- Alcoa Foundation Hall of American Indians: examines Native American history and influence in western Pennsylvania.
- Walton Hall of Ancient Egypt: holds artifacts, video programs, and interactive computer displays.
- Polar World: examines the Inuit and their lives.
- Benedum Hall of Geology: focuses on Pennsylvania while demonstrating how natural forces shape the world.
- Hillman Hall of Minerals and Gems: contains breathtaking displays of gems and crystals.
- Hall of African and North American Wildlife: exhibits animals in their natural habitats.
- Discovery Room: has hands-on exhibits meant for the kids, but who can resist playing?

Tue–Sat 10–5 (Mon 10–5 in Jul and Aug), Sun 1–5. Guided tour Sat and Sun. $6 adults, discounts for senior citizens, students, and children; admission includes Museum of Art. ♿ (East Pittsburgh)

Writers with Pittsburgh Connections

Nelly Bly (investigative journalist)

John Dickson Carr (suspense writer)

Rachel Carson (environmental writer)

Willa Cather (novelist)

Michael Chabon (novelist, *The Mysteries of Pittsburgh*)

Malcolm Cowley (playwright, *Exile's Return*)

Marcia Davenport (novelist, *Valley of Decision*)

Annie Dillard (essayist)

George S. Kaufman (playwright and screenwriter)

Robinson Jeffers (poet)

Colleen O'Shaunessy McKenna (children's writer, *The Truth About Sixth Grade*)

Mary Roberts Rinehart (mystery writer)

Martin Smith (suspense writer, *Time Release*)

Gertrude Stein (experimental writer)

Jane Gray Swisshelm (war correspondent)

Ida Tarbell (history writer)

August Wilson (playwright, *The Piano Lesson*)

Doina Locke

Bessemer converter at Bessemer Court and Transportation Museum

CARNEGIE SCIENCE CENTER
One Allegheny Ave.
Pittsburgh
412/237-3400

The Science Center is great for all ages, especially those who can relax and learn by playing (just don't crowd the kids away). It deservedly bills itself as "an amusement park for the mind," and it is. Even the gift shop is fun to visit. The small café facing the river is a great place to people-watch, river-watch, and rest your weary feet. Rangos Omnimax Theater draws crowds regularly for its top-quality films that offer a fascinating blend of nature, science, technology, and spectacular cinematography. Regulars often go to the Science Center just to see the movies, which change periodically. Daily 10–5 (Sat 10–9). Admission for Science Center, Rangos Omnimax Theater, and Planetarium: $12 adults; Science Center and Omnimax: $10 adults; Science Center or Omnimax

alone: $6, discounts for seniors and children on all tickets. Parking: $3. ⟁ (North Pittsburgh)

HISTORY MUSEUMS

SOLDIERS AND SAILORS MEMORIAL HALL
Fifth Ave. and Bigelow Blvd.
Pittsburgh
412/621-4253

Exhibits, which honor all veterans, include memorabilia from the Civil War and the Persian Gulf War. Black military history is featured. Films cover military history from the Revolutionary War through Vietnam. Mon–Fri 9–3:30, Sat and Sun 1–4. Free. Reservations required for films and guided tours. ⟁ (East Pittsburgh)

DEPRECIATION LANDS MUSEUM
4743 S. Pioneer Rd.
Allison Park
412/486-0563

At the end of the Revolutionary War, the government, rather than paying veterans in cash it didn't have, gave them parcels of land, which most of them sold. Speculators grew rich from the veteran's need for cash. The museum is housed in a small log cabin just off Route 8, set in the midst of the lands that were given away. Sun 1–4. Donation requested. (North Pittsburgh)

FORT PITT MUSEUM AND BLOCKHOUSE
Point State Park
Pittsburgh
412/281-9284

Fort Pitt was built by the victorious British on the site of the French Fort Duquesne. The Blockhouse, erected in 1764, is the only structure remaining from the original fort. The museum building is a reconstruction of a portion of Fort Pitt. It covers Pittsburgh's earliest history, colonial days, and the French and Indian War. A reconstructed trapper's cabin with its meager furnishings recalls everyday life in eighteenth-century western Pennsylvania. Museums open Wed–Sat 10–4:30, Sun 12–4:30. $4 adults, discounts for seniors and children. Blockhouse open approximately the same hours as museum. Free. & (Downtown Pittsburgh)

MEADOWCROFT MUSEUM OF RURAL LIFE
Meadowcraft Rd.
Avella
724/587-3412
Only 35 miles from downtown Pittsburgh, Meadowcroft Museum can take you back more than 14,000 years at its archaeological dig and then bring you back to nineteenth-century western Pennsylvanian farm life—quite a trip for one day. Meadowcroft's nineteenth-century village includes a one-room schoolhouse, a sheep barn where you can spin wool, and a log home where children can play games that children played in the 1800s. A three-day summer daycamp program explores the archaeological site, prehistoric life in Pennylvania, and nineteenth-century rural life. Memorial Day–Labor Day Wed–Sat 12–5, Sun 1–5, May–Memorial Day and Labor Day–Oct weekends 12–5. $6.50 adults, discounts for children. Most areas are wheelchair-accessible. (South Pittsburgh)

ROUND HILL EXHIBIT FARM
Round Hill Rd.
Elizabeth
412/384-8555 or 412/384-4701
This working farm was founded in 1790. The brick farmhouse was built in 1838. Intended to allow children of

the 1990s to get a close look at a real farm, Round Hill has livestock, including dairy cows, a park, a duck pond, and a picnic area. Daily 8-dusk. Free. (East Pittsburgh)

HARMONY MUSEUM
Town Center
Harmony
724/452-7341
The town of Harmony was settled in 1804 by a communal religious society known as the Harmonists or Rappites, after their leader George Rapp. The town was later acquired by the Mennonites. The museum demonstrates what life was like in the Harmony Society of the nineteenth century. Wandering around the decorated buildings and shops is delightful at Christmas, when artisans and craftspeople are hard at work in period dress. Harmony is worth the drive of less than an hour north on I-79. Sun, Mon, Wed, and Fri 1–4 (Tue–Sun 1–4 Jun–Sept). $3.50 adults, discount for children. (North Pittsburgh)

OLD ECONOMY VILLAGE
13th St. off Ohio River Blvd.
Ambridge
412/266-4500
Originally the town of Economy, Old Economy Village was built by the Harmonists between 1824 and 1830. Sixteen of the original 200 structures on the 6.5-acre plot can be visited. Buildings of interest include the Leader's Home, the Museum, the Mechanics Building, and a store. The Museum is the second-oldest continuously used museum in the country. Old Economy Village has been designated a National Historic Landmark Village. Tue–Sat 9–5, Sun 12–5. $5 adults, discounts for seniors, children, and families. & (West Pittsburgh)

Mysterious Pittsburgh: Mysteries with Pittsburgh Connections

Karen Rose Cercone: *Steel Ashes, Blood Tracks, Coal Dust*

Edie Claire: *Never Buried*

K. C. Constantine: *Sunshine Enemies, The Man Who Grew Slow Tomatoes*, others

Tom Lipinski: *The Fall-Down Guy, Glass Coffin, A Picture of Her Tombstone*

Barbara Paul: *Inlaws and Outlaws*, others

Mary Roberts Rinehart: *The Case of Jennie Brice*

Martin Smith: *Time Release, Shadow Image*

FRICK ART AND HISTORICAL CENTER
7227 Reynolds St.
Pittsburgh
412/371-0606
The Frick is a six-acre complex based around Clayton, the Henry Clay Frick home, the last of the fabulous millionaires' mansions that defined Point Breeze in the late nineteenth century. Andrew Carnegie, George Westinghouse, and H. J. Heinz were neighbors of the Fricks. The grounds include Clayton, the Carriage Museum with antique carriages and autos, and a visitor's center in the children's two-story playhouse. Tue–Sat 10–5:30, Sun 12–5. $5 adults, discounts for seniors and students. Reservations required for a guided tour, which costs $5. (East Pittsburgh)

SENATOR JOHN HEINZ
PITTSBURGH REGIONAL
HISTORY CENTER
1212 Smallman St.
Pittsburgh
412/454-6000
Housed in the newly renovated 1898 Chautauqua Lake Ice Company building, the seven-story Regional History Center is a visually impressive blend of contemporary and vintage architectural features. Whether busloads of schoolchildren or serious researchers, visitors find themselves in a well-planned exhibition and with no excuse for boredom. The first floor contains a real 1947 trolley parked outside the small café and the gift shop. There is a Discovery Place especially for children. Adult visitors to the extensive library archives are welcome. However, coats, bags, and purses must be placed in lockers before entering. Gloves are provided for handling photographs. Sun–Mon 10–5. $6 adults, seniors and children discounted. &
(East Pittsburgh)

PHOTO ANTIQUITIES
531 E. Ohio St.
Pittsburgh
412/231-7881
This tiny jewel of a museum and gallery, dedicated to the history of

photography and the display of vintage photos, might be overlooked if you walk by too fast. It is on the second floor, above Bernie's Camera Shop, and a single doorway marks the entrance. Once upstairs, the visitor must slow down to examine the walls and showcases covered with examples of early photographic art, including daguerreotypes, albumen-coated plates, Magic Lantern slides, and stereopticon 3-D pictures. A separate room is devoted to early views of Pittsburgh. Mon–Sat 9–5. Admission and a guided tour: $4. (North Pittsburgh)

BESSEMER COURT AND TRANSPORTATION MUSEUM
Station Square
Pittsburgh
This "museum" is entirely outdoors. Visitors stroll along the riverfront and view a collection of pieces salvaged from the wreckage of Pittsburgh's industrial days. An enormous Bessemer converter is mounted and graced with a plaque explaining the significance of the Bessemer process of making steel, invented in England, and brought to Pittsburgh by Andrew Carnegie. The scale of the pieces leads to an understanding of the nineteenth-century description of Pittsburgh as "Hell with the lid taken off." Free admission. Parking $1. ♿ (South Pittsburgh)

TOUR-ED MINE
Bull Run Rd.
Tarentum
724/224-4720
Tour-Ed Mine does not look like your typical tourist attraction, but then again, it's not. It was a working open-pit coal mine until the vein ran out. The tour begins deep within the mine, after a one-half-mile ride in an old coal car. Imagining what it must have been like for the miners is rather difficult, until the guide briefly extinguishes all the lights. The utter and complete darkness is quite impressive and not for the claustrophobic. Above ground, there is

Carnegie Museum of Art, p. 101

Carnegie Museum of Art

a small museum exhibiting a company store and a miner's log cabin. Memorial Day–Labor Day daily 1–4. $6 adults, $3 children (North Pittsburgh)

OTHER MUSEUMS

PITTSBURGH CHILDREN'S MUSEUM
10 Children's Way
Pittsburgh
412/322-5058
Interactive exhibits, puppet shows, and a hands-on silk-screening studio where kids can make their own works of art are just a few of the attractions designed to appeal to children up to 12 years of age. Stuffee, a seven-foot-tall soft-sculpture mascot, is a great favorite, both in the museum and when he travels to area schools and turns himself inside out to teach human anatomy. The museum is located in the Old Post Office at Allegheny Center, itself a visual and historical treat. Mon–Sat 10–5, Sun 12–5. Closed Mon in summer. $4 adults, discounted for seniors and children. Half price on Thur. (See also Chapter 7: "Kids' Stuff.") (North Pittsburgh)

STEPHEN FOSTER MEMORIAL
University of Pittsburgh
Pittsburgh
412/624-4100
As unlikely as it seems, composer Stephen Foster ("My Old Kentucky Home") was actually a native of Pittsburgh. It is appropriate that his memorial, the only museum in the country dedicated to an American composer, celebrates American music and contains a museum, library, and auditorium. The auditorium is used for concerts, productions from the university's Theatre Arts Department, and a

program of nineteenth-century American music. Mon–Fri 9–4. Closed on university holidays. Free. Guided tours by reservation (must be made one month in advance): $1.50 adults, discounts for seniors and students. (East Pittsburgh)

ART GALLERIES

NORTH HILLS ART CENTER
3432 Babcock Blvd.
Ross
412/364-3622
This intimate gallery is a visual treat in an unlikely setting: the hodgepodge of businesses along Babcock Boulevard, which never quite seems to achieve true boulevard status. The small retail shop carries a varied selection of reasonably priced pieces by local artists. ⅙ (North Pittsburgh)

PITTSBURGH CENTER FOR THE ARTS
6300 Fifth Ave.
Pittsburgh
412/361-0873
Pennsylvania's largest arts center is housed in neo-Georgian splendor in the former Charles Marshall mansion, built in 1911. The nearby Scaife house, a wedding present from Richard B. Mellon to his daughter Sarah, and the 10.5 acres of Mellon Park are reminders of the sumptuous past. Exhibitions, classes, outdoor concerts, recitals, and conferences keep the center in lively contact with the local, national, and international art world. The art shop extends that contact to the general public. (East Pittsburgh)

SOCIETY FOR CONTEMPORARY CRAFTS
2100 Smallman St.
Pittsburgh

Campbell's Soup Can at the Andy Warhol Museum, p. 100

412/261-7003
More than 200 nationally known artisans in media ranging from acrylics to wood display their work in this modest building. Some of the pieces are for sale. The society has a retail shop in the Fifth Avenue Arcade, offering a wild mixture of pieces that are both decorative and useful, from herbal soaps to blown glass. The Smallman Street location also has a small café to help weary Strip shoppers unwind. (East Pittsburgh)

**SWEETWATER CENTER
FOR THE ARTS
200 Broad St.
Sewickley
412/741-4405**
The balcony gallery features local artists in various media. The former Post Office building also houses the Sewickley Historical Society and offers classes year-round for children and adults. Summer art camps are a major part of the calendar. The center also hosts a European movie series on Friday night. Admission is free; there is a charge for classes and the film series. (North Pittsburgh)

**WOOD STREET GALLERIES
601 Wood St.
Pittsburgh
412/471-5605**
Nestled in the center of downtown, this small gallery is perched above the Wood Street T station. Not only is the concept of art in a subway rather unique but the music piped into the station is all-classical public radio programming. (Downtown)

Kennywood Entertainment

7

KIDS' STUFF

Of course, there would be plenty for kids to like in Pittsburgh. It is, after all, Mister Rogers' Neighborhood.

At the beginning of this century, children were not yet protected by child labor laws, and life was hard for everyone, especially for children who worked in Pittsburgh's mines and factories. But through all the tough times and hard work, Pittsburgh was a family town. It still is. One of the most distinctive characteristics of Pittsburgh's people is their intense dedication to family and home.

The Pittsburgh Children's Museum is entirely dedicated to children's learning and play experiences. Institutions such as the Pittsburgh Zoo, the National Aviary, the Carnegie Science Center, and the Senator John Heinz Pittsburgh Regional History Center also have major interactive educational centers for children. Public parks have wide-open spaces and lots of neat activities, while amusement centers offer variety, the latest games, and protection from the weather.

ANIMALS AND THE GREAT OUTDOORS

PITTSBURGH ZOO
Butler St.
Pittsburgh
412/665-3640
At the Pittsburgh Zoo children feel welcome in the Kids' Kingdom with its walk-through animal yards, sea lion pool, playground, and special attendants to keep both animals and children safe. The Discovery Pavilion is a state-of-the-art interactive learning center. Children marvel at the Aqua-Zoo's huge shark tank and check on longtime zoo personality Chuckles, an Amazon River dolphin. Twilight Zoo, Halloween Zoo Boo, and Zoo Lights are extra-special times for kids at the

zoo. Memorial Day—Labor Day daily 10–6, rest of year daily 9–4:30. $6 adults, $4 ages 2 to 14 and seniors. Parking: $2.50 (East Pittsburgh)

NATIONAL AVIARY IN PITTSBURGH
Allegheny Commons West
Pittsburgh
412/321-4359
Children can feel as free as the birds as they walk through the large Tropical Marsh Land Room, watching birds swim under the small bridge or fly overhead to perch in the lush foliage. More than 250 exotic birds live in re-created habitats. Interactive displays and involved volunteers help younger children relate to the birds and habitats through crafts projects. Daily 9–4:30. $4 adults, $2.50 ages 2 to 12, $3 over 60. & (North Pittsburgh)

MUSEUMS

CARNEGIE MUSEUMS PERFORMING ARTS DEPARTMENT
Forbes Ave. and S. Craig St.
Pittsburgh
412/622-3131
Children have been coming to the Carnegie for Shakespeare and children's performances since 1988. A version of *A Midsummer Night's Dream*, specially adapted for children, is presented in March. After the play, children can tour behind the scenes and ask questions about the production. Free admission to the Museums of Art and History is included. Box lunches may be ordered in advance. Sat at 11 a.m. $6. & (East Pittsburgh)

CARNEGIE MUSEUM OF NATURAL HISTORY

4400 Forbes Ave.
Pittsburgh
412/622-3131
Dinosaurs are probably what people think of first when they think of the Carnegie Museum of Natural History, and well they should, what with the museum's 10 full skeletons, now including a new stance for T. rex. Children (and many adults) find dinosaurs endlessly fascinating. But the Carnegie has much more than dinosaurs. It has the new Alcoa Exhibit of Native American Life, the Benedum Hall of Geology's interactive exhibit explaining Pennsylvania's geological history, and, especially for children, the Discovery Room for hands-on learning. Tue–Sat 10–5 (Mon–Sat in July and Aug), Sun 1–5. $6 adults, $4 students with ID and children ages 3 to 18, $5 seniors. (East Pittsburgh)

CARNEGIE SCIENCE CENTER
One Allegheny Ave.
Pittsburgh

Kennywood, p. 117

Kennywood Entertainment

Ten Best Places to Take Children in Pittsburgh

by Pat Poshard, the mother of twins and editor of *Pittsburgh Parent, Pittsburgh Grandparent,* **and** *Around & About Pittsburgh*

1. Pittsburgh Zoo in Highland Park
2. Fireworks displays at the Point
3. Pittsburgh City, Allegheny County, and Pennsylvania State Parks
4. Amusement parks—Kennywood for the roller coasters and rides, Sandcastle for water slides, and Idlewild for Storybook Forest and scenic picnic spots
5. The Carnegie—natural history and art museum displays, Science Center, and library
6. Seasonal family displays—PPG Place Santa's Holiday Exhibit, Carnegie Science Center Miniature Railroad, Three Rivers Arts Festival
7. Fiddlesticks children's concerts by the Pittsburgh Symphony Orchestra
8. Meadowcroft in Avella for a living American history lesson
9. Local community libraries for reading and storytelling
10. Pittsburgh Children's Museum

412/237-3400
With an amusement park's abundance of fun and engaging activities (don't tell the kids it's educational), a spiral ramp to race from floor to floor, and an Omnimax theater, the Carnegie Science Center is more than enough to wear out even the most active youngsters. Early Learners' Landing and Science Pier is reserved for younger children. SciQuest demonstrates the physics of earthquakes, tornados, and wind. Daily 10–5 (Sat 10–9). Admission for Science Center, Rangos Omnimax Theater, and Planetarium: $12 adults; Science Center and Omnimax only: $10 adults; Science Center or Omnimax alone: $6; discounts for seniors and children on all tickets. Parking: $3. ♿ (North Pittsburgh)

FRICK ART AND HISTORICAL MUSEUM
7227 Reynolds St.
Pittsburgh
412/371-0606
Family Days bring parents and children to Clayton, the Henry Clay Frick mansion that is generally not recommended for younger children. Specially trained teen docents lead the

tour and assist with games and hands-on craft activities. Dressing up in period costumes and role playing lets the children get the feeling of a Victorian-era childhood. Programs in summer and at Christmastime re-create those special times in the Frick household. First and third Sat 9:30–11:30. $10 adult with one child; $5 each additional child. (East Pittsburgh)

PITTSBURGH CHILDREN'S MUSEUM
10 Children's Way
Pittsburgh
412/322-5058
This museum is designed specifically with children up to 12 years of age in mind. The wonderfully renovated Old Post Office is a fascinating building, with sculpture and architectural fragments scattered around the grounds, an outdoor café, and a majestic Victorian interior. Luckey's Climber, a two-story climbing adventure, awaits exploration. Stuffee, the locally renowned seven-foot puppet/

mascot, provides entertaining anatomy lessons. Puppets from *Mister Rogers' Neighborhood* and Jim Henson's *Labyrinth* and *Dark Crystal* are on hand for more fun. Summer Mon–Sat 10–5, Sun 12–5, rest of year Tue–Sat 10–5, Sun 12–5. $4 adults and children, seniors discounted, under 2 free. Half price Thur. ♿ (North Pittsburgh)

SENATOR JOHN HEINZ PITTSBURGH REGIONAL HISTORY CENTER
1212 Smallman St.
Pittsburgh
412/454-6000
To capture the interest of all visitors, especially its younger ones, the former Chautauqua Lake Ice Company building has been carefully renovated with display areas that are both accessible and informative. The Walk through Time exhibit brings selected historical periods to life with walk-through, life-size dwellings and furnishings. Discovery Place, an in-

Teen Faves
by Peter La Russa, age 13

1. Kennywood Park
2. Sandcastle Water Park
3. Paintball at the Strip District
4. Cosmic bowling at Funfest in Harmarville
5. Laser tag at Funfest
6. Miniature golf at Wildwood Highlands
7. Go-carting at Wildwood Highlands
8. Ice-skating at Schenley Park
9. Skiing at Boyce Park
10. Outdoor movies at Flagstaff Hill in Schenley Park in summer

Carnegie Science Center, p. 110

teractive learning center geared toward elementary-school children, lets them touch, read, and play with historical displays. Real-life stories of children from Pittsburgh's past are presented with some of their toys, clothes, and photographs. A small theater shows videotaped oral histories of local residents. Mon–Sun 10–5. $6 adults, children and seniors discounted. ♿ (East Pittsburgh)

PUPPETS AND THEATER

PITTSBURGH INTERNATIONAL CHILDREN'S THEATER
Various locations
412/321-5520
Pittsburgh International Children's Theater presents live performances from around the world for children ages 4 through 12. Shows are performed at various locations throughout the Pittsburgh area including the North Hills, South Hills, Monroeville, Moon Township, and the Cultural District. The subscription series runs October

through March. Single-performance tickets are readily available at the door or in advance by calling 412/321-5520. In May, the five-day International Children's Theater Festival is held in West Park, adjacent to Allegheny Center on the North Side. Children ages 3 through 14 will love the excitement of puppet shows, storytellers, and circus acts.

PRIME STAGE THEATRE FOR YOUTH AND FAMILIES
Charles Gray Auditorium
CLO Academy
Pittsburgh
412/771-7373
Prime Stage presents four shows a year and collaborates with the Carnegie Library, the Pittsburgh Symphony, the Pittsburgh Pirates, the Pittsburgh Holocaust Center, and the Girl Scouts to develop productions by local and nationally known playwrights. Workshops at various middle schools are used to develop material and to acquaint students with theater productions in the making. The series of

four plays for children and families runs from May through December. $10 adults, $6 students and seniors. ♿ (North Pittsburgh)

STORES KIDS LOVE

BRUSTER'S OLD-FASHIONED ICE CREAM & YOGURT
2569 Brandt School Rd.
Wexford
724/934-0840
Kids love making the agonizing choice between ice cream flavors, toppings, cones, sprinkles, and everything else that makes us "all scream for ice cream." Wednesdays are Crazy Hat days: wear a crazy hat, buy a single-scoop cone—and get a free second scoop. On Banana Thursday, bring your own banana and your banana split is half-price. The Wexford store is the second location for this old-fashioned ice cream stand that started as Jerry's Curb Service in Bridgewater, Pennsylvania, and has since gone national. (North Pittsburgh)

THE DISNEY STORE
Ross Park Mall
North Hills
412/635-7470
You don't have to be a kid to love shopping here. The racks and shelves are filled with adult and children's clothing beautifully decorated with assorted characters from Disney animation. With a Disney video always on view in the back of the store, kids can stay and watch, browse for themselves, or help Mom or Dad shop. Jewelry, clocks, accessories, videos, and books are just some of the Disney-themed merchandise to delight young shoppers. Prices are moderate to expensive. Other Disney Store locations are in South Hills Village Mall, the Monroeville Mall, and West Mifflin. (North Pittsburgh)

WQED STORE OF KNOWLEDGE
Monroeville Mall
Monroeville
412/374-1255
WQED is Pittsburgh's public television station, and its name on the store lets you know that what's inside is supposed to be educational. But that doesn't mean that it can't be fun at the same time. Rocket kits, puzzles, small toys demonstrating scientific principles, and even stuffed animals make this a wonderland with a price tag, although prices are not too steep. WQED Store of Knowledge can also be found in Ross Park Mall in the North Hills and in South Hills Village Mall. (East Pittsburgh)

S. W. RANDALL TOYES & GIFTS

806 Ivy St.
Pittsburgh
412/687-2666
An abundance of light, lots of bright colors filling the tall front windows, and a sense of whimsy make this toy store a fun place to visit. Well-made, simply designed toys by Brio, Playmobil, and Lego encourage hours of imaginative play. Cute and cuddly stuffed animals and toys clamor for attention. Dolls, board games, and balls in all shapes, colors, and sizes are old standbys that never fail to entertain. Other S. W. Randall stores are located in Station Square, downtown, and Squirrel Hill. (East Pittsburgh)

RESTAURANTS KIDS LOVE

CHUCK E CHEESE'S
3800 William Penn Hwy.
Monroeville
412/856-5044
This noisy, fun-filled, child-centered national chain restaurant has two locations in the Pittsburgh region, one in Monroeville (East Pittsburgh) and one in Bridgeville (South Pittsburgh). Chuck E Cheese, the giant rodent whose smiling face graces the outdoor signs, appears periodically, and mechanized puppets perform in a short musical revue. The large arcade has kid-size games that are paid for with Chuck E Cheese's tokens, also good for buying trinkets. Cartoons are shown steadily. Pizza, soft drinks, and, if you're with a party, birthday cake are available. Also at 1025 Washington Pike, Bridgeville, 412/257-2570. (East Pittsburgh)

EAT 'N' PARK RESTAURANTS
412/443-7280
With about 40 locations around the Pittsburgh area open 24 hours a day, Eat 'n' Park restaurants are easily

accessible. Eat 'n' Park has fun with food, with offerings like milkshakes, burgers and fries, and bacon and egg Breakfast Smiles for the kid in each of us. Each child gets a free Smiley Face cookie.

PLAY AREAS

CENTER FOR CREATIVE PLAY
5 Station Square East
Pittsburgh
412/281-8886, ext. 46
With over 1,000 toys to play with or borrow from the lending library and with complete wheelchair accessibility, the Center for Creative Play offers fun for children of all ability levels, from infancy to eight years of age. A colorful ball pit, jungle gym, and ride-on toys are great for active play. Children's imaginations are challenged with puppet play, dress-up role playing, and a three-story playhouse. The center has five computer stations with plenty of educational software and games. One computer reserved for adult use has Internet access.

Pittsburgh Zoo, p. 109

Pittsburgh Zoo

Children must be accompanied at all times by an adult. Closed Wed and Sun (except the first Sun of each month). $3 over age one. & (South Pittsburgh)

DISCOVERY ZONE FUNCENTER
Monroeville Mall
Monroeville
412/373-3090
Discovery Zone is an indoor playground, with plenty of tubes to crawl through, rope nets to climb, tunnels to navigate, a Pit of Balls to surf through, and slides to go down. The Mega Zone is reserved for children over age five. There is a Mini Zone where toddlers are free to play without older children. The DZ Café offers a kid-friendly menu: pizza, hot dogs, wings, breadsticks, chips, popcorn, and cotton candy. Everyone under the age of 18 must stay with an adult. Open daily. $7.99 general admission (adult free with a child), $4.99 under 38 inches, under age one free. (East Pittsburgh)

FUN FEST ENTERTAINMENT CENTER
2525 Freeport Rd.
Harmarville
412/828-1100
Laser lights, strobe lights, black lights, "fog" rolling over the lanes, glow-in-the-dark bowling pins, and live DJs make "Cosmic Bowling" hot. Kids love it. Laser Storm is also a kid and family favorite. All ages can team up to play laser tag against other teams and the computer in an eerie, challenging environment. Scorekeeping is computerized. Open daily. Bowling: $2 per game per child, $2.50 per game per adult, $3 per game per person Sun. Reservations required. Laser Storm: $4.75 per game per person, $5.25 per game after 6 p.m. (North Pittsburgh)

FUN FORE ALL
8 Progress Ave.
Cranberry
724/779-2270
This family entertainment complex features a huge video arcade. Bumper Boats, a Pro Track racing course with banked curves and hairpin turns, and a Rookie Track for younger drivers let everyone in on the action. For younger children, a soft-play area gives them plenty of time to roll, climb, and slide. Outdoors, two miniature golf courses present unusual challenges for golfers, whether you know how to play or not. Baseball and softball batting cages are there for practice and fun. Open daily. Go-cart $4 adults, $3 children; miniature golf $5 adults, $4 children. (North Pittsburgh)

GOLF WORLD
3458 Harts Run Rd.
Glenshaw
412/767-4320
The miniature golf course draws children and adults to Golf World, but once there, other "worlds" beckon. Hoops World challenges all comers to sink 10 baskets with the fewest tries. Recorded sports commentaries and music add to the fun. Food World is easy—go to the order window and choose from a full line of fast-food options. Last but not least is Ice Cream World, where the "flurries"— milkshakes blended with your choice of candies or cookies—are the best. (North Pittsburgh)

SAFARI SAM'S
8001 Rowan Rd.
Cranberry
724/779-1991
Safari Sam's is an indoor, all-weather, two-story playground with a super video arcade. Let the kids burn off excess energy in the soft-play area,

slides, ball pit, and more. Toddlers have their own play area with balls and slides, just like the big kids. All children must be accompanied by an adult. The full-service menu offers kids their all-time favorite foods. Sun–Thur 10–9, Fri–Sat 10-10. $4.95 ages 5 and up, $3.95 ages 2 to 4, free for adults and children under 2. (North Pittsburgh)

WILDWOOD HIGHLANDS
2330 Wildwood Rd.
Hampton
412/487-5517
This family amusement center has fun for everyone, with go-carts, bumper boats, and a 28-tee driving range. A deluxe miniature-golf course has a magic castle, fountains, and waterfalls. Go-carts turn into Grand Prix racers on the track's banked curves and turns. Woody's Den is strictly for the younger set, with a four-level soft-play funhouse and kid-size go-carts and bumper boats. Wildwood Highlands is located in the North Hills on the Yellow Belt between Route 8 and North Park. Mon–Thur 11–11, Fri–Sun 11–12. Miniature golf $4.50 adults, $3 ages 4 to 10, $1.50 ages 3 and under; other attractions $1.50–$4.50 per ride. (North Pittsburgh)

THEME PARKS

KENNYWOOD
4800 Kennywood Blvd.
West Mifflin
412/461-0500
Kennywood has over a hundred years of history, but kids don't come for history, they come for the rides—the wilder the better! Kennywood, "Coaster Capital of the World," has some of the wildest. It has 31 major rides, including three wooden coast-

ers, a steel coaster, and a water coaster. The little ones have 14 special rides of their own in Kiddieland. There's also the Turnpike "drive-your-own-car" ride, a miniature train, and Noah's Ark. May–Labor Day daily 11–10. $19.95 ride-all-day weekends, $16.95 ride-all-day weekdays, $4.95 non-riding, free for age 3 and under but Kiddieland rides require tickets. See also Chapter 5: "Sights and Attractions." (South Pittsburgh)

SANDCASTLE
1000 Sandcastle Dr.
Pittsburgh
412/462-6666
Sandcastle's 15 water slides are designed for fun and excitement, and kids love them. Some kids like to race while tubing on the Lazy River. The youngest children splash happily in the Tad Pool. Wet Willie's Waterworks is a multilevel play structure. For a separate price, try the Formula 1 Speedway and OASIS miniature golf. June–Aug daily 11–6. $8.50–14.50. See also Chapter 5: "Sights and Attractions." (South Pittsburgh)

SIGHTSEEING

GATEWAY CLIPPER FLEET CRUISES
9 Station Square Dock
Pittsburgh
412/355-7980
On the Good Ship Lollipop Cruise, Lolli the Clown makes sure the whole family has fun, especially the younger children. Gateway also offers a Lock 'N' Dam Adventure Cruise with "zany explorers" and a Magical Family Fun Cruise with magic shows, clowns, and music. Cruises May–Nov. $4–$8.25. (South Pittsburgh)

8

PARKS, GARDENS, AND RECREATION AREAS

Southwestern Pennsylvania has a rugged natural beauty that the inroads of civilization, heavy industry, and urban growth have not been able to completely obliterate. The Pittsburgh area has a wealth of parks, city and county, all readily accessible. State parks are as close as the Point. McConnell's Mill, Moraine State Park, and Raccoon State Park, although not within Allegheny County, are less than two hours from downtown Pittsburgh.

The city park system is anchored by Mary Schenley's 1898 donation of 300 acres—Schenley Park in Oakland—as well as the gifts of other industrial giants and civic leaders. At the turn of the century, trolley lines carried people to the parks in droves for Sunday outings. It's hard to imagine today, but those parks were "in the boondocks" then. Now they are well within city limits and surrounded by concrete and brick.

The Pittsburgh Parks Conservancy is working to restore the city's four regional parks (Schenley, Frick, Riverside, and Highland) to their former glory. Estimates set the tab at $20 million to improve Schenley Park alone. Plans include repairing erosion and salt damage to roads, improving parking and traffic congestion, and eliminating weeds that are choking out more desirable plantings. Planners would also like to jazz up the parks' images—to reflect their glory days and remind park-goers of their histories.

CITY PARKS

City of Pittsburgh Parks are open to all, free of charge, from dawn to dusk.

Special facilities, such as swimming pools and golf courses, require small admission fees. For information about the facilities or activities, call the

Parks and Recreation Department, Citiparks, at 412/255-2676. For special events call 412/255-8984.

FRICK PARK
Braddock Ave. and Beechwood Blvd.
Pittsburgh

Frick Environmental Center, located along one of the many hiking trails in Frick Park, offers visitors opportunities to explore nature and have fun. Educational programs and seasonal events, such as a wildflower walk, are offered year-round. Ball fields, soccer fields, and tennis courts are complemented by a lawn bowling area in the northernmost section of the park. Small children will enjoy the playgrounds, including the Blue Slide playground near Beechwood Boulevard. Frick Park is located on Forbes Avenue in Squirrel Hill. ㅤ (East Pittsburgh)

HIGHLAND PARK
Stanton, Bunkerhill, and Highland Aves.
Pittsburgh

One of the city's four main regional parks, Highland Park offers more than enough for a full day of fun. The Pittsburgh Zoo is the main but by no means the only attraction in this park. (See also Chapter 5: "Sights and Attractions and Chapter 6: "Kids' Stuff.") Apart from the zoo, the park offers a marvelous wooden play structure where kids can climb, crawl, and swing to their hearts' content. Lighted tennis courts see plenty of action. The wintertime ice-skating rink becomes summertime's deck hockey rink to keep skaters moving all year-round. ㅤ (East Pittsburgh)

MARKET SQUARE
Smithfield St.
Pittsburgh

Phipps Conservatory, p. 126

More of a "parklet," this open square in the center of downtown Pittsburgh draws people like a magnet at lunchtime, especially on a beautiful day. Granted, it is surrounded by restaurants, some venerable, some greasy. The old-timey wood and wrought-iron park benches, patio tables and chairs, and high-back wooden rocking chairs lure even the most intense Type-A personalities for a few moments of peace and nourishment, whether take-out or brown bag. One of the best people-watching outposts in town, Market Square also draws crowds for political rallies (Jimmy Carter spoke here once) and a lunchtime concert series on a small stage. Wednesday night jazz, Thursday movies, and Friday evening concerts draw crowds through summer. ㅤ (Downtown Pittsburgh)

MELLON PARK
Fifth and Shady Aves.
Pittsburgh

Formal gardens distinguish this 10.5-

My Favorite Environments in Pittsburgh

by Dr. Franklin Toker, author of *Pittsburgh/An Urban Portrait*, University of Pittsburgh Press, 1994. He is a professor of the History of Art and Architecture at the University of Pittsburgh.

1. **Heinz Architectural Center in the Carnegie Institute:** *"I love everything about it."*

2. **WQED Studios:** *"WQED maintains the civic dignity of the other Oakland buildings in a way that few modernist structures achieve."*

3. **Allegheny County Courthouse:** *"Its interior courtyard is the most stunning thing in Pittsburgh, and it's just about the only thing that they haven't changed on the building."*

4. **Rose garden and grounds at Mellon Park:** *"They've preserved the plans from when R. B. Mellon lived there."*

5. **Flagstaff Hill:** *"It's totally manmade, but looks absolutely natural. It's gorgeous."*

6. **Evergreen Hamlet in the North Hills:** *"It's one of my favorite environments because it was very well done in the first place and is still well maintained true to the original design . . . . You feel immediately enveloped in the 1850s, when it was built. There is a great respect for nature."*

7. **Commercial streets of Bloomfield:** *"I like it for the life, the scale, the "busyness." It has a lived-in sense. That vitality is not an accident."*

8. **Three Rivers Heritage Trail:** *"It starts near the Heinz plant. I just like to commune with the water as I walk or run on the trail."*

---

acre park, once the estate of Richard B. Mellon. The house, a wedding gift to his daughter, Sarah Mellon Scaife, is on the Fifth Avenue edge of the park and is now part of the Pittsburgh Center for the Arts. Summer concerts on the lawn of the Scaife House always draw attentive crowds. The park also offers a large play area for children, basketball courts, tennis courts, and ball fields. ♿ (Downtown Pittsburgh)

MELLON SQUARE
Smithfield St.
Pittsburgh
Located on Smithfield Street between Sixth Avenue and Oliver Street, Mellon Square offers a respite from office buildings and traffic. A fountain, formal

landscaping, and benches provide a soothing backdrop to the architectural marvels surrounding the one-block plaza. Not to spoil the mood, but Mellon Square caps a much-needed subterranean public parking structure. & (Downtown Pittsburgh)

POINT STATE PARK
Allegheny and Monongahela Rivers
Pittsburgh
Taking advantage of its strategic location at the mingling of the Allegheny and Monongahela Rivers, Point State Park affords visitors the best view of the rivers, their banks, and downtown Pittsburgh. The park's fountain, one of the world's tallest, spikes its waters 150 feet up into the sky like an exclamation point, and sometimes sprays the unwary on the windward side of the plume—welcome on a hot summer day. The approach to the park is through a short tunnel. The Block House and the Fort Pitt Museum offer historical perspective. (See also Chapter 5: "Sights and Attractions.") & (Downtown Pittsburgh)

PPG PLACE SQUARE
Fourth Ave. and Market St.
Pittsburgh
A study in concrete and stone, this open area surrounded by the six towers of PPG Place would seem cold and sterile except for the sparkling glass of the surrounding structures, which seems to bring the square to life. A fine, sunny day can induce people to linger a while at the outdoor tables before dashing back to work or into #2 PPG for a little shopping. & (Downtown Pittsburgh)

RIVERVIEW PARK
Perrysville Ave. (Rt. 19)
Pittsburgh

The standout feature of this large city park with a beautiful hilltop setting is the Allegheny Observatory, which houses the University of Pittsburgh's 13-inch telescope. The observatory is open to the public one day a year at an Open House in October. The public swimming pool, one of 32 run by Citiparks, can be reached by calling 412/323-7223. Play areas, tennis courts, and ball fields are also available. & (North Pittsburgh)

ROBERTO CLEMENTE MEMORIAL PARK
North Shore Dr.
Pittsburgh
This low-key memorial to a revered ballplayer is located near Three Rivers Stadium. A larger-than-life bronze statue in the park shows Roberto Clemente in action. Clemente, an 18-year Pittsburgh Pirate who helped the team to its 1972 World Series win, was killed in a plane crash on December 31, 1972. He had been on a humanitarian mission to deliver aid to disaster victims in Costa Rica. The park, a narrow strip of well-landscaped riverbank on the north shore of the Allegheny River, has a paved walkway, a water-taxi dock, and a small pier and offers fishing, biking, and boating. (See also Chapter 5: "Sights and Attractions.") (North Pittsburgh)

SCHENLEY PARK
Schenley Dr.
Pittsburgh
Nestled between Oakland and Squirrel Hill, due south of Carnegie Mellon University, and southeast of the Pitt campus, Schenley Park provides a wonderful large green space in a congested, highly populated community. From Flagstaff Hill, the site of summertime concerts, movies, and plays, to the artificial Panther Hollow

Lake, the terrain is picturesque. Trails offers challenges to hikers. Phipps Conservatory anchors the northwestern approach to the park. Nearby, a large playground and swimming pool offer summer fun, while a skating rink takes care of the winter season. Call the rink at 412/422-6523 for hours of operation. Players will find ball fields and tennis courts between Panther Hollow Road and Overlook Drive. An 18-hole public golf course and clubhouse are at Forbes and Schenley Drives in the northeast corner of the park; call 412/622-6959 for further information. Cross-country skiers are welcome to use the golf course when the snow falls. ᕃ (East Pittsburgh)

SCULPTURE COURT AT ALLEGHENY LANDING
North Shore Dr.
Pittsburgh

At the far end of Roberto Clemente Memorial Park, near the Sixth Street Bridge, is a large, colorful work of abstract art that virtually invites children to climb on it and play. Other sculptural installations are meant to be walked through and around, to be viewed up close and at a distance. The art is set among fabulous river views and buildings, including the new Alcoa Building with its wavy front of undulating glass. At one end of the park, the Vietnam

Memorial evokes powerful emotions of homecoming. (North Pittsburgh)

WEST PARK
Western Ave.
Pittsburgh

On the North Side, just a few blocks away from Allegheny General Hospital, Allegheny Center, and Mercy Providence Hospital, West Park fronts West North Avenue. Just a block from the street, yet almost unknown, is a delightful urban jewel of a pond, Lake Elizabeth, which boasts a bridge with two lovely arches. Joggers, cyclists, picnickers, and urban philosophers treasure the beauty and peace of the park, while children find their fun on the playground equipment. The National Aviary in Pittsburgh provides another interesting diversion and a bit of quiet time for the whole family. The gift shop offers many delights for the younger set, most of them small and very reasonably priced. (See also Chapter 7: "Kids' Stuff.") ᕃ (North Pittsburgh)

COUNTY PARKS

There are nine Allegheny County parks, covering a total of 12,000 acres. Only the larger ones have extensive recreational facilities, but each has much to offer outdoor enthusiasts. For

Elizabeth Lake in West Park

detailed information on county parks, call 412/350-7275.

BOYCE PARK
Frankstown Rd.
Plum
412/271-2717
Downhill skiing and a wave pool are special features of Boyce Park's 1,096-acre facility. Skiing facilities include four tow ropes, a snow-making machine, and rental equipment. Instruction is also available. The ski lodge can be used year-round; call 412/733-4656 for information. Call the Nature Center at 412/327-0338 for information on talks and special children's programs. (See also Chapter 5: "Sights and Attractions" and Chapter 10: "Sports and Recreation.") (East Pittsburgh)

DEER LAKES PARK
Mahaffey Rd.
Frazier Township
724/265-3520
Three artificial lakes make for plenty of good fishing and boating. Ball fields and picnic facilities lead to even more fun on Deer Lakes Park's 1,191 acres. The park is also the site of the Wagman Observatory. (See also Chapter 5: "Sights and Attractions.") (North Pittsburgh)

HARRISON HILLS PARK
Freeport Rd.
Natrona
724/295-3570
At 501 acres, Harrison Hills Park is one of the smaller county parks. The Rachel Carson Trail begins here and goes from Harrison Hills across the North Hills to North Park. It is maintained through the efforts of the American Youth Hostels, the Western Pennsylvania Conservancy, and other groups. Don't miss the awe-inspiring scenic overlook. From the vantage point of the bluff in the park, you can see the Allegheny River, Westmoreland County, Armstrong County, and Butler County. (North Pittsburgh)

HARTWOOD
215 Saxonburg Blvd.
Allison Park
412/767-9200
A full round of horse-riding events such as show jumping competitions, charity polo matches, and trail riding, make Hartwood a little different than most county parks. The 639-acre site of a former estate, Hartwood also offers tours of its restored Tudor-style mansion, a drive-through light show, hayrides, and summer theater and concerts. (See also Chapter 5: "Sights and Attractions.") (North Pittsburgh)

NORTH PARK
E. Ingomar Rd. and Babcock Blvd.
North Hills
724/935-1971
The largest park in the county system, North Park has one of the largest

swimming pools in the world. It has an Access Trail for those with impaired mobility, and the Rachel Carson Trail connects the park with the Rachel Carson Homestead in Springdale. Marshall Island is a favorite snacking spot for ducks and geese, who come for stale bread offered by friendly humans. Miles of hiking trails, bike paths, and horse paths cross the park's 3,010 acres. Call the naturalist at the Latodami Nature Center, 724/935-2170, for information about its programs. (See also Chapter 5: "Sights and Attractions" and Chapter 10: "Sports and Recreation.") (North Pittsburgh)

ROUND HILL PARK AND EXHIBIT FARM
Rt. 48
Elizabeth Township
412/384-8555
Set up in 1965 with a working exhibit farm added in 1968, Round Hill Park

gives children fresh-air fun and lets them see where their vegetables, milk, eggs, and meat come from. Guided tours are a fun way to get the inside story, but reservations are required. Also on-site is the historic Scott House. The park covers 1,100 acres. (See also Chapter 5: "Sights and Attractions.") (East Pittsburgh)

SETTLER'S CABIN COUNTY PARK
Greer Rd.
Robinson
412/787-2750
Settler's Cabin Park is best known for its wave pool. But with 1,290 acres, there's plenty of room for tennis courts and diving pools, too. The Settler's Cabin is a log cabin, rebuilt in the 1970s, on the site of the Glass-Walker-Ewing house, part of the original land-grant program. A five-year plan is in the works for the Western Pennsylvania Horticultural Society to develop a Botanical Garden Center

North Park Lake, p. 123

Doina Locke

Why So Many Movie Companies Film in Pittsburgh

Brownstones	*Landmarks*
Mills, mines, and factories	*Courtrooms*
Woods, fields, and caves	*Bridges and tunnels*
Bars and nightclubs	*Farms, farmhouses, and barns*
Suburban houses	*Industrial areas*
Offices	*Cafes and diners*
Train stations and railroads	*Downtown*
Estates and mansions	*Jails and prisons*
Parks, lakes and golf courses	*Amusement parks*
Small towns	*Inclines*
Stadiums and arenas	*Victorian facades*
Hospitals and clinics	*Bathhouses*
Churches	*Morgues*
Country roads	*Zoos*

(courtesy of the Pittsburgh Film Office)

on close to 400 acres here. (See also Chapter 5: "Sights and Attractions" and Chapter 10: "Sports and Recreation.") (West Pittsburgh)

SOUTH PARK
Corrigan Dr. and Brownsville Rd.
South Hills
412/835-5710
South Park, Allegheny County's second largest park with nearly 2,000 acres, has two golf courses, one with nine holes and one with 18. Both courses share the same clubhouse. South Park's other amenities include a wave pool, ice-skating rink, and tennis courts. Call the nature center at 412/835-4810 for information about special programs and children's classes. (See also Chapter 5: "Sights and Attractions" and Chapter 10: "Sports and Recreation.") (South Pittsburgh)

WHITE OAK PARK
Rt. 48
White Oak
412/678-3774
The least developed of the county parks, 810-acre White Oak Park looks most like what Pittsburgh's earliest settlers and the Native American tribes must have seen. Trails run through deep woods and up steep hills graced by trillium and other wildflowers. There is an historical marker on the site of Fort Ryerson from colonial times. A workshop at Angora Gardens raises Angora rabbits. A shop sells gift items such

as Angora knit mittens and flower crafts. (East Pittsburgh)

GARDENS

BEECHWOOD FARMS NATURE RESERVE
614 Dorseyville Rd.
Fox Chapel
412/963-6100
Nature lovers delight in the five miles of hiking trails winding through 90 acres of woodlands, open fields, and thickets. Ponds enhance the setting's natural beauty. The Audubon Society of Western Pennsylvania has its headquarters at Beechwood Farms and makes ongoing improvements, including a half-acre demonstration site with 1,500 plants native to the region. The facility includes an environmental education center with a natural history library and bird observation room. Trails open daily from dawn to dusk. Education center open Tue–Sat 9–5, Sun 1–5. Free. (North Pittsburgh)

PHIPPS CONSERVATORY
Schenley Park
412/622-6914
At 2.5 acres, Phipps Conservatory is the largest greenhouse in the country. When it was built in 1893, it was the first large-scale enclosed botanical garden in the United States. The gracefully curved glass structure holds an aquatic garden, children's garden, Japanese courtyard garden, perennial garden, Victorian garden, and others. Special flower shows mark the spring, fall, and Christmas seasons. Tue–Sun 9–5. $4 adults, $5 for special shows; discounts for children and seniors. ♿ (East Pittsburgh)

RODEF SHALOM BIBLICAL GARDENS
4905 Fifth Ave.
Pittsburgh
412/621-6566
Set on the grounds of a beautiful Reform Jewish synagogue and an architectural design marvel in itself, this one-third-acre garden contains over 150 varieties of plants grown in Biblical times. Allow at least 30 minutes to savor the peace and serenity of the plantings and the small stream that flows through the garden. June–Sept 15 Sun–Thur 10–2, Sat 12–1, Wed 7–9. Free. (East Pittsburgh)

Doina Locke

9

SHOPPING

Because of the many distinct neighborhoods within Pittsburgh and the many boroughs and townships in Allegheny County, shopping districts evolved outside of downtown long before the advent of suburban shopping malls. Specialty ethnic foods and products are more widely available here than in many other metropolitan areas, thanks to Pittsburgh's diverse ethnic heritage.

Joseph Horne & Company was Pittsburgh's first downtown department store, established in 1849. In 1879 Kaufmann's Department Store moved downtown from the South Side. Horne's and Kaufmann's dominated downtown and anchored shopping malls through the years. Today, only the Kaufmann name remains. Downtown shopping is undergoing a renaissance, and there are now three large downtown department stores—Kaufmann's, Lazarus (which bought Horne's), and Saks Fifth Avenue—within easy walking distance of each other. Several large office complexes, such as PPG Place, One Oxford Center, and Fifth Avenue Place, serve as bases for clusters of other retail shops.

Elsewhere, major retail districts are found in Shadyside, Squirrel Hill, Oakland, South Side, Station Square, and the Strip District. Large suburban shopping malls include Ross Park Mall, the Galleria, the Monroeville Mall, South Hills Village Mall, and Waterworks Mall. Prime Outlets at Grove City are within an hour's drive north from anywhere in Pittsburgh on I-79.

SHOPPING DISTRICTS

Downtown

Downtown Pittsburgh is also called "the Golden Triangle" because it fits neatly into the region bounded by rivers on two sides and Grant Street on the third. Because of suburban shopping malls, downtown is no longer the place to shop and be seen. However, thanks to two urban renaissances, shopping downtown is seeing a resurgence in popularity. Kaufmann's still maintains its downtown store, complete with a large outdoor clock, a traditional meeting point. Saks and Lazarus, an Ohio-based company that bought out the Joseph Horne Company stores, both have large stores downtown.

FIFTH AVENUE PLACE ARCADE SHOPS
Fifth Avenue and Liberty
Pittsburgh
Large marble-faced planters filled with trees and shrubs and fitted with bench-size ledges invite people to sit and relax while waiting for a bus or taking a breather from shopping. The two-story tall portal in brass and glass lends elegance to the shops on the main floor. The food court and shops on the mezzanine overlook the first-floor courtyard. Generous plantings, wrought-iron tables and chairs, five-globed "street lamps," and plenty of marble and shiny brass make a nice balance between old-fashioned and modern mall design. Shops include Chico's, specializing in moderately priced casual fashions for women with a southwestern flair, Sam Goody records, the Coach Store for top-quality, top-price leather goods, Betsy Ann Chocolates, Ylang Ylang for young and hip clothing and accessories, Saxon Fine Jewelry, and the Society for Contemporary Crafts store, featuring budget-priced handiwork—from wooden riverboat whistles to soft sculpture and blown glass. (Downtown Pittsburgh)

RODIER PARIS
One Oxford Centre
Pittsburgh
412/355-0864

Doina Locke

Homemade pies in the downtown shopping district, p. 127

Rodier Paris presents elegant, sophisticated women's clothing exclusively from the Rodier line. Providing executive and professional women with classic pieces with distinctive flair is the store's goal. Rodier's is noted for its scarves and belts designed to complement the collections. The basis of its line is "Kasha" knit fabric, a washable wool/acrylic blend. (Downtown Pittsburgh)

Station Square

Located on the far side of the Monongahela River, across the Smithfield Street Bridge from downtown, this former PL&E railroad car repair barn attracts window shoppers and serious shoppers alike with its select mixture of more than 50 fine shops and restaurants. A dance club, a comedy club that draws local and national comedians, and a stage for lobby concerts keep Station Square a busy place both night and day. Unique gift items, enchanting decorations, and bustling holiday crowds make Station Square a special Christmastime attraction.

CRYSTAL RIVER GEMS
Station Square Shops
Pittsburgh
412/391-5310
Stunning amethyst geodes, delicate stone carvings, crystals, and polished stones fill this small, tightly organized shop with eye-catching splendor. Excellent specimens of fossilized plants and marine life are displayed to advantage in the shop's large window walls. (South Pittsburgh)

HEINZ HEALEY'S MEN'S APPAREL
Station Square Shops
Pittsburgh
412/281-5115
Fine men's clothing and accessories are attractively displayed in this intimate shop where excellent service comes naturally. A most unusual bonus in a men's apparel shop is a fabulous half-price ticket service that can't be beat. (See Chapter 11: "Performing Arts.") (South Pittsburgh)

LANDMARKS STORE
Station Square Shops
Pittsburgh
412/765-1042
The book and gift shop of the Pittsburgh History and Landmarks Foundation is the place to go for something uniquely Pittsburgh—whether it be a book, video, postcard, vintage photograph, or souvenir featuring Pittsburgh's own Mr. Rogers. Whimsical carvings, architectural casts, and mugs add to the mix of Pittsburgh memorabilia. (South Pittsburgh)

POOR RICHARD'S
TOBACCO SHOP
Station Square Shops
Pittsburgh
412/281-1133
The most discriminating cigar aficionado will be pleased with a choice from Poor Richard's. Fine quality tobacco in all its forms can be found, as well as smoking equipment and accessories. (South Pittsburgh)

ST. BRENDAN'S CROSSING
Station Square Shops
Pittsburgh
412/471-0700
Wonderfully warm woolens, nubby knits, and Celtic charm are the special offerings to be found at St. Brendan's Crossing, an Irish import store. Women's fine fashions and accessories by Irish designers are featured. Fisherman's knit sweaters and cozy woolen wraps called *ruans* are also notable. (South Pittsburgh)

PITTSBURGH CENTER
FOR THE ARTS
Station Square Shops
Pittsburgh
412/642-9227
Works by local artists are spotlighted in a sleek, sophisticated gallery setting. Oil, acrylic, glass, wood, and clay are some of the media used in the pieces on display in this attractive, well-lit store. All works are for sale. This is the place to start collecting art at very reasonable prices. (South Pittsburgh)

Carson Street Shops

Restaurants, bookstores, nightspots, antique shops, tattoo and piercing parlors, fashions for skateboarders and slackers, and specialty shops fill the nineteenth- and early twentieth-century storefronts on the south bank of the Monongahela River.

BALCER BAKERY
2126 E. Carson St.
Pittsburgh
412/431-9906

This old-fashioned bakery with slanted glass display cases and a back wall of bread shelves is the last of 11 bakeries that once lined East Carson Street. Order an elaborate wedding cake or pick up a bag of cookies; you won't be able to resist that wonderful bake-shop aroma. (South Pittsburgh)

CITY BOOKS
1111 E. Carson St.
Pittsburgh
412/481-7555

Over 25,000 books jam City Books' two floors, connected by an old-fashioned metal spiral staircase. Some of the books are new; most are fine-quality collectible used hardbacks. The store buys used books, also. Espresso, sandwiches, and pastries are available. (South Pittsburgh)

HANDWOVEN ON CARSON
2013 E. Carson St.
Pittsburgh
412/488-0112

Sue Carson handweaves cloth of natural fibers and fashions timeless clothing designs in this shop. Rugs, pillows, and wall art are also created on the premises. (South Pittsburgh)

NOW & THEN ANTIQUES AND COLLECTIBLES
1023 E. Carson St.
Pittsburgh
412/431-1373

Here you can buy or sell a wide variety of vintage toys, jewelry, furniture, and glassware. Collectors will find old advertisements, neon signs, and household items. (South Pittsburgh)

PATAK DESIGNS
1220 E. Carson St.
Pittsburgh
412/431-3337

Dramatic fine jewelry is custom made on the premises. Collectors can find rare crystals, gem-quality cut stones, fossils, and mineral specimens. You can also bring in gems for identification or cutting. Expert jewelry repair work is done here as well. (South Pittsburgh)

PERLORA
2220 E. Carson St.
Pittsburgh
412/431-2220

Here you'll find contemporary and ultra-modern furniture in a modern industrial showroom with an exposed steel stairway. The store approaches design with an unstuffy, offbeat whimsy—advertising its wares with slogans such as "If Mr. Spock were a chair," or "If Robin and Marian were a loveseat." (South Side)

PITTSBURGH GUITARS
1409 E. Carson St.
Pittsburgh
412/431-0700

With all the live bands performing up and down Carson Street, it's no wonder that Pittsburgh Guitars is located here. You can buy, trade, or sell a guitar or any other band equipment at the shop. (South Pittsburgh)

RANDY'S ALTERNATIVE MUSIC
1210 E. Carson St.
Pittsburgh
412/481-7445

Randy carries new and used CDs, tapes, and records—but not just any old music. He has recordings you can't find anywhere else in the city. (South Pittsburgh)

ST. ELMO'S BOOKS & MUSIC
2208 E. Carson St.
Pittsburgh
412/431-9100

This shop is a wonderland of New Age, spiritual, and mystical books and paraphernalia. The racks are filled with an eclectic mix of musical, environmental, and meditation CDs and tapes. Fascinating selections of incense and jewelry are clustered about the store. (South Pittsburgh)

SILVER EYE CENTER FOR PHOTOGRAPHY
1015 E. Carson St.
Pittsburgh
412/431-1810

An undistinguished storefront on a not-quite-with-it building houses a gallery that has long been devoted to photographic art. The gallery itself is little more than a white box, the better to focus attention on the works of photographic artistry. (South Pittsburgh)

South Craig Street Shops

There's always bustling foot traffic up and down South Craig Street because it's within a couple blocks of Pitt, CMU, Carnegie Institute, and Carnegie Library, to name just a few of the activity centers in Oakland. Students, faculty, professionals, and just plain folks are drawn to the many exotic boutiques and specialty shops and to the trendy coffeehouses and restaurants.

CALIBAN BOOK SHOP
410 S. Craig St.
Pittsburgh
412/681-9111

Here you'll find rare and scholarly books. (East Pittsburgh)

HISTORY
424 S. Craig St.

Shops in Sewickley, p. 135

Pittsburgh
412/681-4884

A most unusual mix of cultures and interests is reflected in the stock of History, on the corner of South Craig Street and Forbes Avenue, and of History II, its sibling store located a few doors down Craig Street. Primitive masks hang on one wall, a model of the "new" T. rex lunges on a countertop, collector-quality mineral specimens and Bronze Age artifacts fill a glass case, thousands of beads fill bins in the corner, and large-scale statues peer out the windows in a browser's wonderland. The store captures the eclectic, intellectual curiosity of Oakland. (East Pittsburgh)

IRISH DESIGN CENTER
303 S. Craig St.
Pittsburgh
412/682-6125

Imports from Ireland fill the corner shop of the Craig Center Building. Bulky, cream-colored, knit fishermen's sweaters, Irish linen shirts and blouses, woolen skirts, and woven woolen wraps present a hearty, natural fashion look. Decorative and functional items such as goblets, ceramic bowls, and banners with Celtic designs are moderately priced and beautifully made. (East Pittsburgh)

MADE BY HAND FINE CRAFTS
303 S. Craig St.
Pittsburgh
412/681-8346
You'll find high-quality signature pieces by artists and artisans from all over the country. Jewelry, picture frames, whimsical novelty clocks, goblets, and ceramic bowls are some of the items displayed in this tiny, sophisticated showroom. Prices are reasonable. (East Pittsburgh)

PAPYRUS DESIGNS
319 S. Craig St.
Pittsburgh
412/682-3237
Gorgeous gift wrapping paper by the sheet or roll, ribbons, and gift bags along with fine stationery and cards are featured at Papyrus Designs. Unique desk accessories and handsomely bound date books, address books, and journals are enough to inspire even the most disorganized person to bring order to chaos. (East Pittsburgh)

TOP NOTCH ART CENTER
411 S. Craig St.
Pittsburgh
412/683-4444
The giant #2 pencil sticking through the upper level facade points the way to Top Notch Art Center. A discount art supply store, Top Notch offers up to 50 percent off manufacturers' suggested retail prices. Custom framing services are available, or you can buy matting and framing supplies to do it yourself. (East Pittsburgh)

WATERMELON BLUES
311 S. Craig St.
Pittsburgh
412/681-8451
It has the cluttered look and the charming appeal of an upscale general store. Small novelty items, gourmet snacks and food mixes, and trendy home accessories clamor for your attention as you browse through the bins and shelves. For casual gifts and something to keep the children amused, Watermelon Blues is a good place to visit. (East Pittsburgh)

Shadyside

Once "out in the country" and northeast of neighboring Oakland, this former streetcar suburb at one time had millionaires and industrial giants in residence, but now has some of the city's nicest sidewalk shopping. Several blocks of Walnut and Aiken Streets and Ellsworth Avenue are lined with wildly eclectic specialty shops, galleries, and restaurants. Shadyside once held exclusive rights to these fine shops but the "malling" of America has extended to Pittsburgh, and the vast majority of the retailers also have outlets in at least one suburban mall. Parking is limited to on-street metered spaces, a few lots, and a small parking structure.

THE CLAY PLACE
Mineo Building, Second Floor
5416 Walnut St.
Pittsburgh
412/682-3737
Two surprisingly large areas showcase American contemporary sculptures and functional ceramics in this second-floor gallery, founded in

1973. Monthly showings feature local and nationally known artists. The retail shop carries small ceramics, books, and pottery equipment. (East Pittsburgh)

FEATHERS
5520 Walnut St.
Pittsburgh
412/621-4700
Fine household linens, quilts, and furnishings devoted to making a comfortable "nest" fill this shop, located in the Theatre Building on Walnut Street. Luxurious down comforters and pillows recall European tradition and workmanship. (East Pittsburgh)

GLASSWORKS
5418 Walnut St.
Pittsburgh
412/682 5443
For the most exclusive names in crystal, such as Baccarat, Lalique, Orrefors, and Swarovski, check out Glassworks' wide selection. Hand-painted furniture and ceramic and glass giftware with a bit of whimsy add a light touch to the selections. (East Pittsburgh)

JOURNEYS OF LIFE
810 Bellefonte St.
Pittsburgh
412/681-8755
Step off Shadyside's main street to step out of the mainstream for a short, nurturing visit to Journeys of Life. Two stories of books, music, cards, jewelry, and home accessories assist in the journey to recovery, wellness, and personal growth. You don't have to be a "New Ager" a "New Waver," or new at anything to find something of interest here. (East Pittsburgh)

SW RANDALL
TOYES & GIFTS

806 Ivy St.
Pittsburgh
412/687-2666
The two-story glass-fronted fantasy design of this store draws shoppers with its sunny whimsy. Inside, brightly colored kites, stuffed animals, and toys and more toys delight children and adults. The store carries a large supply of Brio and Playmobil sets. Other stores are located in Station Square, Downtown, and Squirrel Hill. (East Pittsburgh)

TOADFLAX INC.
5443 Walnut St.
Pittsburgh
412/621-2500
The entire store is filled with a profusion of flowers to brighten any day. Buy an arrangement or make your own—either way it's tough to choose. Toadflax also carries gardening books and accessories and beeswax candles. You'll be sure to find exactly the right gift for that very special someone in your life. (East Pittsburgh)

Squirrel Hill

The sidewalks are always filled with pedestrians in this bustling shopping district lining both sides of Murray Avenue, east of Oakland. It is rumored that the best bagels and the best deli meats can be found here in this predominantly Jewish neighborhood. Restaurants, coffee shops, stores, a movie theater, a post office, and the Jewish Community Center keep things busy.

ADELE'S LADIES APPAREL
5876 Forbes Ave.
Pittsburgh
412/421-1991
Elegant high fashion, designer's trunk showings, and sophisticated

accessories are Adele's stock in trade. If you have an important event coming up and cost is no object, the sales staff at this upscale shop can help you put together the perfect look. Be forewarned: to browse is to lust—at least in Adele's—after fashion, not sex. (East Pittsburgh

LITTLE'S SUPER SHOE STORE
5850 Forbes Ave.
Pittsburgh
412/521-3530
Little's proclaims itself to be "Pittsburgh's Largest Shoe Store" and carries a huge assortment of styles and sizes, from men's 6–18, AA–EEEE to women's 4–13, AAAA–EE. The whole family should be able to find footware here. (East Pittsburgh)

Robinson Town Centre

This sprawling outdoor mall, a complex of shops and major stores, is located at the junction of Route 22/30 and Route 60. IKEA was one of the original anchor stores. Kaufman's, Kohl's, Super KMart, Wickes Furniture Showroom, and Pier 1 Imports have also established major stores here. Restaurants such as Red Lobster, Dingbats, and Quaker Steak &

Lube have found the Robinson Town Centre area to be a good location.

IKEA PITTSBURGH
2001 Park Manor Blvd.
Robinson
412/747-0747
IKEA is a major department store specializing in Scandinavian-style furniture and contemporary home accessories at bargain prices. It combines showroom floors with pick-your-own warehouse shopping. Most pieces require assembly; delivery and assembly are extra. Parents can shop in peace while their small children enjoy a supervised play area featuring a ball pit. Hungry shoppers can relax in the dining room and enjoy (what else?) Swedish meatballs. (West Pittsburgh)

PIER 1 IMPORTS
Robinson Town Centre
Robinson
412/788-9477
Wicker, pottery, gauze, glass, and brass—as far as the eye can see. Pier 1 offers international shopping with the emphasis on Asian and Latin American wares. Accent pieces, dinnerware, furniture, and clothing fill the store with bright colors and natural materials. (West Pittsburgh)

Sewickley

Reputed to be the wealthiest suburb of Pittsburgh, Sewickley displays a modest, quaintly charming face to the world through its business district. Old-style street lamps, a lush Victorian-style gazebo, and discreetly distinct storefronts portray a small-town Main Street that never was. To maintain that aura of yesteryear, the indoor Nickelodeon Mall carries the name of the first movie theater, which opened in downtown Pittsburgh in 1907. The many intriguing shops, covering an amazing variety of retail items and services, remain a secret undiscovered by many Pittsburghers.

BIRD IN THE HAND GALLERY
427 Broad St.
Sewickley
412/741-8286
After 30 years in the same location,

The Open Mind

Doina Locke

owner Katharine N. Amsler uses every available surface for displaying the works of local artists and a large selection of primitive South American pieces. Be sure to venture into the back room and the upstairs galleries for a rich visual experience. You won't want to leave empty-handed. (North Pittsburgh)

CREATIVE THREADS
431 Broad St.
Sewickley
412/741-1933
Any slogan or design can be machine-embroidered to order on T-shirts, sweatshirts, denim, or canvas, whether you buy it here or bring in your own. The shop carries a wonderful selection of items for golfers, gardeners, and babies. (North Pittsburgh)

NATASHA'S
551 Beaver St.
Sewickley
412/741-9484
Lose yourself in the opulence of vintage clothing from the wealthy. The bride who wants her "something old" to be a gown or headpiece will find an enormous selection. Evening clothes, lingerie, and hats are fun to try on. Natasha also has a display case of fabulous Russian icons. (North Pittsburgh)

THE OPEN MIND
439 Beaver St.
Sewickley
412/741-1888
Alternative medicine, wholistic living, angels, yoga, and meditation are just some of the topics covered by the books, magazines, tapes, and CDs lining the walls of this combination bookstore and center for spiritual and philosophical exploration. Healers, counselors, and teachers

use the second-floor facilities for classes and consultations. Auras, tarot cards, and books are read here. (North Pittsburgh)

TRAVELWARES
429 Broad St.
Pittsburgh
412/741-6100
High-quality leather goods, casual accessories for men and women, and unusual jewelry fill this store to capacity, but with just enough room left over for leisurely browsing. This is the spot to visit for unique gifts and collectibles, for someone special or for yourself. But Travelwares is not a gift shop; it is more a survival outfitter for upscale trekkers in the suburban "wilderness."(North Pittsburgh)

Wetting Your Whistle

The legal drinking age in Pennsylvania is 21, but the state closely regulates alcohol consumption even for adults. Bars and restaurants may serve alcohol until 2 a.m, but Sunday service in restaurants is limited to a predetermined ratio of food to alcohol.

The state also strictly enforces drunk-driving laws with regular police checkpoints. A person is considered to be driving under the influence of alcohol in Pennsylvania if his or her blood-alcohol content is 0.10 percent or higher.

Beer is sold through distributors by the case only. To buy beer on Sunday or by the six-pack, you must go to a bar or restaurant that sells beer to go. These places can sell you only one six-pack at a time, but you can get a maximum of four by leaving the store and returning for each of the remaining three.

State liquor stores, known as state stores, are the only places to buy bottles of wine and spirits. It is helpful to know your spirits, however, because store employees are not supposed to make recommendations. Some of the best-stocked state liquor stores are located in One Oxford Centre, downtown, 412/565-7689; Perry Shops in the North Hills, 412/364-2330; and The Waterworks, Aspinwall, 412/487-4844, which has a notably good wine selection.

To find the nearest beer distributor, check the Yellow Pages. For the nearest state liquor store, look in the state government section of the White Pages.

Strip District

This former wholesale warehouse district, where trains once brought in fresh produce and carried out specialty steel, is still a bustling district selling the freshest produce, meat, and seafood. Specialty ethnic and gourmet foods and ingredients—in general, things that can't be found elsewhere —are all jammed together where shoppers can jostle and push, search and comparison shop, and get a deal on the freshest and the best of the best. Saturday is the Strip's busiest retail day. If you can't handle crowds, try shopping during the week.

BENKOVITZ SEAFOODS
2300 Smallman St.
Pittsburgh
412/263-3016
The store offers fresh seafood, a large center deli case stocked with prepared seafood specialties, a full line of breads, seasoning, and pastas, freezer cases of frozen shrimp, fish fillets, and prepared gourmet entrées and appetizers. It's always jammed at lunch with a huge crowd. Parking is convenient in the small lot. (East Pittsburgh)

ROBERT WHOLEY'S & CO. INC.
1501 Penn Ave.
Pittsburgh
412/261-3377
Long a Pittsburgh tradition, the Wholey's fish sign marks the largest seafood wholesale and retail operation in town. The two-story retail store carries fresh fish, clams, lobsters, and their relatives on ice downstairs and a jam-packed kitchenwares shop upstairs. There's a dining room for folks who want to eat their famous fish sandwiches in rather than take-out. (East Pittsburgh)

PRESTOGEORGE FINE FOODS
1728 Penn Ave.
Pittsburgh
412/471-0133
Known for high-quality fresh-roasted coffee beans, PrestoGeorge draws customers from all over the region for coffee. Racks of specialty pastas, fresh bread, and Italian foods tempt the crowds of dedicated Strip shoppers. (East Pittsburgh)

PENN AVENUE POTTERY
1905 Penn Ave.
Pittsburgh
412/281-9394
Mention the pottery shop with the studio and kiln in the back, and people ask, "Do they still have those wonderful terra-cotta tile faces?" The answer is yes, and the faces have to be seen to be believed. Minimalist, expressive, and whimsical, they'll bring a smile to your face. Wonderful designs, gorgeous glazes, and an appreciation of the unusual characterize the beautifully crafted items for sale. (East Pittsburgh)

PENNSYLVANIA MACARONI
2012 Penn Ave.
Pittsburgh
412/471-8330
You wouldn't think there were that many different kinds of olive oil, but there are. Nor will you believe the number of cheeses, breads, sausages, and other mouth-watering components of Mediterranean cooking available here. (East Pittsburgh)

Lebanon Shops

Mt. Lebanon's Washington Road is lined with numerous stores, many of them one-of-a-kind, in small strip malls. Along Beverly Road, a couple dozen shops clustered on both sides *of the street create a charming Main Street-style shopping area.*

PERKINS GENERAL STORE
308 Beverly Rd.
Mt. Lebanon
412/561-3131
Out of town or in your own home, it always helps to have the right tool or thingamajig for the job. If Perkins doesn't have it, it wasn't what you needed in the first place—and they have the thing you do need. (South Pittsburgh)

OTHER NOTABLE STORES

BERNIE'S PHOTO CENTER
525 E. Ohio St.
Pittsburgh
412/231-1717
The best in photography equipment can be bought, sold, rented, or repaired at this North Side camera shop. Film, accessories, processing, and advice are readily available. For inspiration, visit the photographic museum,

Photo Antiquities, next door and up a flight of stairs. (North Pittsburgh)

HART'S DESIRE/
BOOKWORKS CAFÉ
3400 Harts Run Rd.
Glenshaw
412/767-0344
A formerly deserted machine shop was converted into a wonder of richly polished wood, leaded glass, a cappuccino machine, and gourmet goodies in the Bookworks Café bookshop and the separately owned Hart's Desire boutique. The boutique presents unique fine home furnishings and accessories in a distinctive setting that includes wrought-iron gates between areas, a second-floor mini-loft, and the upright trunks of an oak and an elm. Full-size wooden fireplace mantels and huge wood-framed mirrors provide architectural interest, but are also for sale. Bookworks offers a wonderful selection of books, greeting cards, and stationery. Children's books are found in a balcony reached by a spiral staircase. (North Pittsburgh)

A vendor sells cheese in the Strip District, p. 137

Jeff Greenberg/GPCVB

LITTLE DICKENS' BOOK STORE, A BOOKSTORE FOR CHILDREN LTD.
634 Allegheny River Blvd.
Oakmont
412/828-9005
You'll find a full line of books just for children. The owner stocks books that she has hand-selected for quality and beauty. (East Pittsburgh)

MYSTERY LOVERS' BOOKSHOP AND CAFÉ
514 Allegheny River Blvd.
Oakmont
412/681-3700
Not only does it carry the most complete inventory of mystery, true crime, and suspense novels in the area, but Mystery Lovers' Bookshop also has the largest lineup of touring mystery authors on either side of the Allegheny River. You'll find reference works and how-tos for writers, in addition to the who-dunnits. Junior sleuths love the Boxcar Mystery and Goosebumps series fan clubs, storytellers, and theme breakfasts. The café serves cappuccino, espresso, select teas, and a sinfully tempting line of gourmet desserts. MLB also serves as the community center for mystery enthusiasts, discussion groups, and writers. A favorite gift item is "The Pittsburgher," a basket filled with Pittsburgh-based mysteries, Hershey's kisses, Clark bars, and an MLB T-shirt or mug. The place is a booklover's delight—floor to ceiling—and if they don't have it, they'll get it for you, whether it's a mystery or not. (East Pittsburgh)

RECORD-RAMA SOUND ARCHIVES
Pines Plaza, 1130 Perry Hwy.
North Hills
412/367-7330
Collectors or fans in search of a very special recording begin (and often end) their search here. The shop has over 2.5 million sound recordings. So if it's not here, it probably doesn't exist. This extensive collection includes contemporary hits, CDs, tapes, and records. The shop also takes orders by phone or fax, and will mail orders anywhere. (North Pittsburgh)

THE RUBY SLIPPER
716 Allegheny River Blvd.
Verona
412/826-1250
The Ruby Slipper is a tiny jewel box of a store where you can find moderately priced jewelry that doesn't look just like everyone else's. Truly exceptional, original fine gemstone jewelry is what they do best. If you prefer, you can have your own design custom made. (East Pittsburgh)

MAJOR DEPARTMENT STORES

KAUFMANN'S
400 Fifth Ave.
Pittsburgh
412/232-2000
Kaufmann's is the oldest name in Pittsburgh retailing. It sells moderate to expensive fashions, jewelry, cosmetics, and household furnishings. Look for tremendous savings at special storewide sales. Other locations can be found at seven major regional mall locations, including Century III, Monroeville, Ross Park, and South Hills Village. (Downtown Pittsburgh)

KOHL'S
North Hills Village Mall
Ross
412/358-8730
Kohl's moved to Pittsburgh in 1997, with six locations throughout the area. The Minnesota-based chain

offers moderately priced brand-name clothing and accessories for men, women, and children. (North Pittsburgh)

LAZARUS
Ross Park Mall,
McKnight Rd.
Ross
412/635-5900
The Ohio-based company that bought out longtime Pittsburgh department chain Joseph Horne's Company has seven stores in area mall locations, including Century III, Monroeville, and South Hills Village. The historic downtown location is closed, but a new store near Saks on Fifth Avenue opened in November 1998. Lazarus offers large selections of moderate-to high-priced clothing, jewelry, shoes, accessories, and home furnishings. (North Pittsburgh)

JCPENNEY
Monroeville Mall, Rt. 22
Monroeville
412/373-2620
This national chain maintains locations at Century III Mall and Ross Park Mall, in addition to several other malls throughout the region. Penney's also offers catalog shopping; you can order by phone, by mail, or in person at the store. (East Pittsburgh)

SEARS ROEBUCK AND CO.
300 South Hills Village Mall
Bethel Park
412/831-6599
Sears is a national chain with locations in Ross Park Mall and in Monroeville and West Mifflin. It offers both in-store and catalog shopping. It also offers a variety of services, including automotive and appliance service centers. (South Pittsburgh)

SHOPPING MALLS AND OUTLET CENTERS

AIR MALL
Pittsburgh International Airport,
Airside
Findlay Township
800/ITS-FAIR
This bustling mall inside an international airport is uniquely Pittsburgh. There's sophisticated shopping at more than 100 stores and restaurants at in-city prices—their promise to the shopper. The Nature Company, Victoria's Secret, Eckerd's Drugs, and the Pennsylvania Gift Shop can provide whatever you may have forgotten to pack. (West Pittsburgh)

CENTURY III MALL
Rt. 51, Rt. 885, and Lebanon
Church Rd.
West Mifflin
412/653-1220
Lazarus, Kaufmann's, JC Penney, and Sears co-anchor the mall with Wickes Furniture and TJ Maxx. A large food court, over a dozen specialty food stores, and three restaurants (Elby's Big Boy, Ruby Tuesday, and the Ground Round) make this suburban mall especially taste-tempting. Over 180 specialty shops also make this one of the biggest shopping complexes in the area. (South Pittsburgh)

GALLERIA
Rt. 19 and Gilkeson Rd.
Mt. Lebanon
412/561-4000
Upscale and sophisticated, the Galleria is the home of "some of Pittsburgh's finest fashion stores," including Larrimor's and J. S. Altman Haberdashery for men, Mondi, Chico's, Lillie Rubin, Venetia Boutique, Talbots, H. Baskin Clothiers, Ann Taylor, and Episode for women, and

A Tale of Two Suburbs

As the suburbs gained population in the past quarter century, major arteries connecting the city and the suburbs sprouted retail businesses—until they all resembled continuous strip malls. McKnight Road (Route 19) in the North Hills and William Penn Highway (Business Route 22) in Monroeville are two of the most congested routes. Jersey barriers, which prevent left turns between intersections, and intersections where U-turns are prohibited further complicate driving from one business to another on these roads, even during off-peak driving times. During rush hours and on weekends, allow plenty of time for travel on these roads and keep your map handy. Your best bet is to plan your shopping for off-peak times.

Banana Republic for both. Restoration Hardware offers vintage-style brass hardware and fittings, rustic outdoor accessories, fixtures, and furniture to tempt decorators of any era. Williams-Sonoma outfits the well-equipped gourmet kitchen. Tutto Bella flowers, Today's Tiffany Glass Co., Renaissance Gallery, and the Pittsburgh Center for the Arts offer further home-decorating marvels. Galleria Cinemas has six screening rooms. Mark Pi's China Gate, Hot Licks, Ruby Tuesday, and the London Grille offer fine dining to round out the mix of 54 shops and restaurants. (South Pittsburgh)

MONROEVILLE MALL
Rt. 22
Monroeville
412/243-8511

The Monroeville Mall is one of the largest in the area, with 180 specialty stores, three department stores, and the obligatory food court so shoppers can stay longer at the mall. One of the larger stores is the Burlington Coat Factory Warehouse located in the Mall Annex. (East Pittsburgh)

PRIME OUTLETS AT GROVE CITY
I-79, Exit 31
Grove City
724/748-4770

There are over 130 outlets in this sprawling, seven-cluster complex surrounded by parking lots. The attractive center has wide sidewalks, a children's playground, and a small, nicely landscaped marsh garden. Such nationally known upscale names as Saks Fifth Avenue, Evan Picone, Polo/Ralph Lauren, Mikasa, Sony, Bose, Coach, and Corning-Revere are represented. Prices are always discounted, but are slashed even lower for seasonal sales. (North Pittsburgh)

ROSS PARK MALL
McKnight Rd.
North Hills
412/369-4400

Abercrombie & Fitch, Williams-Sonoma, Pottery Barn, Banana Republic, and Godiva Chocolatier appeal to upscale shoppers at this glossy, bustling suburban mall. The bright and airy second-level food court encourages people-watching while you enjoy a meal or snack from any of over a dozen taste-tempting vendors. Kaufmann's, Lazarus, JCPenney, and Sears are the anchoring department stores. Kiosks and special-interest exhibitions add colorful variety. Get your ears pierced, your watch batteries changed, or have a glamor photo taken. (North Pittsburgh)

SOUTH HILLS VILLAGE MALL
Rt. 19 and Ft. Couch Rd.
Bethel Park
412/831-2900
This attractive, indoor suburban mall offers shoppers a wide variety of goods and services, with anchor tenants Kaufmann's, Lazarus, and Sears. The large food court is centrally located between Kaufmann's and Lazarus and appeals to both kids and adults. A movie theater, professional offices, and a U.S. Post Office complete the service-oriented mix. After the shopping is over, Roxy is the place to stop for food, drinks, and a little jazz. (South Pittsburgh)

WATERWORKS MALL
Freeport Rd.
Pittsburgh
412/366-2252
A Giant Eagle supermarket, TJ Maxx, Radio Shack, Lechter's kitchen furnishings, Marshall's, Waterworks Cinema, several small dress shops, and fine restaurants are just some of the mix of businesses that line the huge parking lot to form an outdoor mall. Damon's the Place for Ribs and Abaté Fine Seafoods offer exciting family dining, while Wendy's serves those who are too rushed to linger for long. (North Pittsburgh)

Doina Locke

10

SPORTS AND RECREATION

Football and hockey reign supreme here. Season tickets are often hard to find at any price. Fans are enthusiastic and loyal, but they expect their teams to deliver. Steeler fans look forward to the year the team earns "one for the thumb," a coveted fifth Super Bowl ring. Everyone in town was a Penguins fan when Mario Lemieux led the team to a Stanley Cup victory.

The Pirates are one of the oldest Major League Baseball teams and have won numerous world championships and division titles. The team continues to draw attention by fielding hardworking, competitive players.

Collegiate sports fans have plenty of good teams to follow. The University of Pittsburgh's Panthers are recognized nationally in football and men's and women's basketball. Duquesne University has gained considerable national attention for its basketball and lacrosse programs. The Robert Morris College football team, though fairly new, is building an outstanding reputation.

With three rivers and plenty of hills and mountains, boating and skiing are naturals for recreation. With more than 26,000 boats registered, Allegheny County has the largest inland boat registration in the country. Fishing, water-skiing, jet skiing, and pleasure boating are popular, while avid sailors love to take their boats to Lake Arthur in Moraine State Park.

PROFESSIONAL SPORTS

Auto Racing

LERNERVILLE SPEEDWAY
Rt. 356

Sarver
724/353-1511 or 724/353-1350
Even though it's about an hour north of downtown, Lernerville is not too far for dedicated dirt-track stock-car racing fans. Twice a year, local sprint-car

racers get their chance to compete with the big names. Races April–Aug Fri 7:30. $10 adults, discounts for seniors and children. (North Pittsburgh)

PITTSBURGH'S PENNSYLVANIA MOTOR SPEEDWAY
Rt. 22, Noblestown exit
Imperial
412/695-0393
Stock-car racing on a dirt track draws the fans on Saturday nights. The season ends with an exciting Pittsburgher 100 with a $21,000 purse. March–Sept Sat 7. $10 adults, discounted for children. (West Pittsburgh)

Baseball

PITTSBURGH PIRATES
Three Rivers Stadium
400 Stadium Circle
Pittsburgh
412/321-2827 or 800/BUY-BUCS
(800/289-2827)
Owner Kevin McClatchy changed the team, its logo, and its manager when he bought the franchise. Attendance has been increasing for the relatively young and inexperienced Pirates, who bring hard work and excitement to the game. A new stadium is in the works. Look for specials games such as Bat Day, Cap Day, and Pirates T-shirt Day, when some of the earliest fans get "freebies." Tickets $5–17; an additional $1 use ticket must be purchased at the stadium. ♿ (North Pittsburgh)

Football

PITTSBURGH STEELERS
Three Rivers Stadium
400 Stadium Circle
Pittsburgh
412/323-1200
Pittsburgh is known for the toughness of its football and hockey fans, who

demand (and often get) great teams. The Steelers were the first football team to win four Super Bowl rings, and they've come close again. Since 1972, every home game has been a sellout. A new 65,000-seat football stadium is scheduled for completion in 2001. Even though loyal fans make tickets hard to get, it's worth a try. ♿ (North Pittsburgh)

Hockey

PITTSBURGH PENGUINS
Civic Arena, 66 Mario Lemieux Pl.
Pittsburgh
412/642-PENS (642-7367) or
412/323-1919
The two-time Stanley Cup–winning Pittsburgh Penguins are on the ice at the Civic Arena. The legendary Mario Lemieux has retired, but fans are looking to Jaromir Jagr for plenty of shots on goal. (Downtown)

Harness Racing

LADBROKE RACING—THE MEADOWS
Race Track Rd.
Meadow Lands
412/563-1224
While enthusiastic fans make the hour-long drive to The Meadows race track, many prefer the off-track betting facilities at six Ladbroke locations, two of which are in Allegheny County, one in Harmarville (North Pittsburgh), the other in Moon Township (West Pittsburgh). Races are simulcast from major tracks around the country. Patrons may place their bets and enjoy the racing action and a fine meal for a full evening's entertainment. Simulcast races daily. For more off-track betting information, call 724/225-9300 or 412/563-1224. (West Pittsburgh)

Fishing in Pittsburgh

At least 13 varieties of freshwater game fish are found in the Ohio, Allegheny, and Monongahela Rivers. North Park and South Park Lakes are stocked with trout by the state. North Park Lake is also a major bass fishery, and panfish such as bluegills and perch are abundant in its waters. Deer Lakes County Park has three artificial lakes, also stocked by the state, and offers plenty of good fishing. A fishing license is required for anyone over age 12.

COLLEGE SPORTS

Allegheny County is home to 31 colleges and universities. The University of Pittsburgh football and basketball teams compete in the Big East Conference, which garners national attention.

Basketball

DUQUESNE UNIVERSITY DUKES AND LADY DUKES
A. J. Palumbo Center
Pittsburgh
412/396-6568 (men's)
412/396-6565 (women's)
The Duquesne University Dukes men's basketball team competes in the Atlantic Ten Conference against schools such as Temple, George Washington, and Rhode Island. The team also plays a popular annual non-conference game against city rivals the University of Pittsburgh Panthers. Home games are played at the A. J. Palumbo Center on the college's campus "on the bluff," just outside downtown along Forbes Avenue. Duquesne's new coach Darelle Porter has injected new life into the struggling Dukes and promises to restore

the team's prominence. $5 general admission, $15 courtside seats. For more information, call 412/232-3853. (East Pittsburgh)

ROBERT MORRIS COLLEGE COLONIALS
Charles Sewall Center
Moon Township
412/262-8295
The Robert Morris College Colonials men's basketball team competes in the Northeast Conference. Since 1981, the Colonials have made five trips to the NCAA tournament and are the only team in their conference to have won a game at the annual event. The team plays home games at the Charles L. Sewall Center on the college's campus in Moon Township, 15 miles west of Pittsburgh. Tickets: $5 adults, $2 for children under 8. For more information, call 412/262-8264. (West Pittsburgh)

UNIVERSITY OF PITTSBURGH PANTHERS
Fitzgerald Field House
Pittsburgh
412/648-8300
The Pitt Panthers men's basketball team plays in the nationally ranked Big East Conference against perennial

powers Connecticut, Georgetown, St. John's, Syracuse, and Villanova. Panther home games are played either at the venerable Fitzgerald Field House, which provides an intimate but raucous collegiate environment, or—against more prominent opponents—at Civic Arena on the northern edge of downtown. Under the energetic leadership of head coach Ralph Willard, the team continues to produce players bound for the National Basketball Association, such as Billy Knight and Charles Smith. Tickets $12–$17. For more information, call 412/648-8304. (East Pittsburgh)

Football

DUQUESNE UNIVERSITY DUKES
Arthur J. Rooney Memorial Field
Pittsburgh
412/396-5584
The Duquesne University Dukes play football in Division I-AA of the Metro Atlantic Athletic Conference against powerhouses such as Georgetown, St. John's, and Iona. A renewed commitment to the football program and the efforts of head coach Greg Gattuso have helped the Dukes pull off two conference championships during the past four years. Home games are played at the new Art Rooney Athletic Field on the campus along Forbes Avenue in downtown Pittsburgh. The field, which features a removable bubble, also is used as the winter practice field for the Pittsburgh Steelers. Tickets $7. For more information, call 412/232-3853. (East Pittsburgh)

ROBERT MORRIS COLLEGE COLONIALS
Charles Sewall Center
Moon Township
412/262-8295

When the Colonials appeared on the scene in 1994, former National Football League head coach Joe Walton put his stamp on the program. Walton has guided the team to a total of 30 victories in its first four seasons of Division I-AA play. Home games are played at Moon Stadium. Tickets $5–$7. For more information, call 412/262-8449. (West Pittsburgh)

UNIVERSITY OF PITTSBURGH PANTHERS
Pitt Stadium
Pittsburgh
412/648-8300
Each fall, the Pitt Panthers football team competes against nationally ranked teams in the Big East Conference. Home games are played at Pitt Stadium in Oakland, roughly 10 minutes from downtown. The Panthers have been the launching pad for numerous NFL stars, including Mike Ditka, Tony Dorsett, Dan Marino, and Curtis Martin. Tickets $6–$15. For ticket information, call 412/648-8304. (East Pittsburgh)

Roberto Clemente statue outside
Three Rivers Stadium

Doina Locke

On Horseback

There are horse-show rings at North Park and South Park and a dressage and show-jumping area at Hartwood. The national caliber Hartwood show-jumping festival in June and the polo matches in September benefit local charities. There are marked bridle trails through the woods and meadows of North Park, South Park, Boyce Park, and Settler's Cabin Park. Some private riding stables nearby rent horses for the day.

RECREATION

Biking

ALLEGHENY CYCLING ASSOCIATION (ACA)
4208 Post St.
Pittsburgh
412/266-8481
While biking on Pittsburgh streets is hazardous, many cyclists enjoy the winding suburban roads in the rest of Allegheny County. Biking through city and county parks is also popular. Commuters, fitness cyclers, and those who ride for fun rejoiced at the opening of a paved bike path from the County Jail parking lot to Schenley Park, snaking between the Boulevard of the Allies and the Parkway East. Another local biking association is the Western Pennsylvania Wheelmen (WPW) Bicycle Club, 412/782-1341 or 412/372-5429. (East Pittsburgh)

SOUTH PARK BMX TRACK
Rt. 51 and Curry Hollow Rd.
West Mifflin
412/831-3620
One of the top two bicycle motocross race tracks in the country, South Park BMX track provides riders with thrills and excitement. The South Park track has hosted a Fourth of July race with top national competitors, but it still offers fun for racers at all levels. (South Pittsburgh)

Boating

With three rivers, it should be no surprise that Pittsburghers are enthusiastic boaters. However, boaters must coordinate their travels with lock and dam schedules. Free information on boating on Pittsburgh's rivers is available from the U.S. Army Corps of Engineers, Federal Building, 1000 Liberty Ave., Pittsburgh 15222. The Pittsburgh Safe Boating Committee publishes a Guide to the Three Rivers, which contains maps of the rivers and lists docks, ramps, marinas, and restaurants.

Lake Arthur, Moraine State Park's 3,225-acre artificial lake, is a favorite with area sailors. For those who don't own their own, sailboats can be rented by the hour or the day from the boathouse on Lake Arthur's south shore. For information, call Moraine State Park in Butler County at 724/368-8811.

TIP

For information about recreational opportunities for the disabled, contact the following organizations:

Three Rivers Adaptive Sports–Chapter of Disabled Sports USA
P.O. Box 38235, Pittsburgh, PA 15238

National Handicapped Sports and Recreational Association
451 Hungerford Dr., Suite 100, Rockville, MD 20850, 301/217-0968

Keystone Paralyzed Veterans of America
800/775-9323

NORTH PARK BOATHOUSE
Pearce Mill Rd.
North Park
724/935-1968
Rowboats, canoes, and paddleboats can be rented at the North Park Boathouse for use on 75-acre North Park Lake. Mandatory life jackets are also available. For added water safety, a certified lifeguard is on duty seven days a week during summer. No motorboats are allowed on the lake, but there are public launching ramps for other boats. (North Pittsburgh)

Bowling

AMF MT. LEBANON LANES
1601 Washington Rd.
Mt. Lebanon
412/854-0600
With a total of 52 lanes with automatic scoring and the added attraction of bumper bowling, Mt. Lebanon Lanes is the largest bowling facility in western Pennsylvania and eastern Ohio. Reflections Lounge and a snack shop keep the bowlers going. A live DJ adds to the excitement on Wednesday, Friday, and Saturday night. (South Pittsburgh)

FUNFEST ENTERTAINMENT
CENTER
2525 Freeport Rd.
Harmarville
412/828-1100
Cosmic bowling originated in Pennsylvania and has taken off all over the country, with satisfyingly loud rock music, black lights, glow-in-the-dark pins, and "fog" rolling out onto the alleys. Funfest also has Laser Storm, impromptu teams battling it out at Laser Tag in staged battle areas. A snack bar and a lounge refresh the hungry and the weary. (See also Chapter 7: "Kids' Stuff") (North Pittsburgh)

HOLIDAY LANES
Rt. 286
Plum
724/327-3535
The Holiday Lanes complex includes 36 lanes with automatic scoring, an 18-hole miniature golf course, an arcade, and a billiards room. The Holiday Lounge and a snack bar help the

athletes keep up their strength. (East Pittsburgh)

AMF NOBLE MANOR LANES
2440 Noblestown Rd.
Greentree
412/922-4622

Indoors at Noble Manor Lanes, you'll find 40 lanes with automatic scoring, billiards, and pinball. Outdoors, you'll find 18 holes of miniature golf and six batting cages. When you need a refreshment break, try the snack bar or the Chatterbox Lounge. (West Pittsburgh)

Fitness clubs

AIRPORT FITNESS
Pittsburgh International Airport,
Airside
Findlay Township
412/472-5231

Its airport location is a boon to frequent travelers who often find themselves with long layovers. Equipment such as treadmills, stair-steppers, exercise bicycles, and rowing machines and strength machines guarantee a maximum efficiency workout. No workout clothes? You can rent clean shorts, shirt, socks, and shoes for $4. Saunas, showers, toiletries, and towel service help restore your travel-ready appearance. Daily 6–10. $11.25 per single visit. Memberships and 10-visit punch cards available. (West Pittsburgh)

BALLY TOTAL FITNESS
551 Blazier Rd.
Wexford
724/934-5959

While this spacious, well-maintained location is a favorite with regulars, other locations in Penn Hills and Monroeville have swimming and racquetball facilities in addition to the full spectrum of aerobic and strength equipment. Visitors are welcome from out-of-town health clubs with reciprocal membership in the National Health Club Association. (North Pittsburgh)

THE CITY CLUB
119 Sixth St.
Pittsburgh
412/391-3300

This busy downtown health club offers a stress-relieving, three-lane, 22-meter heated swimming pool, a steam room, sauna, Nautilus equipment, and free weights. Visitors can also play racquetball, squash, handball, or basketball. One-day passes $12. (Downtown Pittsburgh)

CLUB JULIAN 24 HOUR FITNESS
101 Corbett Ct.
Ross
412/366-1931

A fitness club that's open 24 hours a day is a rarity. Club Julian has a swimming pool, aerobic fitness equipment, free weights, and a sauna. The location, adjacent to Northway Mall is very convenient for folks in the North Hills. Visitors must come in with a member. (North Pittsburgh)

DOWNTOWN ATHLETIC CLUB OF PITTSBURGH
1 Bigelow Sq.
Pittsburgh
412/560-3488

This convenient location is a full-service health club with a swimming pool, Nautilus and cardiovascular workout machines, free weights, aerobics classes, a sauna for women, and a steam room for men. Club membership is required. Single-visit passes for guests of the William Westin Penn Hotel or Pittsburgh Marriott City Center cost $10; inquire at hotel front desk about discounts. Open daily. (Downtown Pittsburgh)

EXECUTIVE FITNESS CENTER AT THE DOUBLETREE HOTEL
1000 Penn Ave.
Pittsburgh
412/560-6406
A hotel-based downtown location, swimming pool, full range of strength-training and cardiovascular fitness equipment, aerobic classes, sauna, steam room, and showers mean there is no excuse for not staying fit while on the road or slaving away in the city. Membership is required; visits are free for Doubletree Hotel guests, $12 per day for visitors who are not staying at the Doubletree. Open daily. (Downtown Pittsburgh)

PARKWAY CENTER INN HEALTH & POOL CLUB
875 Greentree Rd.
Pittsburgh
412/922-7070
You can keep fit on the road with the Parkway Center Inn's Health & Pool Club swimming pool, weight room, stepper and rowing machines, Life Cycle training circuit, and treadmills.

Top off your fitness routine with a little relaxation in the hot tub, saunas, or men's steam room. Free for Parkway Center Inn guests. Open daily. (West Pittsburgh)

Golf

DEER RUN GOLF COURSE
4321 Monier Rd.
Gibsonia
724/265-4800
Located in the suburbs north of Pittsburgh, this 18-hole public course is a par 72 with a yardage of 6,300 feet from the white tees. Open daily. Greens fees discounted Mon–Thur. (North Pittsburgh)

GRANDVIEW GOLF CLUB
1000 Clubhouse Dr.
North Braddock
412/351-5390
Overlooking the scenic Monongahela River, the Grandview Golf Club is an 18-hole course rated at par 71. The challenging course caters to advanced golfers. It features scenic views of downtown Pittsburgh and Kennywood Park across the river. (East Pittsburgh)

Discs Are Flying

Flying Disc (or Frisbee) Golf is an organized sport with leagues and open competitions all over the country. Sometimes known as Ultimate Frisbee, the sport has enthusiasts in Pittsburgh who welcome visitors, newcomers, and new members to their organizations. The Pittsburgh Summer Ultimate League is for city teams with members between the age 15 and 35. For more information, call the Pittsburgh Flying Disc Society at 412/734-0321.

MEADOWINK GOLF COURSE
4076 Bulltown Rd.
Murrysville
724/327-8243
Roughly 20 minutes east of downtown Pittsburgh, the Meadowink Golf Course in Murrysville offers 18 holes of golf rated at par 72. The total yardage for this course is about 6,200. Greens fees discounted Mon–Thur. (East Pittsburgh)

NORTH PARK GOLF COURSE
Kummer Rd.
North Hills
724/935-1967
Golfers consider this 18-hole golf course a great quality public course. With a paved cart path making all holes easily accessible, the course is playable under less than perfect conditions. Carts are available but not required. (North Pittsburgh)

OAKMONT EAST
Hulton Rd. and Rt. 909
Oakmont
412/828-5335
The sister course to the famous Oakmont Country Club course, which has hosted numerous major championships, Oakmont East is an 18-hole course rated at a par 72 with a total yardage of 5,720. The cost for 18 holes of golf is low on weekdays and only slightly higher on weekends. Clubs are available for rental. (East Pittsburgh)

PITTSBURGH NORTH
GOLF COURSE
3800 Bakerstown Rd.
Gibsonia
724/443-3800
Located in Gibsonia in the North Hills, the Pittsburgh North Golf Course offers golfer 27 unique holes along with some wonderfully scenic wooded

The City Club, p. 149

Doina Locke

rolling hills. Weekend cost for 18 holes is double the weekday fee. (North Pittsburgh)

SCHENLEY PARK GOLF COURSE
Forbes and Schenley Dr.
Pittsburgh
412/622-6959
The only golf course located within Pittsburgh's city limits, the 18-hole Schenley Park Golf Course is less than 10 minutes from downtown. It is a par-67 course with a total yardage of less than 5,000. Clubs and carts available for rental. No tee time reservations are accepted. (East Pittsburgh)

SOUTH PARK GOLF COURSE
East Park Dr.
Library
412/835-8784
Both a nine-hole and an 18-hole public golf course share the clubhouse at South Park. A paved track means that carts can be used even when the greens are wet. Winter golf is, of course, weather dependent but is very popular. (South Pittsburgh)

Hiking

County and state parks all have well-marked hiking trails. Maps are available at park administration offices. Check with Rail to Trails at 717/238-1717 for information on railroad rights-of-way that have been converted to hiking and biking trails. For those who prefer urban hiking, pick up a map from the Greater Pittsburgh Tourist and Convention information booth and take a walking tour of the city.

NORTH PARK
E. Ingomar Rd. (Yellow Belt)
North Hills
724/935-1766

North Park is a hiker's dream: miles of paved paths, blazed trails through the woods, and in-park roads that can be safely shared by cars, walkers, joggers, in-line skaters, and cyclists. The five-mile paved path around North Park Lake is a scenic joy, but good weather can clog the lane as strollers, fitness walkers, dog walkers, runners, cyclists, in-line skaters, and joggers with strollers try to navigate the path. On nice days, there's a little more elbow room on the road that starts at the North Park swimming pool and loops past Pie Traynor baseball field. North Park also has an Access Trail for those with mobility problems, such as the wheelchair bound. The Rachel Carson Trail, a hiking trail maintained by the AYH, Western Pennsylvania Conservancy, and other volunteer organizations, extends from the Harrison Hills County Park across the North Hills to end at North Park. (North Pittsburgh)

Ice-skating

BLADERUNNERS ICE COMPLEX
66 Alpha Dr.
Harmarville
412/826-0800

Fans often spot Pittsburgh Penguins practicing at Bladerunners, and that just adds to the fun. Other locations are in Cranberry and Bethel Park. (North Pittsburgh)

NORTH PARK ICE SKATING RINK
Pearce Mill Rd.
North Hills
724/935-1780

The Best Baseball Team Ever

In the 1930s, Pittsburgh was represented in the Negro National League by two of the country's best teams: the Pittsburgh Crawfords, sponsored by the Hill District's Crawford Grill, and their toughest opponents, the Homestead Grays. Rob Ruck, author of Sandlot Seasons, *describes the 1936 Pittsburgh Crawfords as "possibly the best baseball team ever assembled for regular season play." Five members of that team, which included Satchel Paige and Judy Johnson, ultimately made it into the Baseball Hall of Fame.*

TIP

For River Weather Information, call 412/644-2890. For River Warning Conditions, call 412/578-8076.

The large outdoor rink at North Park is used for hockey, skating lessons, and public skating in winter only. The second-floor party room in the refreshment pavilion is available for rental year-round. (North Pittsburgh)

SCHENLEY PARK SKATING RINK
Overlook Dr.
Pittsburgh
412/422-6523

This outdoor rink is a year-round facility, used for ice-skating and ice hockey in winter and in-line skating and roller hockey from May 1 through Labor Day. (East Pittsburgh)

SOUTH PARK SKATING RINK
Corrigan Dr.

South Hills
412/833-1199

South Park's outdoor ice-skating rink is available for winter use only. Ice time is scheduled for skating lessons, hockey leagues, and public skating. (South Pittsburgh)

In-line Skating

Pittsburgh has an active community of in-line skaters who hold weekly group skates for all skill levels. Newcomers are welcome. Call Steve at 412/591-3644 for information about the Three Rivers In-Line Skate Club or Pittsburgh's National Skate Patrol. Schenley Park Rink has in-line skating May through mid-September; call Eric Van at 412/422-6523 for information.

North Park Swimming Pool, p. 156

Doina Locke

Attention: Soccer Fans

The Pittsburgh Riverhounds, a professional outdoor soccer team, began play in spring 1999 in Bethel Park Stadium. The Riverhounds are members of the United Soccer Leagues, a 30-team league established in 1986. The team's regular May-through-September playing season consists of 28 games. For information, call 412/381-GOAL or 412/381-4625. For tickets call 888/ETM-TIXS

V.I.P. SOUTH PARK
Corrigan Dr.
South Park
412/833-5258
This privately owned recreation complex within South Park offers roller and in-line skating, swimming, and 18 holes of miniature golf with one general admission ticket. If you don't have your own, you can rent skates for a small fee. There are picnic tables and a refreshment stand, also. (South Pittsburgh)

Laser Tag

LASER STORM
7715 McKnight Rd.
Ross
412/364-3473
Whether you bring your own combat team or hook up with other players, the battle's always fierce. Once you have strapped on your equipment and entered the battle zone, strobe lights, barriers, fog, and automated snipers make it tough to score hits on the other team without taking too many hits for your team. Scorekeeping is automated. (North Pittsburgh)

FUN FEST ENTERTAINMENT CENTER

2525 Freeport Rd.
Harmarville
412/828-1100
A favorite with the kids, laser tag also makes for family fun. An elaborately staged playing area includes fog, music, and flashing lights. Mechanized "sentries" also fire to complicate the action. Scorekeeping is computerized, and the team with the most hits made and least hits received wins. (See also Chapter 7: "Kids' Stuff.") (North Pittsburgh)

Paintball

In recent years, paintball has grown dramatically in popularity, in Pittsburgh and around the country. The region has both indoor arenas and outdoor gaming fields. Three Rivers Paintball, a nationally recognized playing site, hosts the annual Zap International Amateur Open. Teams come from as far as Brazil, Australia, and Japan. In 1997, the open drew 80 ten-man teams and more than 60 five-man teams.

PAINTBALL SPORTS ARENA
1600 Smallman St.
Pittsburgh
412/434-6900

Making the best of a converted industrial location, Paintball Sports Arena has two indoor arenas, with a total of 30,000 square feet of gaming area. Since part of the fun of this sport is its glorious messiness, the showers and locker rooms are more than welcome amenities. Players can prepare for combat on the practice range and in the pro shop, while non-combatants can take advantage of the observation deck. (East Pittsburgh)

THREE RIVERS PAINTBALL
250 Rochester Rd.
Cranberry
724/775-6232

Airport Fitness, p. 149

Doina Locke

Paintball is essentially a "capture the flag" game, played with CO_2-powered paintball guns, messy but with a relatively low risk factor. Three Rivers has open public games every weekend. Players must be 10 or older; sessions are 4.5 hours long. Three Rivers provides all equipment and protection, including full face mask and goggles. Each gaming field is supervised and refereed at all times. (North Pittsburgh)

Skiing

BOYCE PARK SKI LODGE
Pierson Run Rd.
Plum
412/733-4656

With snow-making capabilities, Boyce Park may extend a ski season from mid-December to early March, dependent on cooperation from winter weather. Four tow ropes and rental equipment are available. Beginners can sign up for lessons. Ticket prices are very affordable. For information on ski conditions, call 412/733-4665. (East Pittsburgh)

Swimming

The Department of Parks and Recreation (Citiparks) operates 31 outdoor swimming pools. City residents and non-residents may purchase single-day and year-round admission. For

Do the Wave: Area Wave Pools

Boyce Park Wave Pool, Frankstown Road, Plum, 412/325-4677 or 412/325-4667

Settler's Cabin Park Wave Pool, Ridge Road, Settlers Cabin Park, 412/787-2667 or 412/787-2668

South Park Wave Pool, McConkey Road, South Hills, 412/831-0810 or 412/831-0811

---

information call 412/594-4645. Citiparks operates one indoor pool year-round, the Oliver Bath House. For information call 412/431-8380. The county park system maintains pools at North Park, South Park, Boyce Park, and Settlers Cabin Park in summer.

NORTH PARK SWIMMING POOL
South Ridge Dr.
North Hills
724/935-1951
The handsome stone bathhouse and refreshment stand make the facility look like a country club. The pool, at 135 by 350 feet and with a capacity of 2.5 million gallons of water, is one of the largest in the world. It has viewing stands for swim meets and qualifying trials, twisting water slides, and a kiddie wading pool graced by a delightful mushroom-shaped fountain. (North Pittsburgh)

Tennis

NORTH PARK TENNIS AND PLATFORM TENNIS COURTS
Pearce Mill Rd.

North Hills
724/935-5270
With 17 tennis courts, there's usually one available, and if you have to wait, it won't be for long. Advance reservations are not accepted anyway. For diehard tennis lovers, there are three platform courts for winter-only play. A small fee is charged. (North Pittsburgh)

SOUTH PARK TENNIS COURTS
Corrigan Dr.
South Hills
412/833-5558
South Park has 33 courts, so tennis lovers can usually find a free court. No advance reservations accepted. A small fee applies. (South Pittsburgh)

SETTLER'S CABIN TENNIS COURTS
Greer Rd.
Settler's Cabin Park
412/787-2824
There are six tennis courts at Settler's Cabin Park and they're open seven days a week. A small fee is charged per person. (West Pittsburgh)

11

PERFORMING ARTS

The Pittsburgh Cultural District is a 14-block area bounded by Liberty Avenue, the Allegheny River, Tenth Street, and Stanwix Street. Within that area are located the Benedum Center for the Performing Arts, Heinz Hall, the Byham Theater, and the Harris Theater. As the cultural district has flourished, so too have nearby restaurants, pubs, and nightclubs, their numbers on the increase.

The Cultural District has been developed as a complement to the city's traditional cultural center in Oakland. There, the performing arts departments of the colleges and universities have provided opportunities for eager young singers, actors, dancers, choreographers, composers, writers, and directors to learn their craft and hone their skills.

THEATER

ANTONIAN THEATRE
Carlow College, 3333 Fifth Ave.
Pittsburgh
412/578-6000
The 915-seat Antonian Theatre is the venue for an eclectic mix of stage, musical, dance, and choral performances by local and national companies, including the Pittsburgh Opera. Ticket costs vary and sales are handled by each production company. The Antonian is also the home of the Carlow College Theatre Group; for

information and tickets call 412/578-6652. Closed June–Aug. Call 412/578-6685 for general performance information. ♿ (East Pittsburgh)

CARNEGIE MELLON SCHOOL OF DRAMA SHOWCASE OF NEW PLAYS
Kresge Theatre, College of Fine Arts Building
Carnegie Mellon University
Pittsburgh
412/268-2407
Top actors drawn from the Carnegie Mellon School of Drama student

body and faculty and local professional talent perform in the five-production winter season and the summer Showcase of New Plays. The winter season includes a mixture of drama and musical productions. A Studio Theatre series of eight sit-down readings is held in July. Winter season Sept–May Tue–Sat at 8. Summer Showcase performances Fri and Sat at 8, Sun at 2. Studio Theatre readings are free, but donations are appreciated. & (East Pittsburgh)

CITY THEATRE
57 S. 13th St. and Bingham St.
Pittsburgh
412/431-2489
The City Theatre Company presents a full season of works by playwrights such as Athol Fugard, Steve Martin, and David Mamet and adapted works such as *The Chosen* from the story by Chaim Potok. The City Theatre is also the venue for performances by other groups such as the Pittsburgh Irish & Classical Theatre. (South Pittsburgh)

CIVIC LIGHT OPERA
Benedum Center for the
Performing Arts, 719 Liberty Ave.
Pittsburgh
412/281-3973 or 412/456-6666
Its humble origins are as lighthearted as its performances. The opera began

in 1946 as an open-air theater in Pitt Stadium. Later, the CLO graduated to a canvas tent near the Civic Arena, then under construction. Next the group moved into a home under the Civic Arena's retractable roof. Today, having outgrown the Civic Arena, the opulence of the Benedum only adds to the glitter of CLO's full-scale Broadway productions. Past productions have included *Gypsy*, *Miss Saigon*, *The Phantom of the Opera*, *Les Miserables*, and *Carousel*. & (Downtown Pittsburgh)

KATZ PERFORMING ARTS CENTER
Jewish Community Center
5738 Darlington Rd.
Pittsburgh
412/521-8011
The Jewish Community Center and its Katz Performing Arts Center is the venue for concerts, dinners, recitals, talent shows, literary talks, preschool and after-school programs, and other events. Kol Isha, Pittsburgh's Jewish women's theater group, mounts its productions here, also. As described by a member, the JCC is "the mecca of Jewish life, not only in Squirrel Hill, but in the entire metropolitan region." & (East Pittsburgh)

KUNTU REPERTORY THEATRE
3TO1 Forbes Quadrangle
230 S. Bouquet St.

Pittsburgh
412/648-7548

Kuntu Repertory Theatre is a coalition of talented individuals from both the student body and faculty of the University of Pittsburgh Theatre Arts Department and from the neighboring community. Their mission is to introduce the theater experience, primarily historical drama, to the community and to integrate a rich ethnic heritage with contemporary life. Performances are presented in facilities and public schools throughout the city. (East Pittsburgh)

LESTER HAMBURG STUDIO THEATRE
S. 13th St. at Bingham St.
Pittsburgh
412/431-2489

The Lester Hamburg Studio Theatre, located adjacent to the City Theatre at the corner of South 13th Street and Bingham Street, is a black-box theater seating 99. (A black-box auditorium is a plain black room in which the stage can be arranged with the audience on three sides, with the audience facing the stage, or any other way that best suits a production.) The season generally runs May through September. (South Pittsburgh)

OPEN STAGE THEATRE
City Theatre
57 S. 13th St.and Bingham St.
Pittsburgh
412/257-4056

Using the City Theatre as its venue, the Open Stage Theatre presents local talent in top-quality, thought-provoking productions. According to artistic director Ruth Willis, nearly half of Open Stage Theatre's 33 productions since its inception in 1992 have been Pittsburgh premieres. (South Pittsburgh)

PITTSBURGH IRISH & CLASSICAL THEATRE
805 Hazelwood Ave.
Pittsburgh
412/521-2937

The Pittsburgh Irish & Classical Theatre was formed in 1996. Founders Stephanie Riso and Andrew Paul aimed for collaboration between local and national theater professionals to present both modern and classical works of primarily Irish, English, and other European writers. Three plays are presented each season, in venues that match the performance, such as the City Theatre, the Pittsburgh Playhouse, and the Lester Hamburg Studio Theatre. (East Pittsburgh)

PITTSBURGH PUBLIC THEATRE
Allegheny Square
Pittsburgh
412/321-9800

Located in the historic Allegheny Regional Branch of the Carnegie Library, the Pittsburgh Public Theatre has a strongly contemporary, yet intimate, character. With its stark black-box configuration, the stage

Heinz Hall, p. 167

GPCVB

can be arranged to suit the individual production. The contrast of the brightly lit stage with the black interior of the auditorium always makes the space seem cozy, not claustrophobic. & (North Pittsburgh)

PITTSBURGH SAVOYARDS
568 Lincoln Ave.
Pittsburgh
412/734-8476
Using public schools and Carnegie Free Libraries for performances, the Pittsburgh Savoyards have brought affordable theater to children for many years. Gilbert and Sullivan comedies are an audience favorite.

PLAYHOUSE OF POINT PARK COLLEGE
222 Craft Ave.
Pittsburgh
412/621-4445
The Playhouse of Point Park College is the home of four exceptional performance companies: Point Park College Theatre Company, Playhouse Theatre Company, Playhouse Dance Theatre, and Playhouse Jr., which has celebrated its 50th anniversary. These four companies stage excellent performances in the three theaters under the Playhouse roof. Past productions have included *A Chorus Line*, the dance classic *Cinderella*, *You're a Good Man, Charlie Brown*, and the much-loved children's story *The Wind in the Willows*. Season runs Oct–Aug. Personal amplifiers for the hearing impaired and signing for selected performances are available; please call in advance. & (East Pittsburgh)

PITT THEATRE
University of Pittsburgh
Pittsburgh
412/624-7529
Pitt Theatre presents university theater

students, working in conjunction with faculty and professional actors, in the 600-seat Stephen Foster Memorial Theatre and the 90-seat Studio Theatre in the basement of the Cathedral of Learning. Studio Theatre Mainstage, Mini-Mainstage, and Workshop productions are all open to the public. The current three-year celebration, "American Century!" begins with the dynamics of family and homecomings, considers American enterprise and its philosophy, then turns to "Stories Told and Retold," American literary classics that have been adapted for the stage. & (East Pittsburgh)

QUANTUM THEATRE
6334 Crombie St.
Pittsburgh
412/422-3823
Founder and producing director Karla Boos believes in the impact of nontraditional performance sites when presenting innovative, challenging theater. For that reason, Quantum Theatre presentations are site-specific, performed at locations all over the city, in the spirit of installation art. For more than eight years, renowned works by Pinter, Shakespeare, and others have shared seasons with new works and those having world, American, or regional premieres. (South Pittsburgh)

SALTWORKS THEATER
2553 Brandt School Rd.
Wexford
724/934-2820
Since 1981, Saltworks Theater has specialized in providing uplifting family entertainment with a message. Using both professional and amateur performers, Saltworks Mainstage Productions have featured classics, comedies, musicals, and dramas in the Orchard Hill Chapel. Saltworks'

The Pittsburgh Cultural Trust and WQED Pittsburgh collaborate to provide a 24-hour information hotline for events in Pittsburgh and the region: 800/PHON-ART (800/746-6278).

touring group of professionals stages up to 200 productions per year in school auditoriums and churches in Pennsylvania, West Virginia, Ohio, and New Jersey. (North Pittsburgh)

UPSTAIRS THEATRE
4809 Penn Ave.
Pittsburgh
412/361-5443

For over 12 seasons, the Upstairs Theatre has offered nontraditional off-Broadway productions. The nine-show season includes comedy, drama, and the occasional musical. The theater has a capacity of about 100. Despite its name, the theater does have wheelchair access. No performances in Aug. Parking available next to the building. ♿ (East Pittsburgh)

MUSIC AND OPERA

BACH CHOIR OF PITTSBURGH
Church of the Ascension,
Ellsworth Ave. and Neville St.
Pittsburgh
412/682-2224

With a repertoire encompassing music from the Renaissance through the contemporary era, the Bach Choir of Pittsburgh collaborates with other musical organizations for the richest possible musical experiences. The highlight of the season is the Good Friday presentation of Mozart's "Requiem" at the Church of the Ascension in Oakland. (East Pittsburgh)

CHATHAM BAROQUE
James Laughlin Music Center,
Woodland Rd.
Chatham College Campus
Pittsburgh (Oakland)
412/365-1867

Chatham Baroque, recipient of one of only three prestigious grants awarded to resident chamber music ensembles in the nation, performs seventeenth- and eighteenth-century music on period instruments, including baroque violin, viola da gamba, lute, baroque guitar, and theorbo. The ensemble tours the eastern United States and presents a series of four concerts from October through May. Single tickets are available by mail or at the box office. ♿ (East Pittsburgh)

MENDELSSOHN CHOIR OF PITTSBURGH
3228 Nottingham Dr.
Pittsburgh
412/823-4188

Celebrating its 90th anniversary in 1998, the Mendelssohn Choir of Pittsburgh offers a three-concert subscription season from October through May. Music director and conductor Robert Page leads the Mendelssohn Choir, which performs in the Carnegie Music Hall in Oakland. Single performance tickets are usually available. Order by mail or phone. (East Pittsburgh)

PITTSBURGH CHAMBER MUSIC SOCIETY
P.O. Box 81066
Pittsburgh
412/624-4129

For more than 38 seasons, the Pittsburgh Chamber Music Society has brought internationally and nationally renowned chamber ensembles and guest artists to the Carnegie Music Hall. Past performers have included the Juilliard String Quartet, the Tokyo String Quartet, and the Beaux Arts Trio. The Society's six-concert season extends from October through April. Single performance tickets are generally available. (East Pittsburgh)

PITTSBURGH NEW MUSIC ENSEMBLE
Duquesne School of Music
600 Forbes Ave.
Pittsburgh
412/261-0554

Founder David Stock has taken this resident ensemble of Duquesne Uni-

versity through more than 23 seasons of cutting-edge musical innovation. Drawing primarily from American music but also from all over the world, the ensemble introduces Pittsburgh to the avant-garde of all styles of music, from jazz to country and beyond. At the start of the 1998–1999 season, the New Music Ensemble moved to its new venue at the Katz Performing Arts Center in the Jewish Community Center in Squirrel Hill. (East Pittsburgh)

PITTSBURGH OPERA
711 Penn Ave.
Pittsburgh
412/281-0912

The Pittsburgh Opera was established in 1939, and it is now ranked among the top opera companies in the country. World-renowned Tito Capobianco became the opera's artistic director in 1984. That year, the Pittsburgh Opera became one of the first companies to project simultaneous English translations above the stage, a hugely popular innovation. The permanent home of the company

Pittsburgh Public Theatre, p. 159

Unicorn Stock Photos/Jean Higgins

Pittsburgh Film Trivia

- *Producer George Romero (*Night of the Living Dead, Day of the Living Dead, Dawn of the Dead*) is from the Pittsburgh area. Extras from Allegheny and Washington counties "had a ball" playing zombies for his film; some were reluctant to get out of character when filming was over.*
- Mrs. Soffel, *starring Diane Keaton and Mel Gibson, was based on Pittsburgh's true story of the warden's wife who fell in love with a convict and helped him escape.*
- Gung Ho *stars Pittsburgh's own Michael Keaton.*
- *Award for weirdest title:* Blood Sucking Pharaohs of Pittsburgh. *Second place:* The Fish That Saved Pittsburgh

and the Pittsburgh Opera Orchestra is the Benedum Center for the Performing Arts. The opera presents four productions from October through April. (Downtown Pittsburgh)

PITTSBURGH SYMPHONY ORCHESTRA
Heinz Hall, 600 Penn Ave.
Pittsburgh
412/392-4900
With music director Mariss Jansons receiving a warm welcome to the city in 1997, the Pittsburgh Symphony has exceeded its own standard of musical excellence. The PSO performs at Heinz Hall September through May, before going on tour. The PSO Pops Concert Series, with Marvin Hamlisch as principal conductor, runs October through June. Although the Symphony Association is over 100 years old, it doesn't seem to be feeling its age: the PSO offers both a Fiddlesticks Family Concert Series for children ages 4 to 10 and a Tiny Tots Family Concert Series for children ages 3 to 6. (Downtown Pittsburgh)

RENAISSANCE AND BAROQUE SOCIETY OF PITTSBURGH
303 S. Craig St.
Pittsburgh
412/682-7262
After more than 30 seasons, the Renaissance and Baroque Society continues to bring to Pittsburgh internationally and nationally acclaimed ensembles for performances of early music (medieval, Renaissance, baroque, and early classical). Concerts are generally held in the 750-seat Synod Hall, located directly behind St. Paul's Cathedral at 125 North Craig Street in Oakland. Single-performance tickets or "series samplers" are usually available for the eight-performance subscription series season. (East Pittsburgh)

RIVER CITY BRASS BAND
P.O. Box 6436

On Location in Pittsburgh

Just a few of the many movies made in the Pittsburgh area:

1996	Assassination File	**1990**	Silence of the Lambs
	The Christmas Tree	**1988**	Blood Sucking
	Desperate Measures*		Pharaohs in Pittsburgh
	The Journey		Dominick and Eugene
1995	Diabolique		Monkey Shines: An Experiment in Fear
	Kingpin		Prince of Pennsylvania
1994	Boys on the Side*		Tiger Warsaw
	Houseguest	**1987**	Robocop
	The Piano Lesson	**1986**	Gung Ho
	A Promise Kept: The Oksana Baiul Story	**1985**	Day of the Dead
	Sudden Death	**1984**	Mrs. Soffel
1993	Breathing Lessons	**1983**	All the Right Moves
	Finnegan's Wake	**1982**	Creepshow
	Only You		Flashdance
	Milk Money*	**1981**	The Steeler and the Pittsburgh Kid
	Roommates	**1979**	Dawn of the Dead
	The Stand*		The Fish that Saved Pittsburgh
1992	The Cemetery Club	**1978**	The Deer Hunter
	Citizen Cohn	**1977**	Slapshot
	Hoffa	**1968**	The Night of the Living Dead
	Innocent Blood	**1958**	Some Came Running
	Striking Distance	**1951**	Angels in the Outfield
1991	Bob Roberts	**1947**	The Unconquered
	Lorenzo's Oil	**1914**	The Perils of Pauline
1990	Darrow		
	Night of the Living Dead: The Remake		

* Filmed partially in Pittsburgh

412/322-7222

The immensely popular River City Brass Band, under the musical direction of Denis Colwell, has been rewarded for its high degree of professionalism and dedication to taking music "to the people." The band has seen increasing subscriptions for its November through May season. Its venues include the Carnegie Music Hall in Oakland, public school auditoriums in the North Hills, the South Hills, and Monroeville, and the Palace Theatre in outlying Greensburg.

Y MUSIC SOCIETY
5738 Forbes Ave.
Pittsburgh
412/521-8011

Known for introducing artists such as Vladmir Horowitz to Pittsburgh at the beginning of their illustrious careers, the Y Music Society presents concerts, performances, and recitals at the Carnegie Music Hall in Oakland. Founded in 1926, the society is the longest continuously running musical performance series in the city. ♿ (East Pittsburgh)

DANCE

DANCE ALLOY
5530 Penn Ave.
Pittsburgh
412/363-4321

Originally an outgrowth of the Pittsburgh Dance Council, the Dance Alloy was founded in 1976 as a resident repertory company that would integrate local talent with the regional and national professional dance community. Mark Taylor, a choreographer and teacher who had his own dance company in New York, leads the contemporary troupe during its season at a variety of area locations, including the Byham Theater, and during tours across the country. Visitors can drop by to see open rehearsals and works in progress at the Neighborhood Dance Center at 5530 Penn Avenue in the Friendship neighborhood. (Downtown Pittsburgh)

PITTSBURGH BALLET THEATRE
2900 Liberty Ave.
Pittsburgh
412/281-0360

The Pittsburgh Ballet Theatre performs at the Benedum Center for the Performing Arts. Classical masterpieces, modern dance classics, and world premieres of original works have been featured. A lavish production of *The Nutcracker* is a perennial favorite with children and their parents in December. The PBT was founded in 1969. (Downtown Pittsburgh)

PITTSBURGH DANCE COUNCIL
719 Liberty Ave.
Pittsburgh
412/355-0330

The Pittsburgh Dance Council presents a subscription series of performances by nationally and internationally renowned companies. Such acclaimed groups as Pilobolus, Alvin Ailey, and Riverdance have appeared under the auspices of the council. Programs are presented at the Benedum Center for the Performing Arts and the Byham Theatre. (Downtown Pittsburgh)

CONCERT VENUES

A. J. PALUMBO CENTER
Duquesne University
Pittsburgh
412/391-1111

Located on the campus of Duquesne

Benedum Center for the Performing Arts

University in downtown Pittsburgh, the A. J. Palumbo Center is used primarily for the college's indoor sporting events such as basketball. While the building does not provide the best acoustical environment, its 5,000-seat capacity has nevertheless made it a popular venue for intimate concerts by medium-sized national music acts that pass through Pittsburgh. There is generally an abundance of reasonably priced parking at nearby lots, as well as on-street metered parking. ♿ (Downtown Pittsburgh)

BENEDUM CENTER FOR THE PERFORMING ARTS
719 Liberty Ave.
Pittsburgh
412/456-6666
Formerly the Stanley Theatre movie house, the renovated building is now home to the Pittsburgh Opera and Ballet, touring Broadway shows, and other events. Built in 1927, the building's lobby, hallways, and auditorium are opulent and indicative of Pitts-

burgh's early wealth. The auditorium can seat 2,800. The theater's backstage area is nationally renowned for spaciousness and efficiency. ♿ (Downtown Pittsburgh)

BYHAM THEATER
Ft. Duquesne Blvd. and Sixth St.
Pittsburgh
412/456-6666
The former Fulton movie theater, a building that dates to 1907, has been restored to its former glory and an active schedule of stage performances. The Pittsburgh Cultural Trust directs overall operations of this venue, which has a capacity of over 1,300. Dance performances are produced by the Pittsburgh Dance Council and bring to Pittsburgh renowned performers and dance companies. Stage shows are presented at the Byham by Gargaro Productions. Comedy revues and gospel music programs have also appeared on the Byham's stage. ♿ (Downtown Pittsburgh)

CARNEGIE MUSIC HALL
4400 Forbes Ave.
Pittsburgh
412/396-5494
The entrance to the Music Hall, directly across from the Forbes Avenue entrance to the Museum of Natural History within the Carnegie Institue, is a dazzling display of rococo gilt and marble. The Music Hall is the primary venue for presentations of the Y Music Society. The hall is also used by many community, cultural, and educational organizations for lectures, programs, recitals, and performances. The hall can accommodate an audience of 2,000. ♿ (East Pittsburgh)

CIVIC ARENA
66 Mario Lemieux Place
Pittsburgh

412/642-2062 or 642-1800 (information)
412/323-1919 (ticket purchases)
The Civic Arena was the nation's first and largest retractable dome auditorium and represents a remarkable engineering tour de force. The unusual cantilevered black steel section encloses retracting sections of the dome as it opens in two and a half minutes over an area seating up to 18,000. The arena is the home of the Pittsburgh Penguin hockey team, but it also handles large-scale concerts and circus performances. &. (Downtown Pittsburgh)

COCA-COLA STAR LAKE AMPHITHEATRE
Rt. 18
Burgettstown
412/323-1919
Located about 45 minutes west of Pittsburgh, the amphitheatre has become a popular warm-weather venue for major music acts. Reserved seating is available for 7,500. Some seating is located under the stage's overhang, and some tables are available. The least expensive tickets are for lawn seating, which creates a festival atmosphere for concerts and brings the amphitheatre's total capacity to over 20,000. Tailgate parties are permitted in the parking lot, but no food or drink can be brought through the gates. Refreshments are for sale in the amphitheatre. Parking $6. &. (West Pittsburgh)

HEINZ HALL
600 Penn Ave.
Pittsburgh
412/392-4900
This former movie palace was transformed into Heinz Hall in 1971. The exterior design has been called Viennese Baroque. The auditorium holds 2,847. &. (Downtown Pittsburgh)

I. C. LIGHT AMPHITHEATRE
1 Station Square
Pittsburgh
412/232-6200 (information)
412/391-1111 (tickets)
Essentially a huge tent in the parking lot near Station Square just across the river from downtown Pittsburgh, the 5,000-seat I. C. Light Amphitheatre is a popular venue for touring music groups and other performers because of its intimate atmosphere. The tent is also used for special events such as cook-offs and car shows. &. (South Pittsburgh)

ROSEBUD/METROPOL
1650 Smallman St.
Pittsburgh
412/261-4512
Metropol and Rosebud are separate yet neighboring clubs under the same management. Metropol is the ultimate mid-size venue for top national artists. The renovated industrial building offers maximum space for production equipment, sound and light set-ups, on-stage action, and for a full capacity crowd of 1,400. Rosebud can accommodate 400. &. (East Pittsburgh)

12

NIGHTLIFE

Pittsburgh after dark has the urban excitement of clubs and nightspots, the magical landscape of hills, rivers, and bridges outlined in lights, and the inscrutable mystery of narrow streets and unlit, winding suburban roads. As many of the city's neighborhoods undergo revitalization and gentrification, exciting possibilities are being realized. In the Strip District, warehouses and factory buildings are being converted into restaurants, nightclubs, microbreweries, and loft apartments. On the South Side, neglected, badly remodeled Victorian buildings are being rediscovered and handsomely restored to their former glory. Station Square, a railroad station and freightyard, has been restored and transformed into a complex of elegant restaurants, charming shops, and lively nightspots. Downtown's Cultural District is witnessing an exciting synergy between performing arts companies, theaters, restaurants, and nightclubs.

Beyond the city limits, former blue-collar neighborhood bars are drawing people from all over the region with a multitude of alternative, cutting-edge sounds, delicious ethnic foods, good selections of microbrews, and hearty, honest conviviality that transcends all barriers.

DANCE CLUBS

CHAUNCY'S
Commerce Ct. at Station Sq.
Pittsburgh
412/232-0601
The upbeat, sophisticated young crowd that can be found here every night from Happy Hour on unwinds with plenty of dancing, snacks, dinner, and drinks. It may not be *Saturday Night Fever*, but disco rules on Friday and Saturday. The latest Top 40 hits are heard on Monday, Wednesday,

Thursday, and Sunday. On Tuesday, Oldies reign supreme. Open 8–2. (South Pittsburgh)

CLUB HAVANA
5744 Ellsworth Ave.
Pittsburgh
412/661-2025
Seething with hot Latin sounds, Club Havana features a variety of live and recorded music. A Latin jazz band performs on Tuesday, and free salsa and Merengue dance classes are offered from 8 to 10 on Tuesday and Sunday. The extensive drink menu includes a variety of Cuban specialties. A number of appetizers are featured including traditional Latin American tapas. (East Pittsburgh)

COZUMEL
5507 Walnut St.
Pittsburgh
412/621-5100
This second-floor nightspot brings live Latin music and dancing to Shadyside on most Fridays and every Saturday. The dance floor is getting crowded, not only with some really hot Latin American dancers but also with eager newcomers ready to learn. There's plenty of authentic Mexican food and drinks to keep energy levels high. (East Pittsburgh)

DONZI'S
The Boardwalk
1501 Smallman St.
Pittsburgh
412/281-1585
Donzi's is the spacious dance-hall section of the Boardwalk's floating entertainment complex. DJs and bands provide the dance music from Wednesday to Saturday. On Tuesday, dancers move to the throbbing retro beat of "Planet Disco." Friday Happy Hour features a free cookout from 6 to 8. Don't miss the 10:30 Friday fireworks. Tue–Fri 8–2, Sat 5–2. $5 cover charge after 9. (East Pittsburgh)

GATEWAY CLIPPER FLEET
9 Station Square Dock
Pittsburgh
412/355-7980
The Gateway Clipper Fleet—riverboats that cruise the Allegheny, Monongahela, and Ohio Rivers—provides some of the most unique dance clubs in the city. The Captain's Dinner Dance Cruise sails nightly at 6:30 year-round and offers live music. Adult-only Moonlight Dance Cruises sail from 11 p.m. to 1:30 a.m. on selected dates from April through November. Coors Light Showboat Oldies Dinner Dance Cruises, which sail on

Doo-Wop Date

Definition: dinner, a cruise, and a drive-in movie. You don't need a captain's license to do the cruising—just a flashy car with lots of polished chrome. Though most of them were babies in the 1950s, plenty of Pittsburgh-area Boomers are still fond of spending summer evenings showing off their classic cars and big engines. Rock 'n' roll music is often provided by local radio stations that set up mobile units and attract crowds interested in a taste of nostalgia.

During the 10 days of the Mellon Jazz Festival in June, jazz greats can be found at performances and jam sessions till all hours at various locations all over town. Jazz enthusiasts will find this an awesome time to visit Pittsburgh. Check newspaper listings, the free weeklies, or call 412/281-3881 for exact times and locations.

selected dates from March through November, feature hits of the '50s and '60s, performed by live bands. The Boilermaker Jazz Band performs on the Dixieland Chick 'n' Ribs Dinner Cruise on Tuesday and Thursday May through October. The festive Mardi Gras–type Sailabration features a parade, a King and Queen, and Bourbon Street music. For a different sound, try the Bud Light Rhythm & Blues Cruises on select Fridays and Saturdays May through December. Tickets $7.50–$40. Reservations recommended. (South Pittsburgh)

HAVE A NICE DAY CAFE
1700 Penn Ave.
Pittsburgh
412/281-6423 or 201-1200
If "groovy" is your thing, then the Have a Nice Day Cafe and its huge Happy Face is your kind of place. Disco is alive and well here, where a casually dressed, young, and jumping crowd gathers under the disco ball nightly to boogie the night away to live bands and DJs. The club features a full menu for lunch and dinner. $5 cover after 9 on Fri and Sat. (East Pittsburgh)

METROPOL
1600 Smallman St.
Pittsburgh
412/261-2221
The stark atmosphere of exposed steel catwalks, columns, and crossbeams of the warehouse district impart grungy sophistication to "Industrial Dancing." The vast multi-level club can handle crowds of up to 1,400 on the dance floor and the balcony. On Friday and Saturday, there is a free buffet. $5 cover charge. & (East Pittsburgh)

PATIO DECK
The Boardwalk
1501 Smallman St.
Pittsburgh
412/281-3680
Dock your boat (or watch other people dock theirs), then dance under the stars. Dance to disco music on Wednesday and to the oldies on Thursday. Enjoy live bands on the floating stage and watch fireworks on clear, summer Friday nights. Steel bands provide a lively Caribbean and reggae atmosphere on Saturday and Sunday afternoons. Monday is jazz night. Open May–Sept. (East Pittsburgh)

ROSEBUD
1650 Smallman St.
Pittsburgh
412/261-2232
Live bands Tuesday through Saturday and DJ disco on Sunday keep the dancers moving. Thursday is salsa night at Rosebud and Tuesday belongs to reggae. On Friday local bands are showcased, and every Saturday the club presents House of Soul. In warm weather, the large front window walls open for outdoor seating. $5

Pittsburghers (and Western Pennsylvanians) in Show Biz

F. Murray Abraham, actor

Carroll Baker, actress (Johnstown)

Perry Como, singer (Canonsburg)

Bill Cullen, performer, TV celebrity

John Davidson, singer/actor

Ann B. Davis, actress (Ambridge)

Billy Eckstine, jazz great

Barbara Felden, actress

Scott Glenn, actor

Jeff Goldblum, actor (West Homestead)

Charles Grodin, actor/director/writer

Michael Keaton, actor (Coraopolis)

Gene Kelly, actor/dancer/director

Henry Mancini, composer

Dennis Miller, comedian/actor

Joe Namath, football star/actor (Beaver Falls)

William Powell, actor

Fred "Mr. Rogers" Rogers, producer/TV host/minister (Latrobe)

George Romero, producer/director/writer

Lillian Russell, actress

James Stewart, actor (Indiana)

Sharon Stone, actress (Meadville)

Lyle Talbot, actor

Regis Toomey, actor

Bobby Vinton, singer (Canonsburg)

Fritz Weaver, actor

Patricia Wettig, actress (Grove City)

---

cover charge, $3 Tues and Wed specials. ♿ (East Pittsburgh)

SANDBAR
Sandcastle Water Park
Rt. 837 between the
Homestead High Level Bridge
and Glenwood Bridge
W. Homestead
412/462-6666
The perfect place to cool off on a warm summer night is a hot watering hole. Sandbar is part of the Sandcastle Water Park but admission to the park is not necessary. Live bands and DJs provide music Thursday through Saturday, weather permitting. Dress is casual, including bathing suits, because hot tubs and sand volleyball are part of the fun. Open June–Labor Day. $2 cover charge. No one under 21 allowed. (South Pittsburgh)

MUSIC CLUBS

Jazz

THE BOARDWALK
1501 Smallman St.
Pittsburgh
412/281-3680
The Boardwalk is an adult amusement park: a restaurant (Crewser's), a nightclub (Donzi's), and two outdoor bars with service from both Crewser's and Donzi's (Patio Deck) clustered together on barges anchored near the Allegheny River shore. Located west of the 31st Street Bridge, the Boardwalk offers a dock for pleasure boaters who can then come aboard. The Pepsi Floating Stage presents live jazz at 8 on Monday, disco at 9 on Wednesday, Oldies at 8 on Thursday, a stage show Saturday at 9, a Caribbean steel band Saturday and Sunday from 2:30 to 5:30 p.m., and rock on Sunday at 9. (East Pittsburgh)

CRAWFORD GRILL
2141 Wylie Ave.
Pittsburgh
412/471-1565
The legendary Crawford Grill in the Hill District was *the* place to see all the jazz greats of the 1930s, '40s, and '50s. The neighborhood has since suffered the ravages of time and urban renewal (the club advertises secure parking), but there's still live jazz on Friday and Saturday. Delicious soul food and drinks are available Friday and Saturday only. (East Pittsburgh)

FOSTER'S BAR & GRILL
Holiday Inn Select-University
Center, 100 Lytton Ave.
Pittsburgh
412/682-6200
The cozy and casual lounge at this not-so-ordinary Holiday Inn is the setting for Pittsburgh's top jazz artists on Friday and Saturday from 9 p.m. to 2 a.m. On Sunday you can bring your instrument and sit in or just listen from 7 to 11 at the Pittsburgh Jazz Society Jams. On Wednesday from 6 to 7, Jazz for Juniors showcases local performers. (East Pittsburgh)

JAMES STREET PUB
422 Foreland St. and James St.
Pittsburgh
412/323-2222
Located in a beautifully renovated North Side home not far from Allegheny University Hospital, the James Street Pub focuses on adventurous food and great music. You can find jazz here Wednesday until 11, Thursday until 12, and Friday and Saturday until 1. The Banjo Sing-A-Long with the Pittsburgh Banjo Club is a little-known treat for all ages. On Wednesday night, bring your banjo (if you have one) and your voice and join the Sing-A-Long upstairs. (North Pittsburgh)

Penn Brewery

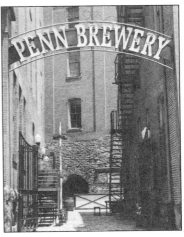

Doina Locke

Moon over Miami—
Palm Trees over Pittsburgh

Drivers exiting I-79 at the Wexford interchange often do a double take when they spot the tropical oasis gracing the BP gas station at the T-Bones shopping plaza on the Orange Belt. Landscapers lend a touch of whimsy to one of the North Hills' busiest interchanges in summer by planting full-grown palm trees among the hardier plants that Pennsylvanians are accustomed to seeing. Capistrano has its swallows; Hinckley, Ohio, has its buzzards; and T-Bones has its palm trees. Landscape artistry or roadside kitsch, the palm trees brighten the rush hour for thousands of commuters when nothing else can.

KANGAROO'S OUTBACK CAFÉ
Robinson Plaza II, Rt. 60 and Park Manor Dr.
Robinson
412/788-9003
Live jazz is the attraction on Thursday at this Australian-themed pub. DJs spin music of the '80s, some R&B, and some rock on Friday and Saturday. At its quietest, this is a very lively place where people come to have fun—and some legendary hot wings. Wednesday is all-you-can-eat ribs and wings night. $2 cover charge Fri and Sat after 9. (West Pittsburgh)

PENN BREWERY
Troy Hill Rd.
Pittsburgh
412/237-9400
The Boilermaker Jazz Band is featured at Penn Brewery year-round. They're joined by various German bands to keep up the lively rathskeller atmosphere from 7:30 to 10:30 p.m. Tuesday through Saturday. The fun moves outdoors to the beer garden in summer. The fall Oktoberfest draws a happy, energetic mob to this former German neighborhood, ready to dance to oompah bands and toast each other with foaming steins. (See also Chapter 5: "Sights and Attractions.") (North Pittsburgh)

TEMPERANCEVILLE TAVERN
424 S. Main St.
Pittsburgh
412/920-1300
Local bands play jazz and blues Wednesday through Saturday at the Temperanceville Tavern, part of the renaissance of the tiny West End neighborhood. Happy Hour draws customers from nearby North Side and downtown. $2 cover charge Wed only. (West Pittsburgh)

Rock and R&B

ELECTRIC BANANA
3887 Bigelow Blvd.
Pittsburgh
412/682-8296

Pittsburgh palm trees, p. 173

The only spot on Bigelow Boulevard with a giant banana surrounded by lightbulbs on its facade is also the place to look for the leading edge of alternative, new wave, psychedelic, and heavy metal sounds. Nationally known acts and the latest in original local bands show up here, too. Sun 7:30–11, Tue–Sat 8–2. No age minimum. Cover begins at $3 Tue–Sat. (East Pittsburgh)

EXCUSES BAR & GRILL
2526 E. Carson St.
Pittsburgh
412/431-4090
An eclectic mix of live blues, R&B, new rock, and old rock keeps the crowd happy at Excuses. Snack on the excellent wings and wash them down with any of 24 imported beers on hand. Thur–Sat 10–2. $2–$4 cover charge. (South Pittsburgh)

GRAFFITI
4615 Baum Blvd.
Pittsburgh
412/682-4210
Graffiti is one of Pittsburgh's best

showcases for top-name performers. The second-floor loft provides an exceptional setting for the hottest acts in hard rock, jazz, country, reggae, traditional Celtic music, and comedy. The multilevel club also has a dance floor, lounge, and restaurant (reservations required). Performances Wed–Sat. Cover charge varies. (East Pittsburgh)

JERGEL'S
3385 Babcock Blvd.
North Hills
412/364-9902
This comfortable, casual restaurant and bar draws a steady multigenerational crowd with its great food, generous drinks, and eclectic mix of live entertainment. Wednesday through Saturday features '60s, '70s, and '80s, rock, R&B, and country. (North Pittsburgh)

LAVA LOUNGE
2204 E. Carson St.
Pittsburgh
412/431-5282

From the dark, black-red front lounge to the spotlighted stage in the back room, the Lava Lounge effectively creates a subterranean, organic environment. Free-form carved wooden chairs and booth dividers, stalactite hanging lamps over the well-stocked bar, and the deep, cushioned "pit" booth keep up the mood. Music starts at 11. $3 cover charge. (South Pittsburgh)

METROPOL
1600 Smallman St.
Pittsburgh
412/261-2221
Glossy, high-tech Metropol is Pittsburgh's premiere venue for local bands, live DJs, and nationally known entertainment. It has set the standard for cutting-edge sound since 1988. The cavernous multilevel converted warehouse can easily handle special event crowds of up to 1,300. Wed–Sat 9–2. $5 cover charge. (East Pittsburgh)

NICK'S FAT CITY
1601 E. Carson St.
Pittsburgh
412/481-6880
The dramatic, high-sheen art deco facade of Nick's Fat City screams '30s nightclub. The young, with-it crowd, however, doesn't; dress is ultra-casual. Inside, the decor features an extensive collection of rock 'n' roll memorabilia. Local bands are featured Tuesday through Saturday. Tue–Sat 8–1:30. $5 cover charge. (South Pittsburgh)

Country and Western

BLOOMFIELD BRIDGE TAVERN
4412 Liberty Ave.
Pittsburgh
412/682-8611
This popular neighborhood tavern features a variety of live bands, from punk to polka, as well as bluegrass, country, rock, and acoustic acts. The music is hearty and so is the food. Specialties are Polish staples—pierogies and kielbasa—and more than 100 varieties of imported beers to wash them down. Daily 11–1:30 a.m. $4 cover for live music. (East Pittsburgh)

How to Talk the Talk

Many native Pittsburghers speak what is affectionately known as *Pittsburghese*, a soft drawl sprinkled with pronunciation and syntax unique to Pittsburgh. In Pittsburghese, *downtown* sounds more like *dahntahn*, something that needs to be done "needs done," and rubber bands are called gum bands. Some North Siders are called *Yunzers*, because when they say *you*, it sounds like *yunz*. To get in on the fun, check out some of the guides to Pittsburghese, such as The *Tongue-in-Cheek Guide to Pittsburgh* by Ken and Jackie Abel.

MOONDOG'S PUB
378 Freeport Rd.
Blawnox
412/828-2040

Don't let its meager appearance fool you—Moondog's is big on showcasing local talent with open-stage nights on Tuesday and Wednesday. The tiny club has a "local bar" feel, but fans come from throughout the Pittsburgh area to hear well-known local rock 'n' roll, country, reggae, and blues performers. (North Pittsburgh)

ROSEBUD
1650 Smallman St.
Pittsburgh
412/261-2232

State-of-the-art technology makes Rosebud one of the best, large-scale venues for top artists, nationally known groups, and hot local bands. Reggae is featured on Tuesday, country on Wednesday, Latin American dance music Thursday, and local bands on Friday. Tue–Sat 11:30–6, Sun 9 a.m.–2 a.m. Cover charge varies. (East Pittsburgh)

Blues and Soul

BLUES CAFÉ
19th St. and Carson St.
Pittsburgh
412/431-7080

Come to the Blues Café for live music, whether blues or jazz, nightly. Saturday at 3:30 p.m. the best local jazz musicians come to jam. Daily 11–2. $2 cover. (South Pittsburgh)

BUFFALO BLUES
2165 S. Highland Ave.
Pittsburgh
412/362-5837

The live music starts at 10:15, and the beat goes on until 2 Tuesday through Sunday night at Buffalo Blues. Hot-

licks, the popular barbecue restaurant at Buffalo Blues, fuels the lively crowd with everything from great hot wings to ribs. Belloma Blues Bombers headline Saturday. Look for Blues Jam Sunday from 9 to 1. $3–$5 cover. (East Pittsburgh)

PUBS AND BARS

CHURCH BREW WORKS
3525 Liberty Ave.
Pittsburgh
412/688-8200

Church Brew Works is a thriving microbrewery and a fine restaurant and pub operating in the lovingly refurbished sanctuary of the former St. John the Baptist Church of Lawrenceville. Beverages are not limited to beer. Imported and domestic wines, Church Brew Works' own ginger ale, and birch beer are also available. (See also Chapter 4: "Where to Eat.") (East Pittsburgh)

GANDY DANCER
Landmark Bldg., Station Square

Have A Nice Day Cafe, p. 170

Doina Locke

Pittsburgh
412/261-1717
This popular after-work stop for professionals, office workers, and even a Pittsburgh celebrity or two crackles with excitement as patrons invest the same energy into their socializing as they do into their work—and Pittsburgh is a hardworking town. Happy Hour from 4:30 to 6:30 Monday through Friday draws a lively, mixed crowd for music, free hors d'ouevres, and fun. The full-service restaurant has great food at good prices. Mon–Thur 11:30–12, Fri and Sat 11:30–2, Sun 2:30–10. (South Pittsburgh)

PENN BREWERY
Troy Hill Rd.
Pittsburgh
412/237-9400
The former Eberhardt & Ober Brewery on Troy Hill, Pittsburgh's historic German neighborhood, is the perfect setting for enjoying an old-style German beer hall—with benches, long tables, and steins of beer. Twelve German-style beers are brewed on the premises. The rathskeller downstairs feels authentic and comfortable. The brick courtyard makes a wonderful summer beer garden. (See also Chapter 4: "Where to Eat" and Chapter 5: "Sights and Attractions.") (North Pittsburgh)

STRIP BREWING CO.
& RESTAURANT

2106 Penn Ave.
Pittsburgh
412/338-2337
This full-service restaurant carries a mix of 15 microbrews for the discerning brew connoisseur or the novice taster. Diners seated on either the first or second floor can view the brewing operation. Other services include a cigar room and humidor. (East Pittsburgh)

VALHALLA MICROBREWERY
& RESTAURANT
12th St. and Smallman St.
Pittsburgh
412/434-1440
This microbrewery and restaurant provides multilevel dining and an outdoor deck for warm weather. Beer vats are part of the decor, and the names of the brews add to the fun: Big Olaf Dunkel, Eric the Red lager, and Pillage Pilsner. (East Pittsburgh)

SPORTS BARS

CLARK BAR & GRILL
503 Martindale St.
Pittsburgh
412/231-5720
Before or after games or shows, this close-to-the-stadium pub is jammed. A great place to spot an athlete, the Clark Bar also has a small sports museum. Its own history shouldn't be ignored. The famous candy bar that

originated in Pittsburgh used to be made in this building, and even though the company is long gone, the name lingers on. This is a good, solid old-time bar, with a black-and-white tiled floor, a long bar, and big, old-fashioned booths. The food is hearty and the desserts are sweet treats. (North Pittsburgh)

WOODSON'S ALL-STAR GRILLE
Station Square
Pittsburgh
412/454-2600
Former Steeler Rod Woodson's place is a good spot to rub elbows with a whole bunch of sports fanatics and athletes. There are lots of huge screens so that no one in any of the five seating areas need miss a single play or any of the action. Lest you forget, sports memorabilia line the walls, hang from the rafters, and fill the gift shop at the entrance. Everyone is welcome—just remember—you're rooting for the home team! (North Pittsburgh)

MOVIE HOUSES OF NOTE

BEEHIVE BIG SCREEN
3807 Forbes Ave.
Pittsburgh
412/687-9428
The Beehive screening room is in the back of a coffeehouse, in what looks like an old, Hollywood-style fake castle. Since it's right on the Pitt campus, it's usually packed with students inside and out. Don't worry; they're harmless. To blend in, dress *very* casually, turn your baseball cap backward, and slouch. (East Pittsburgh)

DEPENDABLE DRIVE-IN
Moon-Clinton Rd.
Coraopolis

412/264-7011
This wonderful slice of American life from the 1950s is still enjoyed in the Pittsburgh area, only cars now are more likely to be loaded with families than teens on a hot date. Theaters program accordingly, emphasizing family-friendly movies to encourage parents to bring children along and take advantage of the per-car, rather than per person, admission charge. (West Pittsburgh)

HARRIS THEATER
809 Liberty Ave.
Pittsburgh
412/471-9700
The primary screening outlet for Pittsburgh Filmmakers, a nonprofit arts organization, Harris Theater shows art-house movies, independent, and foreign films that never make it to regular movie theaters. The theater, along with a few other small movie houses, is also used by Pittsburgh Filmmakers for its Three Rivers Film Festival. (Downtown Pittsburgh)

A fake castle houses Beehive Big Screen.

Doina Locke

Star Gazing

While Pittsburgh may not be New York or Los Angeles, it has three professional sports teams and is frequently the site of major film productions. So plenty of well-known people pass through town. Your chances for a little star gazing are best at:

Woodson's All-Star Grille *(Station Square, South Side)*

Metropol *(Strip District)*

Clark Bar and Grille *(North Side)*

Mario's *(South Side)*

Penguins hockey games *(Downtown)*

Andy Warhol Museum *(North Side)*

Next Decade *(Oakland)*

Gandy Dancer *(Station Square, South Side)*

REX THEATRE
1602 E. Carson St.
Pittsburgh
412/381-2200
Billing itself as "Pittsburgh's Oldest Theater," the Rex shows Hollywood movies but also some independent, foreign, and classic films. Only as wide as a storefront, the tiny lobby presents an uphill climb to the candy counter and the seats beyond. The building's '30s look is so well-preserved that "Dish Night" probably wouldn't be too much of a surprise. $6.50 evenings, $4 before 6. (South Pittsburgh)

SUPER SAVER CINEMAS 8
Northway Mall, 800 McKnight Rd.
North Hills
412/367-1593
Eight screens show budget-friendly, second-run movies in the North Hills. The weekend crowd usually spills over into the mall and creates quite a jam until screening time. Any other time, it's pretty easy to buy a ticket without waiting and find a seat with no problem. The lobby of this well-maintained theater is colorfully lit with bright neon designs. $3.25 adults. (North Pittsburgh)

DINNER THEATERS

BLARNEY STONE
30 Grant Ave.
Etna
412/781-1666
A fixed-price dinner theater package is offered Friday and Saturday evenings and Sunday afternoons for select productions. There is a cover charge for guest artist performances. Tickets cost $15–$20. (North Pittsburgh)

RADISSON HOTEL
101 Mall Blvd.

Monroeville
412/856-5159

A wide-ranging choice of dinner shows are featured at the Radisson Hotel from March through December. Past offerings have included Broadway productions, "Pittsburgh Opry," and an interactive mystery play. The Radisson offers lunch, dinner, and brunch shows. (East Pittsburgh)

COMEDY CLUBS

COMEDY CLUB
Pittsburgh Greentree Marriott
101 Marriott Dr.
Pittsburgh

412/635-0708

Located in the Greentree Marriott, the Comedy Club offers snacks, sandwiches, and drinks and features local talent. Shows Fri and Sat 8:30 and 10:30. Reservations required. (West Pittsburgh)

FUNNYBONE STATION SQUARE
Shops at Station Square
Pittsburgh
412/281-3130

For 16 years, the Funnybone has kept Pittsburghers laughing by showcasing local and national talent. Tuesday is open-stage night. Closed Mon. $1.25–$10 cover charge. (South Pittsburgh)

Doina Locke

13

DAY TRIPS FROM PITTSBURGH

Day Trip: Grove City

Distance from Pittsburgh: 50 miles

When you're in Pittsburgh, don't pass up a chance to take advantage of the out-of-the-ordinary bargains at **Prime Outlets at Grove City**, less than an hour away from Pittsburgh north on I-79. Take the Grove City exit and follow the signs. Remember: there is no sales tax on most clothing and shoe purchases in Pennsylvania.

If you'd prefer to ease into your bargain-hunting day trip, detour through **Zelienople**, about a half hour north of downtown via I-279, north to I-79, then further north to exit 27. Turn left and head for Route 19 and Zelienople, named by the town founder, German aristocrat Baron Dettmar Basse, for his beloved daughter Zelie. Just north of town, the popular **Log Cabin Inn** takes advantage of a picturesque setting with a glassed-in back dining room overlooking a densely wooded hillside. Your best chance of getting a table with a view is before noon or after 1:30. Back in town, on South Main Street, the **Kaufman House** offers good food at reasonable prices and a cozy, small-town cordiality.

On a leisurely visit, take time to visit **Passavant House**, the restored home of Zelie Basse Passavant. The handsome Federal-style building is a window into nineteenth-century life in Zelienople and also has a genealogy library. Just a short way down Main Street, the **Buhl House**, built around 1805, is the oldest building in town.

Now that you're ready for shopping, retrace your route to I-79 and head north. Take exit 31, Grove City, and follow the signs into the spacious parking lot. The outdoor mall is quite attractive, especially since it's only a

PITTSBURGH REGION

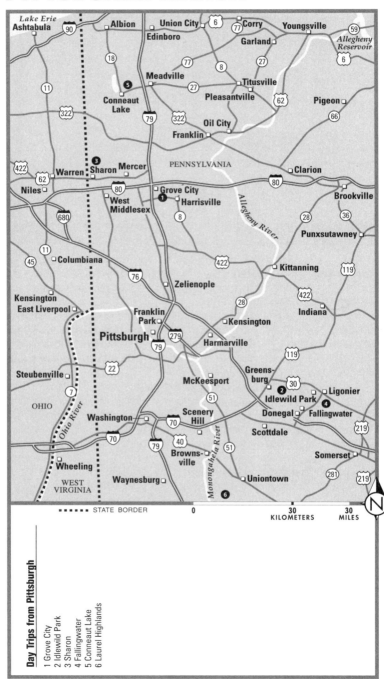

Lake Erie
Ashtabula
Albion
Union City
Corry
Youngsville
Edinboro
Garland
Allegheny Reservoir
Meadville
Titusville
Conneaut Lake
Pleasantville
Pigeon
Oil City
Franklin
PENNSYLVANIA
Warren
Sharon
Mercer
Clarion
Niles
Grove City
Harrisville
Brookville
West Middlesex
Columbiana
Punxsutawney
Kittanning
Zelienople
Kensington
East Liverpool
Indiana
Franklin Park
Kensington
Pittsburgh
Harmarville
Steubenville
Greensburg
McKeesport
Ligonier
Idlewild Park
Fallingwater
Donegal
OHIO
Washington
Scenery Hill
Scottdale
Wheeling
Browns-ville
Somerset
WEST VIRGINIA
Waynesburg
Uniontown

Ohio River
Allegheny River
Monongahela River

STATE BORDER

0   30   30
        KILOMETERS   MILES

N

Day Trips from Pittsburgh

1 Grove City
2 Idlewild Park
3 Sharon
4 Fallingwater
5 Conneaut Lake
6 Laurel Highlands

few years old. A word of warning: orient yourself at one of the kiosk maps or get a map to keep with you, because, with 140 shops such as Off 5th Saks Fifth Avenue, Eddie Bauer, and Sony to choose from, you will either get very foot-weary or frustrated by backtracking.

Prime Outlets Stores are open Monday through Saturday from 10 to 9 and Sunday from 11 to 6. For information, call 724/748-4770. Whatever else you do, depart more than 30 minutes before closing time, because the ways out are limited, and almost everyone wants to get onto southbound I-79. The traffic jams can be horrendous.

Since you're in the area, take the opportunity to visit the **Wendell August Forge**—follow the signs on Route 208 from Grove City. Reportedly the country's oldest and largest operating forge, Wendell August Forge is known for its high-quality workmanship. Prices are reasonable for hand-crafted items; stock up for gift-giving. Tours are given between 8 and noon and 12:30 and 4 Monday through Friday

From Grove City, Route 208 leads west to **Volant**, a nineteenth-century farming community centered around a grist mill on Neshannock Creek. A restoration of the grist mill in the 1980s brought about Volant's transformation into a charming commercial center of about 50 craft, antique, and country shops and restaurants. Most shops are located near the grist mill in historic buildings and in a collection of railroad cars on Main Street. Many items are home-crafted by members of Old Order Amish families living in the nearby New Wilmington area.

Travelers who prefer to stay in bed-and-breakfasts can choose from several north of the Pittsburgh area. In Zelienople, the **Inn on Grandview Bed & Breakfast** is at 310 Grandview Avenue; call 724/452-0469 for reservations. Farther north, **Lynnrose Bed & Breakfast** is located in Grove City at 114 W. Main Street. For reservations call 724/458-6425.

Getting there from Pittsburgh: Take I-279 north from downtown to I-79. To go to Zelienople, take exit 27 and go west to Route 19. To continue to Grove City, stay on I-79 and get off at the Grove City exit, 31. Take Route 208 west to Volant.

Day Trip: Idlewild Park

Distance from Pittsburgh: 60 miles

Ever since 1878, when Judge Thomas Mellon of Pittsburgh began using William Darlington's 350-acre estate, Idlewild, as a resort destination for his Ligonier Valley Railroad, western Pennsylvanians have enjoyed its natural beauty and the amusement park attractions that have been added over the years. Idlewild Park is now the fourth-oldest operating amusement park in the nation and a part of the Kennywood Park Corporation. Judge Mellon and his railroad are long gone, and today's Pittsburghers can make the trip in under two hours via the Pennsylvania Turnpike and routes 711 and 30.

Fred Rogers, the creative genius behind public television's *Mr. Rogers'*

Neighborhood, is a native of nearby Latrobe. He provided the inspiration for Idlewild Park's Mister Rogers' Neighborhood of Make-Believe, where visitors ride a life-sized trolley through the familiar neighborhood filled with animated figures of its well-known residents.

Storybook Forest

There's much more for all ages, from toddlers to seniors. Raccoon Lagoon is an eight-acre range of kiddie rides, while Storybook Forest features costumed characters in attractions that bring nursery rhymes to life. Jumpin' Jungle is an active play zone for youngsters, and Olde Idlewild has 16 amusement-park rides for everyone. Bathing suits are required for the water park, the H2Ohhh Zone. When you're ready to sit for a while, Hootin' Holler is the place, with live entertainment, food, and gift shops. Idlewild Park is open every day except Monday from late May until early September. For information on hours and ticket prices call 724/238-3666.

Back on Route 30, only a half-mile from Idlewild Park is the **Colonial Inn**, a restaurant known for its elegant atmosphere and fine dining. Route 30 also leads to the town of Ligonier and the **Forbes Road Gun Museum**, which has a collection of firearms dating back to 1450.

Casual eating spots in Ligonier include **Ruthie's Diner** on Route 30 and **Big Pap's** on West Main Street. Ruthie's is known for home cooking and great pies, and Big Pap's claims to serve the best Reuben sandwiches in town.

Route 30 is also known as the **Lincoln Highway Heritage Corridor**, one of eight heritage parks in Pennsylvania. The Lincoln Highway was promoted around the turn of the twentieth century as the first transcontinental highway. Although the full transcontinental version was never built, Pennsylvania's Route 30 has many historic points of interest, including museums, restaurants, businesses, and inns.

One such museum, the **Compass Inn Museum** is in Laughlintown, about three miles east of Ligonier. The museum is a log house built in 1799 that served as a tavern and a stagecoach stop for many years. The barn houses vehicles such as sleighs and Conestoga wagons, tools of the blacksmithing trade, and farm equipment. Living history weekends, the third weekend of June, July, and August, offer demonstrations of eighteenth- and nineteenth-century crafts. Call 724/238-4983 for more information. The **Ligonier Country Inn** next door is open for breakfast, lunch, and dinner Tuesday through Saturday. Call 724/238-3651.

Getting there from Pittsburgh: Take the Pennsylvania Turnpike (I-76) to the Donegal exit 9, go east on Route 711 to Route 30, and follow the signs to Idlewild Park. From downtown Pittsburgh, you can reach the turnpike by taking the Parkway East (I-376) to Monroeville.

Day Trip: Sharon

Distance from Pittsburgh: 70 miles

A day trip north of Pittsburgh, such as this one to Sharon, Pennsylvania, offers many intriguing spots that are worth a quick side trip. About a half hour north of downtown by way of I-279 north to I-79 north to exit 27, turn left and you'll find yourself in the historic town of **Harmony**, the original Pennsylvania settlement of George Rapp and his Rappites, or Harmony Society. The Harmonists were a communal, celibate society that flourished in the first half of the nineteenth century, until they all died out. The Harmony Museum is set on the Diamond in the town's center. Guided tours are offered of the museum and other buildings with Harmonist relics.

While you're in Harmony, visit the historic **Harmony Inn**. The food is delicious and, if you're lucky, the mischievous resident ghost might pull a gentle prank like locking a woman in the ladies' room—then again, maybe he won't!

Once again heading north on I-79, take exit 32 to I-80 west, take exit 1, then follow the signs to Sharon and some serious discount shopping. Advertising itself as the world's largest shoe store, **Reyer's Shoes** actually has two locations in Sharon and claims an inventory of over 170,000 shoes, all for sale at less than retail prices. **The Winner**, offering prices up to 70 percent off, is a women's clothing store that takes special care to make

Vocal Group Hall of Fame & Museum, p. 186

William J. Boyd

shopping a pleasant experience, including arranging items by color and providing a comfortable lounge. The Winner offers four floors of clothing that range from casual to formal. Chocoholics beware: Sharon is also the home of **Daffin's Candies**, which has created what some say is the world's largest chocolate bunny, a chocolate castle, and other delights for its Chocolate Kingdom.

Downtown Sharon is also the home of the **Vocal Group Hall of Fame and Museum**, "dedicated to the greatest vocal groups of all time." Ranging all the way back to the early 1800s, the museum's three floors of displays feature memorabilia such as stage costumes, vinyl records, and recorded clips from memorable hits. For further information, call 800/753-1648.

Quaker Steak & Lube serves excellent food in a former gas station filled with automobile memorabilia including cars hanging from the ceiling. The restaurant advertises its delicious, award-winning "killer golden garlic wings—the best anywhere." Locations are popping up elsewhere, such as in Robinson and Cranberry, but the Sharon location is the original, the one that started it all. Call 724/981-7221.

Not more than ten minutes from Sharon, the **Pennzoil Pennsylvania Hall of Fame Motorsports Museum** in West Middlesex has more than 50 cars and motorcycles on display. A special feature is a reproduction of a section of the Daytona Speedway, angled at 31 degrees to give visitors an idea of how steeply the curves are banked on the course. Added attractions are a Grand Prix go-cart track and a Speedway putt-putt golf course, the only miniature-golf course in the area with auto-oriented obstacles. The museum is open daily from 10 to 6. Admission is $8 for adults, but coupons for $2 discounts are widely available. Call 724/528-2277 for further information.

For an unusual vision of the Old South á la *Gone With the Wind*, delicious fine dining, and overnight accommodations, there is **Tara**, a country inn located north of Sharon, off Route 258. For information or reservations, call 724/962-3535.

Getting there from Pittsburgh: *Take I-275 north to I-79. Continue north to exit 32 for I-80 west. Take exit 1 and follow the signs north to Sharon.*

Day Trip: Fallingwater

Distance from Pittsburgh: 60 miles

Legendary architect Frank Lloyd Wright has been proclaimed a genius of American architecture. Two stunning examples of his designs integrating structures with their natural surroundings, Fallingwater and Kentuck Knob, are found within miles of each other in the forested beauty of the Laurel Highlands.

Edgar Kaufmann, owner of Pittsburgh's Kaufmann's Department Store chain, commissioned Wright to build the home at his country retreat set amid 5,000 acres of natural wilderness. The house was built of local sandstone, reinforced concrete, steel, and glass. Construction took three years,

Olde Idlewild Park, p. 184

from 1936 through 1939. The house was set over a waterfall on Bear Run and creates a stunning combination of human-made and natural elements.

Fallingwater was donated to the Western Pennsylvania Conservancy by Edgar Kaufmann Jr. and remains as it was when the family used it. Well-informed docents conduct one-hour tours, and more detailed two-hour tours are available by reservation only. Because of the hilly terrain and numerous stairs, those who may have difficulty with the tour are advised to call in advance. Reservations are strongly recommended, especially on weekends. Call 724/329-8501 for reservations. The café at the visitors center serves a delicious gourmet lunch. The gift shop carries contemporary works of art, pieces incorporating Wright-inspired designs, books, and jewelry in all price ranges.

One-half mile north of Fallingwater on Route 381, the **Bear Run Nature Preserve** offers 20 miles of hiking and cross-country skiing trails on 4,000 acres. The preserve is owned and operated by the Western Pennsylvania Conservancy.

Progressing south on Route 381, just beyond Ohiopyle, follow the signs to **Kentuck Knob**, another Frank Lloyd Wright home, this one overlooking the Youghiogheny River Gorge. Set just below the crest of a mountain, Kentuck Knob is integrated into its setting just as definitively as Fallingwater. Using local fieldstone, tidewater cypress, glass, and copper, Wright designed this home as a hexagon with an open floor plan and wide overhangs. A sculpture garden and informal plantings enhance the home's natural setting.

Kentuck Knob is open for tours from 10 to 4 Tuesday through Sunday and is closed Mondays except for holiday weekends. Reservations are necessary to guarantee admission. In-depth tours are available daily at 8:30 a.m. by reservation only. Children under 9 years of age are not permitted. Call 724/329-1901 for reservations. Kentuck Knob also has a coffee shop, a gift shop, and an orchid greenhouse.

In Scenery Hill on Route 40, west of Route 381, the **Century Inn**, renowned for fine dining, is open for lunch and dinner daily. A national historic landmark, it is one of the country's oldest continuously operated inns. It is closed December 30 through mid-March. Pittsburghers have been known to drive to Scenery Hill just for dinner at the Century Inn, the spectacular scenery along Route 40, and the numerous gift and craft shops nearby. Call 724/935-6600.

Getting there from Pittsburgh: Take the Pennsylvania Turnpike (I-76) east to exit 9, Donegal, go east on Route 31 to Route 381/711, and follow the signs to Fallingwater. To return to Pittsburgh from Scenery Hill, take Route 40 west to I-70, take the (Washington, Pennsylvania) connector west to I-79, head north to I-279, then continue east into downtown Pittsburgh.

Day Trip: Conneaut Lake

Distance from Pittsburgh: 90 miles

Situated on the border between Pennsylvania and Ohio, Conneaut and Pymatuning Lakes have long been a warm-weather destination for Pittsburghers eager for a quick getaway. Roughly two hours north of Pittsburgh, the region lends itself well to day trips or overnight stays.

One of the main attractions on Pennsylvania's largest natural lake is the 106-year-old **Conneaut Lake Park**, a traditional amusement park featuring classic thrill rides, an old-fashioned midway, a water park, a lakefront hotel, and free access to the lake's sandy beaches.

Throughout the season, Conneaut Lake Park offers entertainment such as polka festivals and oldies acts. Fireworks displays are held on Memorial Day, the Fourth of July, and Labor Day. For more information, call Conneaut Lake Park at 814/382-5115.

In the nearby town of Conneaut Lake, travelers will find a nice selection of moderately priced craft shops and restaurants along Main Street. The **Berry Basket** specializes in antiques and floral arrangements, and **Bella Notte** offers an array of unique gifts. A number of quaint eateries, including the **Caddy Shack Restaurant**, the **Lakefront Diner**, and the **Beacon Inn Restaurant and Bakery,** offer moderately priced family dining. For an overnight stay, **Hotel Conneaut** is very affordable.

About 20 minutes west of Conneaut Lake along Route 6 is **Pymatuning Reservoir**, right on the Pennsylvania and Ohio border. Pymatuning Reservoir features a number of free, lifeguarded beaches, as well as rest room and shower facilities.

The first 20 or so feet of the lake has a rocky bottom that can be a little rough on your feet. Surf shoes or snug-fitting waterproof sandals are the best guarantee of pain-free wading and strolling along the beach. A number of fishing areas and private boat rental facilities also dot the reservoir's shoreline.

Visitors to the reservoir's spillway area can purchase bags of stale bread to feed the fish, which are so abundant they leap and swarm over each other to gobble the snacks as soon as they hit the water. The spot is also a refuge for migrating ducks and geese, the **Pymatuning Waterfowl Area**. In season, the birds are as eager as the fish to get at the food, practically walking on top of the jam-packed fish. A nearby museum presents an overview of the array of wildlife living in the region. Admission is free.

***Getting there from Pittsburgh:** Follow I-279 north to I-79 north. Take exit 36B and travel west along Route 322 for about eight miles. Turn right onto Route 18 north and proceed three miles to the park.*

Day Trip: Laurel Highlands

Distance from Pittsburgh: 60 miles

A glimpse of western Pennsylvania's rich history, stunning beauty, and recreational activities is available during a day trip to the Laurel Highlands. The **Fort Necessity National Battlefield** surrounds a reconstruction of a fort built by George Washington in 1754. The base for Washington's first campaign of the French and Indian War, the fort includes entrenchments and other exhibits reconstructed on their original sites. Located near the fort is the Mount Washington Tavern, a fully restored stagecoach inn featuring rooms furnished with nineteenth-century artifacts.

Five miles east of Route 40, the **Laurel Caverns**, the state's largest system of caves, feature more than two miles of underground passageways. The caves, naturally carved out of Loyalhanna limestone, have been explored since the late 1700s.

Guided tours of lighted sections of the cave are conducted by knowledgeable staff members, who provide detailed explanations about how the caverns were formed and preserved. Because of the cool temperature in the cave—a constant 52 degrees—a light jacket or sweater will come in handy. The guided tours take between two and three hours.

For the more adventurous, tours into unlighted sections of the caverns are available. These tours can be strenuous and are not advisable for young children or people with physical limitations. People taking the tours must wear long pants, long-sleeved shirts, and hiking shoes. They also must bring two flashlights or lanterns that use D batteries. Hard hats are provided. For more information, call 724/438-3003.

White-water rafting along the **Youghiogheny River** offers visitors a variety of challenges, including the mild rapids of the Middle Yough, the quick pace of the Lower Yough, or the ultimate white-water experience of the Upper Youghiogheny River. (Note: Youghiogheny is pronounced Yock-uh-gay-nee. The shortened form, Yough, is pronounced Yock.)

Rafting excursions typically depart from Ohiopyle State Park, which can be reached by taking Route 40 from Uniontown to Route 381. The trip downriver can last anywhere from two to seven hours, depending on the package. Several outfitters offer packages that allow visitors to bicycle upriver and make the return trip in a canoe or raft. Outfitters include Laurel Highlands River Tours, 800/472-3846; Mountain Streams, 800/723-8669; and Ohiopyle Trading Post, 888/644-7953.

***Getting there from Pittsburgh:** To get to the Laurel Highlands from downtown Pittsburgh, head south through the Liberty Tunnels, and follow Route 51 to Uniontown and Route 40.*

APPENDIX: CITY·SMART BASICS

EMERGENCY NUMBERS

Police/Ambulance/Fire 911
(Except in Sewickley Heights. Check the telephone directory for emergency numbers if calling from that borough.)

Pittsburgh Poison Center (Mr. Yuk)
412/681-6669

Pennsylvania State Police
Services and Emergency Calls
412/787-2000

United Way HelpLine
(crisis and suicide prevention)
412/255-1155

HOSPITALS AND EMERGENCY MEDICAL CENTERS

Allegheny University Hospital
320 E. North Ave.
412/359-3131

Children's Hospital of Pittsburgh
3705 Fifth Ave.
412/692-5437

Forbes Metropolitan Hospital
of Allegheny University
Medical Centers
225 Penn Ave.
Wilkinsburg
412/247-2000

Magee-Womens Hospital
300 Halket St.
412/641-1000

Mercy Hospital of Pittsburgh
1400 Locust St.
412/232-8111

Mercy Providence Hospital
1004 Arch St.
412/323-5600

Ohio Valley General Hospital
Heckel Rd.
McKees Rocks
412/777-6161

St. Francis Medical Centers
225 Penn Ave.
412/622-4343

Sewickley Valley Hospital
720 Blackburn Rd.
Sewickley
412/741-6600

Shadyside Hospital
5230 Centre Ave.
412/623-2121

Suburban General Hospital
100 S. Jackson Ave.
Bellevue
412/734-6000

UPMC Passavant Hospital
9100 Babcock Blvd.
North Hills
412/367-6700

UPMC Presbyterian Hospital,
Montefiore Hospital, and Eye & Ear Hospital
200 Lothrop Ave.
412/647-2345

UPMC St. Margaret Hospital
815 Freeport Rd.
Aspinwall
412/784-4000

UPMC South Side Hospital
2000 Mary St.
412/488-5500

UPMC Western Psychiatric
Institute and Clinic
3811 O'Hara St.
412/624-2100

Western Pennsylvania Hospital
4800 Friendship Ave.
412/578-5000

RECORDED INFORMATION

Air Quality
412/578-8179

Entertainment Hotline
412/922-5252

Pittsburgh Downtown Partnership
412/566-4190, ext. 1

Pollen Count
800/9-POLLEN or 800/976-5536

Time
412/391-9500

Visitor Info Hotline
800/366-0093

Weather
412/936-1212

POST OFFICE

US Mail Central Mail Facility
800/725-2161

VISITOR INFORMATION

American Automobile Association
412/363-5100 or 800/441-5008

Greater Pittsburgh Convention
and Visitors Bureau Inc.
412/281-7711 or 800/927-8376

Pennsylvania Office of Travel,
Tourism and Film Production
800/VISIT PA or 800/847-4872

Pittsburgh Chamber of Commerce
412/392-4500

Pittsburgh Council for
International Visitors
412/624-7800

Traveler's Aid
412/281-5474

Visitor Info Hotline
800/366-0093

CAR RENTAL (PITTSBURGH INTERNATIONAL AIRPORT LOCATIONS)

Avis
412/472-5200 or 800/831-2847

Budget
412/472-5252 or 800/527-0770

Dollar
412/472-5100 or 800/800-4000

Hertz
412/472-5955 or 800/654-3131

National
412/472-5094 or 800/227-7368

Thrifty
412/472-5288 or 800/367-2277

DISABLED ACCESS INFORMATION

Carnegie Library of Pittsburgh
Library for the Blind and
Physically Handicapped
412/687-2440 or 800/242-0586

Greater Pittsburgh
Guild for the Blind
412/221-2200

Pennsylvania Blindness and
Visual Services
412/565-5240

Pittsburgh Blind Association
412/682-5600

Pittsburgh Hearing, Speech and
Deaf Services (Voice, TTY)
412/281-1375

Pittsburgh Steelwheelers, Inc.
412/781-5700

Radio Information Service
412/488-3944

MULTICULTURAL RESOURCES

Hispanic Chamber of Commerce in
Western Pennsylvania
412/322-5015

Japan Information Center
University of Pittsburgh
412/648-7617

Jewish Community Center
412/521-8010

National Association for the
Advancement of Colored People
412/471-1024

OTHER COMMUNITY ORGANIZATIONS

Allegheny County Department of
Aging Information and Referral
412/350-5460 or 800/344-4319

College for the Over Sixty
University of Pittsburgh
412/624-7308

Lesbian & Gay Film Festival
of Pittsburgh
412/232-3277

BABYSITTING AND CHILDCARE

Adair Associates
412/563-1540

Temps for Tots
412/281-8399

NEWSPAPERS

North Hills News Record
800/874-9994
http://pittsburghLIVE.com

Pittsburgh Post-Gazette
412/263-1100
www.post-gazette.com

Tribune Review
724/834-1151
http://pittsburghLIVE.com

Valley News Dispatch
724/226-1006
http://pittsburghLIVE.com

New Pittsburgh Courier
412/481-8302

City Paper
412/560-2489

Employment Paper
412/481-6397

In Pittsburgh Newsweekly
412/488-1212

Jewish Chronicle
412/687-1000

Pittsburgh Business Times
412/481-6397

Pittsburgh Catholic
412/471-1252

Renaissance News
412/391-8208

MAGAZINES

Mt. Lebanon Magazine
412/343-3407

North Hills Magazine
412/486-1333

*Pennsylvania Health and
Fitness Magazine*
412/784-0750

PITTSBURGH
412/622-1360

Pittsburgh Parent
724/443-1891

Shady Ave.
412/687-5731

BOOKSTORES

B Dalton Bookseller
Station Square
412/261-4680

Barnes & Noble Booksellers
339 Sixth Ave.
412/642-4324

The Bookshelf
Duncan Manor
North Hills
412/367-2021

Bookworks
1139 Freeport Rd.
Fox Chapel
412/782-6661

Bookworks Cafe
3400 Harts Run Rd.
Glenshaw
412/767-0344

Borders Books & Music
Norman Centre II, Rt. 19 and
N. Highland Rd.
South Hills
412/835-5583

Cokesbury
19015 Perry Hwy.
Cranberry
800/835-9804

Jay's Book Stall
3604 Fifth Ave.
412/683-2644

Journeys of Life
810 Bellefield St.
412/681-8755

Lemstone Books
1000 Ross Park Mall
North Hills
412/367-6110

Little Dickens—A Bookstore
for Children Ltd.
634 Allegheny River Blvd.
Oakmont
412/828-9005

Mandala Books
2022 Murray Ave.
412/422-6623

Mystery Lovers Bookshop
514 Allegheny River Blvd.
Oakmont
412/828-4877

Waldenbooks
South Hills Village Mall
South Hills
412/833-2322

RADIO STATIONS

KDKA AM 1020, news, talk, Pirates
KQV AM 1410, news
WQED FM 89.3, classical
WDUQ FM 90.5, jazz, NPR news
WYEP FM 91.3, alternative, public
WLTJ FM 92.9, soft rock
WBZZ FM 93.7, contemporary hits
WWSW FM 94.5, oldies
WDRV FM 96.1, modern hits
WRRK FM 96.9, classic rock
WZKT FM 98.3, top 40
WSSH FM 99.7, adult contemporary

WZPT FM 100.7, '70s and '80s
WORD FM 101.5, Christian
WDVE FM 102.5, rock, Penguins
WWCS AM 540, news
WHJB AM 620, rock oldies
WPIT AM 730, Christian talk
WEDO AM 810, variety
WWSW AM 970, oldies
WASP AM 1130, news, talk
WTAE AM 1250, sports talk,
   Steelers
WJAS AM 1320, big band, sports talk
WPPT AM 1360, talk
WBCW AM 1530, talk
WCJX AM 1550, talk

TELEVISION STATIONS

KDKA 2, CBS
WTAE 4, ABC
WPXI 11, NBC
WQED 13, PBS
WQEX 16, PBS
WCWB 22, Warner Brothers
WPCB 40, Cornerstone

INDEX

Cater to Your Interests on Your Next Vacation

**The 100 Best Small Art Towns in America
3rd edition**
Discover Creative Communities, Fresh Air, and
Affordable Living
U.S. $16.95, Canada $24.95

**The Big Book of Adventure Travel
2nd edition**
Profiles more than 400 great escapes to all corners
of the world
U.S. $17.95, Canada $25.50

Cross-Country Ski Vacations
A Guide to the Best Resorts, Lodges, and Groomed
Trails in North America
U.S. $15.95, Canada $22.50

Gene Kilgore's Ranch Vacations, 5th edition
The Complete Guide to Guest Resorts, Fly-Fishing,
and Cross-Country Skiing Ranches
U.S. $22.95, Canada $35.50

Indian America, 4th edition
A traveler's companion to more than 300 Indian
tribes in the United States
U.S. $18.95, Canada $26.75

Saddle Up!
A Guide to Planning the Perfect Horseback
Vacation
U.S. $14.95, Canada $20.95

Watch It Made in the U.S.A., 2nd edition
A Visitor's Guide to the Companies That Make Your
Favorite Products
U.S. $17.95, Canada $25.50

The World Awaits
A Comprehensive Guide to Extended Backpack
Travel
U.S. $16.95, Canada $23.95

**JMP travel guides are available
at your favorite bookstores.
For a FREE catalog or to place a
mail order, call: 800-888-7504.**

John Muir Publications • P.O. Box 613 • Santa Fe, NM 87504

ABOUT THE AUTHOR

Doina Locke lives in the Pittsburgh area and loves it. She has written hundreds of articles for regional newspapers and magazines, most of them about Pittsburgh, its people, and its points of interest. Locke and her husband, Michael, are the proud parents of Bill, Shane, Michael, and Thomas. Doina N. Locke is shown here with her daughter, D. Shane Locke.

JOHN MUIR PUBLICATIONS
and its City•Smart Guidebook authors
are dedicated to building community
awareness within City•Smart cities.
We are proud to work with the Greater
Pittsburgh Literacy Council as we
publish this guide to Pittsburgh.

Incorporated in 1982 as a nonprofit organization, the Greater Pittsburgh Literacy Council is the largest adult literacy agency in Allegheny County. Led by a staff of professional educators and more than 600 volunteers, GPLC provides reading, writing, math, and English as a Second Language instruction to approximately 2,000 adults annually. In addition, GPLC provides GED (high school equivalency) preparation, workplace skills development, family literacy, welfare-to-work skills, and computer-assisted instruction. GPLC won the Laubach Literacy Award for Excellence in 1998.

For more information, please contact:

Greater Pittsburgh Literacy Council
100 Sheridan Square
Pittsburgh, PA 15206
Phone: 412/661-READ or 412/661-7323
Fax: 412/661-3040
Web site: trfn.clpgh.org/gplc

OPEN UP
A LIFE.

GREATER PITTSBURGH
LITERACY COUNCIL